BARBARA

A late snowfall in Seattle, Washington. The Philips family: Henry, Barbara, and Elsie, standing outside their home. (1922)

BARBARA

UNCHARTED COURSE THROUGH BORDERLINE
PERSONALITY DISORDER

WENDELL AFFIELD

Foreword by
WILLIAM M. PETERSEN MD

WHISPERING PETALS PRESS, LLC

ALSO BY WENDELL AFFIELD

MUDDY JUNGLE RIVERS

A River Assault Boat Cox'n's

Memory Journey of His War in Vietnam and Return Home

HERMAN

1940s Lonely Hearts Search

Chickenhouse Chronicles Book I

PAWNS

The Farm, Nebish, Minnesota, 1950s

Chickenhouse Chronicles Book II

The Philips family. Elsie, Henry, Polly, Barbara
San Fransisco, California (circa 1926)

Published in the United States by Whispering Petals Press, LLC. Printed in the United States of America

Library of Congress Control Number: 2021905420

BARBARA, Uncharted Course Through Borderline Personality Disorder Chickenhouse Chronicles Book III Wendell Affield, Whispering Petals Press, LLC

Although the author and publisher have made every effort to ensure the accuracy of information contained in this book, we assume no responsibility for errors, inaccuracies, omissions, or inconsistency thereof. Any slights of people, places, or organizations are unintentional. Dialogue is reconstructed unless transcribed from diaries and letters.

Paperback ISBN 978-1-945902-08-6

eBook ISBN: 978-1-945902-09-3

Audio book ISBN 978-1-945902-10-9

Foreword by William M. Petersen MD, Bemidji, Minnesota

Photographs are property of the author unless otherwise noted.

Book cover by Damonza at Demonza.com

10 9 8 7 6 5 4 3 2 1 First Edition

ATTENTION CORPORATIONS, UNIVERSITIES, COLLEGES, AND PROFESSIONAL ORGANIZATIONS: Quantity discounts are available on bulk purchases of this book for educational, gift purposes, or premiums for increasing magazine subscriptions or renewals. Special books or book excerpts can also be created to fit specific needs.

For information, contact Whispering Petals Press, LLC: PO Box 652, Bemidji, MN 56619-0652

info@whisperingpetalspress.com

To Barbara
Your story lives on

———

Barbara (Philips) Affield (1920-2010). A short concert
in the old farmhouse, Nebish, Minnesota (1988). Fifty
years after Institute Droissard and Julliard School of
Music. Listen at *https://www.wendellaffield.com/media*

CONTENTS

PART III
DNA DISCOVERIES—MY NEW FAMILY

FROM THE AUTHOR

Two years ago, I thought I was close to completion on my *BARBARA* story, but an amazing thing happened. After seventy years of not knowing who my biological father was, I discovered my paternal biological family. Overnight I suddenly had six new siblings who proved to be accepting and loving—six new siblings who opened their lives to a stranger. I felt compelled—with their blessing—to add Part III to my mother Barbara's story.

August 11, 2020, would have been Barbara's (1920-2010) one hundredth birthday. I'd like her take on this story. I've come to realize that her greatest life-long dread was a deep fear of abandonment. Though unfounded, that fear, through the decades, created enormous obstacles in her relationship with her parents, grandparents, and husbands. I offer the following information so you might better understand Barbara's struggle.

Barbara Philips Affield (left) and her mother Elsie Fratt
Philips at Fergus Falls State Hospital, Minnesota, where
Barbara had been committed. I discovered this first picture
in the chickenhouse among my late grandmother's photos.
(August 1960)

In 2010, after Barbara died, I found this second photo
among my late mother's belongings in the attic of the old
farmhouse. In studying the leafy corn stalks and shadows
in this second photo, I came to realize that it was identical
to the first.

Why did Barbara snip herself out that summer of 1960 while
she was in Fergus Falls State Hospital? Was she angry that Elsie
had not rescued her? No one will ever know the demons Barbara
struggled with that summer after she lost her nine children to the

court system. And then for her mother to leave her in the Fergus Falls hospital—was it the ultimate abandonment?

From the early 1940s onward, my grandmother Elsie wrote that her daughter Barbara was schizophrenic. The "diagnosis" was not correct. Did Elsie use the term to dramatize Barbara's mental disorder? About fifteen years ago, as I began my research, I studied literature about schizophrenia because I knew if I were to tell Barbara's story, I needed to understand the ghosts that haunted her. As I studied schizophrenia, the term "borderline personality disorder" (BPD) kept popping up.

In 1938, the American psychoanalyst Adolph Stern first used the term "borderline" to describe a group of patients who were on the border of psychosis and neurosis, or possibly mild schizophrenia—words my grandmother often used in her diaries and her mental health journals.

After much research and sharing Barbara's history with mental health experts, I've concluded that, had Barbara been evaluated, she might have been diagnosed with borderline personality disorder, an abnormal brain condition that has tormented humans for thousands of years, but was not recognized as a mental disorder until 1980.

Today mental health experts recognize that emotional invalidation during early childhood—usually by the parents—is a factor in the development of BPD. Elsie was not supportive of Barbara and favored her second daughter, who, in fact, was diagnosed with schizophrenia in 1945.

In the early 1930s, the mental health field did not recognize borderline personality disorder, and doctors were unprepared to deal with Barbara's issues as they began to reveal themselves as she moved into adolescence.

Borderline Personality Disorder (BPD)
Diagnostic Criteria301.83 (F60.3)

A pervasive pattern of instability of interpersonal relationships, self-image, and affects, and marked impulsivity, beginning by early adulthood and present in a variety of contexts, as indicated by five (or more) of the following:

1. Frantic efforts to avoid real or imagined abandonment. (**Note:** Do not include suicidal or self-mutilating behavior covered in Criterion 5.)

2. A pattern of unstable and intense interpersonal relationships characterized by alternating extremes of idealization and devaluation.

3. Identity disturbance: markedly and persistently unstable self-image or sense of self.

4. Impulsivity in at least two areas that are potentially self-damaging (e.g., spending, sex, substance abuse, reckless driving, binge eating.) (**Note:** Do not include suicidal or self-mutilating behavior covered in Criterion 5.)

5. Recurrent suicidal behavior, gestures, or threats, or self-mutilating behavior.

6. Affective instability due to marked reactivity of mood. (e.g., intense episodic dysphoria, irritability, or anxiety usually lasting a few hours and only rarely more than a few days).

7. Chronic feelings of emptiness.

8. Inappropriate, intense anger or difficulty controlling anger (e.g., frequent displays of temper, constant anger, recurrent physical fights.)

9. Transient, stress-related paranoid ideation or severe dissociative signs.

FOREWORD

Mental illness has been a part of the human experience since the dawn of civilization. It has repeatedly been referred to in texts millennia old. *BARBARA* is an amazing accomplishment by a lay person, Wendell Affield, to write about the severe mental illness suffered by his mother, Barbara, throughout her life. As a family physician from northern Minnesota, recently retired from thirty-five years of rural medical practice, approximately 40% of my daily medical practice clustered about persons exhibiting signs of, and suffering from, the fallout effects of mental illness. And it is not just the patient who is impacted by this disease. Families, friends, and society as a whole all bear the impact of it...personally, economically, and psychologically. For the purpose of clarification, when I talk about mental illness, I am referring to three basic category types which include Personality Disorders (e.g. Narcissistic, Sociopathic), Mood Disorders (e.g. Major depression, Bipolar Disorder), and Thought Disorders (e.g. Schizophrenia, Psychosis). These conditions all have the similarity of representing a human brain which is not functioning normally. They are distinctly different from each other based on their agreed to psychiatric definitions as elaborated in the American Psychiatric Association Diagnostic and Statistical Manual of Mental Disorders V (DSM-5). These three forms of mental illness can overlap somewhat in a particular patient. But, in general, serious mental illness tends to fall primarily, first and foremost, into one of these three categories.

In 2013, I left my corporate family medicine practice and spent the final (and most meaningful) years of my physician work caring for Veterans in the Bemidji, Minnesota, outpatient VA clinic. This is where I met the author, Wendell Affield. I am a member of the local Veteran's Writers Group, which Wendell has facilitated for the past four years, and provide medical insight to the Veterans related to their risks for health issues associated with their service in the Armed Forces. Wendell acknowledges that he suffers from posttraumatic stress disorder (PTSD) related to battlefield trauma and personal injury during his Vietnam War experience. He was awarded the Purple Heart after incurring a serious life threatening injury when his Navy riverboat was attacked in a Viet Cong ambush. Through his writing about these life experiences, Wendell has found a peace of mind and maturity about personal tragedies which occurred even earlier in his life. His writing has been most impressive to his family and to all those who know him through his significant volunteer efforts in the Bemidji community over the past several years.

Wendell asked me to review this book about his mother, Barbara, from a medical mental health perspective. He was convinced that his mother's primary diagnosis was likely Borderline Personality Disorder (BPD). I was initially skeptical of that notion, in part because his grandmother, Elsie, frequently labeled Barbara as suffering from "schizophrenia," which is a type of Thought Disorder. Patients with Thought Disorder, though they may overlap somewhat with those suffering from Personality Disorders, are in a distinctly different diagnostic category and have very different treatment approaches and care.

Barbara's sister, Polly, who was truly diagnosed with schizophrenia, was periodically hospitalized throughout her adult life.

Wendell has uncovered an amazing wealth of historic documentation of his family's intimate history through the discovery of the "chickenhouse diaries" and other family letters and documents. However, throughout all the resources, never was there uncovered a physician-defined notion that Barbara actually suffered from schizophrenia. The psychiatrists who saw Barbara in the later 1940's, in fact, felt that she suffered from a severe Personality Disorder rather than a primary Thought Disorder. The fact that she was, to some extent, able to participate in the care of her children is certainly more likely to occur in a patient without schizophrenia, though there are milder forms of both Thought Disorders as well as Personality Disorders. Therapeutic intervention for Borderline Personality Disorder in general, is not very successful, and the more severe the illness, the less likely the patient will be successful in overcoming the social consequences of the condition. Wendell's mother Barbara essentially exhibited periods of silence alternating with agitational outbursts for the entirety of her adult life.

The fairly encouraging and amazing advancements of medical science over the past century, particularly with regard to our scientific knowledge of infectious disease, heart disease, diabetes and cancer conditions (to name just a few), have not translated as well into understanding the most complex organ of them all...the human brain. Where we have found "cures" for several medical conditions and successful intervention for life threatening infections, the understanding of, and therapeutic interventions for, mental illness haven't kept pace. In the case of psychiatrically-defined Personality Disorders, successful intervention requires patient willingness to follow a cognitive solution spelled out by the therapist, and adherence to a behavioral modification plan. Medications have not proven effective for these individuals; nor have more seriously invasive brain surgical strategies, such as lobotomy, leucotomy, and most recently, deep-brain stimulation. Many persons with a strong Personality Disorder aren't usually interested in the sacrifices required to allow them to function more successfully, as defined by society in general. Many patients with Personality Disorders are above average in intelligence, and quite good at manipulating others. Other than criminal legal intervention (many do end up here), therapeutic help falls short, as there are simply no easy solutions, especially with those more seriously affected. Such individuals don't view the world as most of us do. They often feel the rules we take for granted simply don't apply to them. I believe this was the case with Barbara. And, the decades that her mother Elsie spent seeking meaningful intervention for her daughter were fruitless, and also depleted the family of important resources. Wendell has often wondered how his mother would fare today with her multifaceted difficulties. I am convinced, that other than being better able to define her mental illness, she probably would not be much better off today than in the 1930's.

Throughout this interesting narrative of Barbara's life, Wendell has assumed the daunting task of verifying his suspicions that his mother, in fact, suffered from a Personality Disorder, and not the diagnosis of the Thought Disorder of schizophrenia. Establishing the correct diagnosis of these two very similar, yet distinctly different major types of mental illness, can test the patience and practical experience of the medical practitioner. Wendell systematically provides the reader with a volume of well-documented signs and symptoms that are associated with the diagnosis of Borderline Personality Disorder. In the absence of information of any serious oppositional notions, especially from any of Barbara's many physicians, I am in agreement with his conclusion about his mother's chronic state of mental illness. In my many years of family practice in the rural setting, where every condition 'under the sun' shows up first, I likely have never observed a more difficult and severely perplexing patient with Borderline Personality Disorder than Wendell's mother Barbara. The effects of her intransigent mental illness seriously affected her nine children, along with their several different fathers, and other family members. After reading this account of his mother's life, I am amazed at Wendell's incredible success in his many endeavors. Perhaps that is the greatest mystery of this poignant story.

William M. Petersen MD
Bemidji, Minnesota
March 4, 2021

This is the year [1934] before Barbara became ill...How great was our loss but it is most difficult to foresee the future when it is an uncharted course?

Elsie Fratt Philips, decades later, in a letter to her mother Idalia

Barbara Ann Philips [front row far right] at Thomas School, Rowayton, Connecticut. (1933-'34)

Lest I Forget

Time, you are cruel,
As cruel as can be,
Today you're my friend
Tomorrow my enemy!
I loath you, Time,
You don't dream and wish,
You never say, "I'll wait,
You didn't quite finish"!
You skimp and save on me,
Like an Irish plaited kilt,
But I don't really hate you,
Won't you change, Lilt?
You snub me so, Time,
You never wait for me,
So all I have of you
Is my diary!

Barbara Ann Philips, sixteen years old
Winter 1936
Darien, Connecticut

INTRODUCTION

The spring of 2010, a few months after Barbara died, my sister Laurel and I unlocked the chickenhouse door on the family homestead near Nebish, Minnesota. When my grandmother Elsie Philips died in 1984, Barbara had her belongings shipped from Seattle, Washington, to the farm. They were first stored in the hayloft of the dairy barn, but after a windstorm blew the barn down, the storm-damaged contents were transferred to the chickenhouse, and Barbara put a padlock on the eighty-year-old building.

From 1991 onward, after the padlock was placed on the chickenhouse door, Barbara would become hysterical if any of her eight children (her ninth child, Randy, had died in an airplane crash in 1978) suggested unlocking it and exploring the contents. The morning Laurel and I removed the padlock in 2010, remnants of our grandmother's calico curtains and wool blankets sagged from broken chicken perches. Manure, straw, and feathers littered the frost-heaved concrete floor. Mold spores and dust that we'd awakened danced in sunbeams that filtered through fly-scat-coated windows. The stench of mouse urine and decay permeated the coop. Laurel brought protective masks. I purchased several large plastic totes to haul our discoveries to my house because our siblings wanted to burn everything.

Laurel standing in doorway of the chickenhouse, at the
farm in northern Minnesota. (Spring 2010)

Laurel and I spent two days methodically working our way through the building. Donned in masks and protective gloves, we started in one corner and began sifting through our family history. The first thing we discovered was my grandmother's urn, tucked beneath a mildewed chair cushion, wedged in a corner outside the chicken-feed hopper. First edition books, many signed by the author, dry-rotted in manure-crusted nesting boxes. I discovered a 1926 leather-bound edition of *Penrod* (1914) by Booth Tarkington—a silk bookmark dangled from page fifty-eight. Furniture disintegrated from dry rot; dovetail joints pulled apart and once-exquisite furniture collapsed sideways like falling dominos.

Beneath a heap of old clothing and newspapers, we discovered several sealed boxes containing the bulk of the letters and diaries. There were thousands of documents. The earliest was a letter dated 1822 written by David Olmsted, who had been a soldier in the Connecticut Provisional Regiment in 1781. It was obvious that Barbara had never looked at the documents. Bundles of letters, held by brittle rubber bands, remained in good condition. Some of the packets were sorted by author, some by year, and some by event. There were seven World War II V-mail messages written by my grandfather while he was on convoy duty in the North Atlantic.

My grandmother was a prolific writer. We discovered reams of her rough drafts and correspondence from the people who replied to her letters. I have a small library of 1940s mental health books and my grandmother's lists of questions for the psychiatrists who treated her two daughters. There were scrapbooks from their European tour in 1937-38. Diaries and pictures spanned decades from the 1890s to the 1980s.

I had newspaper clippings from 1917 to the1970s, scrapbooks, photo albums, legal documents, and letters—thousands of letters. Many pieces were not relevant to my research—correspondence exchanged with strangers, wedding invitations, obituaries—names lost in the mist of time. I've spent more than ten years reading, sorting, and cataloging documents as I unraveled a heart-breaking story.

PART I

THE EARLY YEARS

PRIVILEGED CHILDHOOD

My grandparents, Henry and Elsie Philips, raised in the Pacific Northwest, came from families who had made their mark in banking, real estate, and the timber industry during the late 19th and early 20th centuries. On March 24, 1918, three months after marrying Henry, Elsie was featured on "The World of Society and Woman" section of the *Salt Lake Herald-Republican-Telegram*. The article below her picture began, "Mrs. Henry Olmsted Philips, wife of Lieutenant Philips at Ft. Douglas, is one of the most charming young matrons at the garrison." World War I (WWI) ended later that year and Henry was discharged from the army. He and his bride returned to the family business in Seattle, Washington, and to Whidbey Island where his family owned Greenbank Farm.

In the glow of WWI victory, the United States found itself on the cusp of change. The Roaring Twenties is synonymous with the Golden Age of Radio, "talkies" (sound movies), Spirit of St. Louis and Charles Lindbergh. Financial speculation knew no bounds as the stock market soared. New technology drove over-production of agricultural crops; commodity prices plummeted and forced millions of rural families into cities as industry and technology expanded, pushing the demand for new jobs in manu-facturing.

Young women pushed the bounds of newfound freedom. Smoking cars on trains, once the exclusive domain of men, became integrated as white women were allowed to partake. Beauty parlors mushroomed across the country with the demand for a new hairstyle. With close-cropped hair, shorter skirts, and flapping open boots, liberated young women became "Flappers." Tea Rooms sprang up, catering to the "modern woman." Contrary to the temperance movement, many teahouses surrepti-tiously served alcohol. My grandmother was a 1915 Vassar girl and an early women's rights advocate. She loved her whiskey tonic, which she euphemistically referred to as "Tea." This was the world into which my mother Barbara was born on August 11, 1920.

The first letter in which Elsie mentioned Barbara was stamped Greenbank, Washington. It was written to Elsie's mother, Idalia Fratt, who lived across Puget Sound in Everett. An excerpt:

> *Friday, June 25, 1921:* Dearest Mother, just a note to let you know that we are getting settled slowly but surely. Baby Ann (Barbara Ann) thrives over here—she's fatter than ever and quite brown. We love it here [Greenbank Farm], it is simply marvelous. Loads of love to you, Elsie

By autumn 1921, the young family had moved into a comfortable home in nearby Seattle where they lived for the next few years.

In a 2009 interview, about a year before Barbara died, I asked her what her earliest memory was. She recalled that her crib rested against the west wall beneath an open window on the upper floor of their Seattle home. "Salty Puget Sound and Douglas fir scent drifted into the little room on summer breezes," she told me. "Standing in the crib, I rubbed my fingers against the screen as I reached toward the music that floated up from the open door of the piano conservatory across the street."

Sitting in the shaded Minnesota farmhouse kitchen during that interview, Barbara looked back almost ninety years, sipped her Hills Bros. coffee from a small teacup, and continued, "The music was for me. It filled the room and I felt a warmth."

My Aunt Katherine "Polly," (1922-2006) was born in Seattle, Washington. Elsie wrote in Polly's *Baby Book* that the infant was severely ill with influenza when she was six days old. Shadows of the 1918 Spanish influenza pandemic continued to haunt the country for the next decade. Parents must have been terrified when newborn infants fell ill. Is it possible that Polly's "influenza" with accompanying high fevers affected her developmentally?

I share information about Polly's condition because today, as I mentioned earlier, mental health professionals recognize that emotional invalidation is an early amplifier for borderline personality disorder development. How did Elsie's favoritism toward Polly affect Barbara's emotional development as a young child?

Elsie wrote in Polly's *Baby Book*, "'Pollydoll' learned to walk when she was fifteen months old." To begin walking at fifteen months is beyond the average for this motor development skill. Another comment in the *Baby Book* raises a red flag: Elsie wrote, "At eleven months Polly says, 'Da-Da' and 'Ma-Ma.' At seventeen months she adds only 'bye-bye.' Barbara Ann talks so much she [Polly] doesn't have a chance."

Elsie's comments indicate that very early in Polly's life, Elsie recognized her younger daughter's vulnerability and began to favor Polly over Barbara. Research is divided on the influence an older sibling has on the toddler. In watching my own grand-daughters, the older sister appears to be an asset to the younger sibling's speech development. By seventeen months, a toddler should have a vocabulary of twenty to one hundred words. Did Elsie really blame Barbara for Polly's slow development?

On January 12, 1924, Elsie wrote in Polly's *Baby Book*, "Polly's curls shorn by Barbara Ann. This is a perfect crime as Polly's curls were simply lovely." When I first read the passage, I thought "perfect crime" was a strange word choice to use for a four-year old's actions. It was the first of many times over the next two decades where Elsie's favoritism toward Polly was obvious. As you will see, this partiality escalated throughout their relationship. I believe it's one of the reasons Barbara eventually turned against her mother.

Elsie's 1930s diary entries document an alarming pattern of Polly's forgetfulness and declining academic performance. What caused this cognitive impairment, or was Polly just a negligent teenager? Polly's letters, Henry's letters, and Elsie's diary entries reveal Polly's downward spiral, which escalated in 1940. Polly was diagnosed with schizophrenia in 1945. She spent the rest of her life institutionalized or living with her parents. After Henry died, Elsie became Polly's guardian-conservator and the two lived together.

But back to Barbara's story. In one of my interviews with her, she told me about an evening when she was four and their house burned down while her parents were out. Barbara and her year-old sister Polly were with a babysitter. According to Barbara, the babysitter was upstairs talking out the window to her boyfriend on the lawn below. Smoke spiraled up the staircase; the babysitter panicked and ran out of the house. Barbara dashed from her bedroom into her parents' smoke-filled room. More than eighty years later, she recalled a ladder coming to the window, breaking glass. "A fireman in a white shirt climbed in through the window, picked me up, and handed me out the window to a firefighter on the ladder."

The next afternoon, Barbara toured the damaged house, holding her father's hand. Polly's crib was full of glass where the window had been knocked in when Polly was rescued. In Barbara's bedroom, she discovered that her pajamas had been singed. "The paraffin had melted on my china dolls," she told me. "Their faces were twisted." Earlier in the evening on the day of the fire, Barbara's Aunt Idalia, named after her mother— affectionately known as Daddles and later shortened to "Dee"— and her boyfriend, Charlo, had been downstairs in the living room. Nine decades later, Barbara speculated, "Charlo must have dropped a smoldering cigarette down in the sofa cushions before he left the house."

Barbara told me that the Seattle newspaper accused Henry of burning his own house down to collect insurance money. The young family left Seattle and the scandal. They first settled in New York, where Elsie's younger brother, Nicholas Fratt, lived. Correspondence dated 1923 indicated that Elsie, Henry, and their two daughters lived in White Plains, New York. Elsie commented in a letter to her mother that they could "…hardly wait to settle down on our country estate of old New England." The move was short-lived. Two years later they relocated to the West Coast and Henry became branch manager of his father's real estate loan office in Oakland, California—Calvin Philips & Company.

Old documents hint that Elsie's father, Charles Diller Fratt, who struggled with diabetes, gifted his daughter much of her inheritance to help the young family resettle. In California, Elsie designed and decorated the home they built, including custom-made light fixtures. My grandmother's letters document the many hours her family spent at their country club. I have a silver platter inscribed, "1927, Orinda Country Club, Annual Championship, 3rd Flight, won by Henry O. Philips."

Barbara's early letter, written to her grandmother, Idalia
Fratt. Barbara was six years old. (August 1926)

Dear Grammies,

I've played tennis with my balls and rackets and dusted the house with my ?? mop and had such a good time. I want you to come down here. Love kisses, Barbara Ann

As children, we grew up listening to Barbara blame our grandmother for the family's financial downfall in California. According to Barbara, Elsie was a strong-willed woman and demanded that her brother Norbert be given a position in the Philips real estate loan office, but Henry's father Calvin, with five sons, refused, saying it was a family business. The autumn of 1927, Elsie packed her suitcase and moved back to Everett, Washington, with Barbara and Polly. Then Elsie gave Henry an ultimatum: She and her daughters would return to him if he moved near her brother Nicholas on the East Coast.

Sometimes, to find a larger truth, the biographer must

explore other paths. The following detour clarified a mystery I've pondered for many years as I researched my mother's past.

I recently received ten letters from the folks who now own the Fratt Mansion in Everett. The old letters tell a different story than my mother had told us. Henry had *invited* Norbert to join the firm. Norbert was free-spirited and quite the socializer. His father C.D. Fratt wrote, "I feel very much upset over his [Norbert] being kicked out of Lawrenceville and then being dropped from Cornell...."

In a March 1926 letter, Norbert wrote to his mother about life as a common seaman on a freighter. He spoke of his duties as a deckhand and his upcoming voyage from New York, down through the Panama Canal, and up the West Coast. He concluded the ten-page letter by telling his mother that, "I hope to see Henry when I get to 'Frisco and talk over this job he says I can get there. I think it would be great to settle down near Henry and Elsie. Henry says he could help me lots getting started."

Norbert's letters to his mother document an extravagant lifestyle after he was hired by Calvin Philips & Company. He spent many hours at Orinda Country Club, wooed a young woman he married in 1927, and tried out for the Olympic Club football squad. "They have a great schedule including games in Portland and Honolulu so it would be fine if I could make it. They practice about twice in the week and on Saturdays and Sundays." Norbert made the cut, so was committed to the Olympic Club schedule—so much for business.

Another old letter reveals a fact that I'm sure my mother was never aware of. In a March 1927 letter, Norbert wrote to his father, "Your letter containing the securities and cash arrived last week and also the letter with the dividend check." Eleven pages later, Norbert ended the letter, "I hope you are fine and getting better. Thanks very much for sending the checks and securities. I had no idea there was that much more coming to me as all that." There was no dollar amount listed. Did C.D. and Idalia subsidize each of their children's lavish lifestyles? Is this how Elsie and Henry financed the elegant home in Oakland where they lived for less than two years?

Who can know what happened behind the scenes with Norbert? By autumn 1927, Henry's father Calvin Philips, a strict Quaker, could not have approved of Norbert's work ethic. Twenty months after entering the banking business, Norbert left the Calvin Philips & Company real estate loan business and opened his own office.

Four days after this letter was written, Norbert's father C.D. died. Eighteen months later the stock market crashed, and the United States plummeted into the Great Depression. Did Norbert lose his legacy in the stock market/real estate crash when so many defaulted on loans?

Elsie left Henry to sell the only home they would ever own; fifty years later she lamented the loss of her "Lovely home." Henry closed out their business in California before he traveled east to seek work.

Elsie wrote to her husband:

December 18, 1927: Our own darlingest, this will also be a Merry Christmas letter as it should reach you on Christmas day. How we will miss you and your sweet embraces and kisses. I've decided that the reason we're having all of this trouble now is because we've had such wonderful times when we're together and you can't expect to have everything.

In studying my mother's early life, I could not understand the lavish lifestyle the Philips family lived during the Great Depression. Elsie's father died on February 3, 1928, while she and her daughters were living with her parents. Did Elsie, over the next decade, let her father's legacy trickle away on maids, gardeners, country clubs, and concerts? And in the end, blame her father-in-law? Was a part of that blame transferred to Barbara as she grew older? And yet, all her life, Barbara blamed her paternal grandfather, Calvin Philips, for the family's downfall from their idyllic California life.

In studying thousands of pages my grandmother Elsie wrote, I came to realize that she was a domineering woman and, at times, an unreliable narrator, who often wrote in her diary after the fact so she could put a favorable spin on her own actions.

1929

enry found a position with National Broadcasting Company (NBC) in New York City. Elsie and the girls joined him, and the Philips family settled in Norwalk, Connecticut, from where Henry commuted into the city each day. Barbara and Polly attended private schools. Elsie, through her Vassar alumni connections, soon became active in the political and social world. Over the next two decades, her diaries documented social functions, bridge games, and luncheon dates at the Vassar Club, along with plays, concerts, lectures, political organizing, and community volunteer work.

This letter from Elsie to her mother Idalia in Everett, Washington, illuminated the Philips' lifestyle. Idalia's husband had died eighteen months earlier. Elsie wrote about her two daughters—Barbara was eight, Polly, six.

June 22, 1929: Dearest mother, I'm writing, sitting out on the porch with the children, the country has been wonderful for them. They play beautifully together and are too sweet. At present they are copying some of the art out of one of my books from my course at Columbia. Polly is really very good at it, shortly we are going down to play a little tennis. Barbara, Polly, and I, and then I'm going to take them to an art exhibit by the Guild of the Seven Arts in which I am going to become active when B and P go back to school in the fall. Yesterday was my birthday and although I no longer need to have birthdays, this time I had a lovely one. My present from Henry was a membership in a lovely club here where there is fine swimming in Long Island Sound, golf, tennis, and even riding on Kentucky thoroughbreds. It's the most beautiful spot—200 acres of lawn and green trees and beach and all the softness of Connecticut. The children are thrilled to pieces over it. With hugs and kisses from them and from Nick and Henry and me, Elsie.

Barbara and Polly -- Caption on back: "Two little water nymphs. Try to catch them." (Summer 1929)

Note that Elsie included Nick in her closing. Elsie's brother Nicholas, "Nick," was divorced. He and his three children, Bill, Pete, and Skip, moved in with the Philips family. Less than two months later, on September 3, 1929, the stock market hit an all-time high, then began to decline. On October 29, Black Tuesday struck, and the stock market lost thirty percent of its value. Even as the country spiraled down, the Philips family seemed above it. In the chickenhouse, I discovered this poem, written by Barbara while attending Thomas School in Stamford, Connecticut.

"The little Brook"
Little Brook aren't you fast?
As you scamper past.
How you do bubble along.
I like your pretty little song.

— BARBARA PHILIPS (1929)

Just a happy, inquisitive nine-year-old girl. From outward appearances Barbara, had an idyllic childhood—private schools, country club, maid service, loving parents—but a dark cloud loomed on the horizon.

From left to right: Elsie Philips, Barbara, Polly, Elsie's brother
Nicholas "Nick" Fratt and his sons, Nicholas "Skip," William "Bill,"
and Peter. Hickory Bluff, Darien, Connecticut. (1931)

All her life Barbara loved to play croquet. As children on the
farm in Minnesota, we kids (between working and playing war)
also played croquet several times a week. For us, croquet was
just another form of war—to see how far we could "send" the
opponent's ball. During the game when two balls came together,
the player would place his foot on his ball and strike it with the
mallet, sending the opponent's ball as far as possible—with luck,
into the hog pen. Then the loser had to climb over electric barbed
wire to retrieve his ball before the hogs chewed it.

1932

B y the end of 1932, the stock market had lost ninety percent of its value and the country plummeted into the Great Depression. "The Great Depression" connotates images of Black Thursday when Wall Street stockbrokers leapt from high-rise windows. Ninety years later, sepia images of soup lines and hobos haunt us. Today's homeless families evoke that iconic picture of a mother and her two children. Shadow images of destitute families in *Migrant Mothers: Dorothea Lange's Faces Of The Dust Bowl (1930s)* remind us of the hopelessness of that era. John Steinbeck's *Grapes of Wrath* (1939) is perhaps the best-known symbol of that fateful decade.

In psychological terms, the Great Depression went far beyond economic woes. Men and women lost their sense of self-worth. One of Steinbeck's characters tells another, "They's times when how you feel got to be kep' to yourself." "Inferiority Complex" was the catchall social problem for millions—today recognized as depression. Those who did seek help were exposed to an array of mental hygiene quacks, from newspaper columnists to hypnotists.

As most of the country struggled in the third year of the

Great Depression, Barbara received her first diary—a window into her twelve-year-old world. Barbara, Polly, and Nick's boys were often left alone at home. Inside the front cover, Polly wrote, "Merry Christmas to Barb from Polly, Christmas 1931." Here are a few entries that show Barbara's mindset and worldview.

Second page is a personal record:

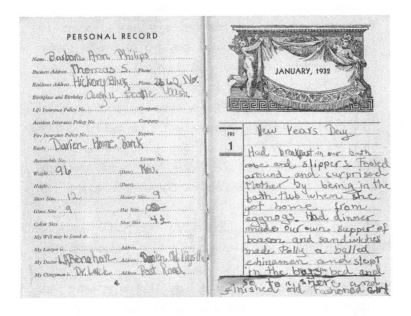

Friday, January 1, 1932: New Year's Day: Had breakfast in our bathrobe and slippers. Fooled around and surprised Mother by being in the bathtub when she got home from eggnogs. Had dinner, made our own supper of bacon and sandwiches. Made Polly a balled Chinamen and slept in the boys' bed and so to snore and finished "Old Fashioned Girl."

The phrase, "and so to snore" appears several times—I

imagine it was little girl code for bedtime. Many of the school day pages are blank. Barbara's diary continues:

> Saturday, January 2: *Went to see the Christmas trees—there weren't any lights on in New Canaan.*
>
> Sunday, January 3: *Went to New York went to the top of the Empire State for luncheon with Donald and John Frothingham afterward.*
>
> Tuesday, January 5: *School started, and we wore our new polo coats to school. They are keen!*
>
> Sunday, January 24: *Had breakfast went to church in Stamford. Had dinner. Took about a 3 mile walk. Came home grownups went out had supper. Wrestled like the Dicks! Traded beds to fool the grownups.*
>
> Saturday, January 30: *Phoned three people for luncheon and none could come, changed beds, I washed Polly's hair and Pol went out to luncheon. Sat by the fire and sewed while Skip read. Dad and Uncle Nick came home to luncheon. Took a walk. Mother and Dad went out to tea.*

I wonder if her daughters knew the "tea" was spiked? Barbara, all her life, was adamantly opposed to alcoholic drinks.

> Monday, February 1: *School all day. That night, Mom and Daddy went out. Uncle Nick stayed with us and Pol and I made a French bed for Mother and Daddy put on their pajamas. Pol sneaked downstairs and got the alarm clock so that we could get up and make breakfast because the maid was out.*
>
> Sunday, February 7: *We have no maid. Worked all morning. Did my math. Patty R. came over, took a walk came home. Skip and Pol surprised us by having supper ready. Fooled around. Daddy and I walked home with Patty and so to snore.*

Thursday, February 11: *School as usual. Haven't had a maid all week so all have helped Mum. Went to music at school without a coat. M.T. almost saw me except all girls crowded around me, etc. and so to snore.*

Friday, April 1: *Went to Washington DC. Drove to Wilmington and battle of Brandywine had dinner slept overnight there.*

Saturday, April 2: *Left Wilmington went to Greenbank Mill and in the afternoon arrived at Washington DC saw capital building, Lincoln Memorial, and Smithsonian Museum, where we stayed at funny little place called Kern. After a lovely dinner we went to see operetta, "Chocolate Soldier."*

The Philips family had owned Greenbank Mills for nearly 100 years. Calvin, Henry's father, grew up there. The family lost Greenbank Mills in bankruptcy in the 1880s. Today, Greenbank Mills & Philips Farm and the National Historic District provide a fascinating glimpse of Delaware life in the late 18th and early 19th centuries. In a 2008 interview, Barbara told me that Calvin had named Greenbank Farm on Whidbey Island, Washington, in memory of Greenbank Mills.

Back to Barbara's diary:

Sunday, April 3: *had breakfast at a swell cafeteria, went to Arlington, Mount Vernon, Potomac River, Washington Memorial, and went to see mother's old friend for Sunday night supper.*

Monday, April 4: *Went to same cafeteria, packed, started on our way. Got arrested but persuaded the cop out of the idea. Stopped for luncheon at a place where the people had been very rich, but now they hadn't a cent. Drove, stopped at Plainfield for dinner. Arrived home quite late after a lovely trip.*

Sunday, May 8: Wow! What a day. For dinner went to see some friends of Dad's he hadn't seen since he was 11. They had two boys 12 and 14. The one 14 was nice, but the one 12 was so shy he got under the table to eat but they both ran away in the afternoon. For supper Donald and John F. came. It certainly was a boyish day.

Sat, June 11: Went to Vassar, stayed at cute house. Went to commencement saw daisy chain and green pastures. All the girls had the same dresses but different colors. Mrs. Eddy, Mrs. Hartely, Gars and Mary and their two beaus and us four and another lady. We had box suppers on the lawn and afterward we saw Chaucer's Prologue and Knights Tale.

Sun, June 12: At Vassar, Breaker [breakfast?] at Pop Over Shop then Ma and Dad to Baccalaureate while we walked all over campus. Went to yummy chimney corners. After that we took a nap at the little house and got ready for supper party at the Wycoffs. They had two girls our age. Went home after lovely trip.

June 12 was the last entry in Barbara's diary—a young girl's attention turned to other things that summer. As others stood in soup lines or went hungry, the Philips family still celebrated traditional holidays. Here is a note that Barbara, just turned twelve a few months earlier, wrote.

Nov. 26th '32
Thanksgiving Menu,

First course

Tomato juice cocktail and hors d' oeuvres, the grownups had a grown up cocktail.

Second Course

Turkey with stuffing

sweet potatoes (southern style)

Cranberry sauce

creamed cauliflower au gratin

Olives and celery

Third Course (Dessert)

Whipped cream dessert with nuts etc.

coffee, fruit, nuts candy cakes

Barbara Philips, Darien, Connecticut. (Winter 1932)

After dinner Barbara went out to play. It may have been a

snowy holiday. In this photo, she stands in the yard, white stocking hat and snowsuit, arms raised as if she is holding ski poles.

There were not many documents from the early 1930s in the chickenhouse. The following letter offers a glimpse of the Philips family as they dealt with financial and relational strains. While visiting at Cedar Gate, Connecticut, Elsie wrote to her mother, Idalia:

> *August 4, 1933*—Dearest Mother, It's perfectly splendid news to hear that the bank business is settled up and you are really coming east as soon as you can get ready. The first of October if we can possibly afford it, we are going to get two smaller houses close together. Henry and Nick have been together far too much for far too long.
>
> The world seems ever full of grief. Just when everything took a turn for the better and the security business began to look as if one might make a living at it once more, the Market is taking a shakedown that lost it all ground it had gained, lost the people all the confidence they had commenced to feel and everything is as dead again as it has been for the past four years. There surely is no lasting joy. Something is always taking it away. I can hear you say, "Children are a lasting joy," and there's some truth to that. I'm overjoyed to have a letter from Bar [Barbara] saying she was tapped for "A.T.C." [Academically Talented Class] the honor society that usually only older girls are chosen for and usually you have to have been there two or three years before you are chosen. Only a very few are chosen—it is a very solemn affair and a very dignified honor. I'm busy getting Barb's and Skip's birthday boxes ready for them. What a season this is. And now Barb is going into her

teens. Old Father Time is turning the pages too fast. Well, we'll all feel better when we get you back here. Love in abundance, Elsie.

The letter started on such a positive note, however, Idalia's "bank business" was not "settled up." After her husband died in 1928, Idalia took out a loan, through a bank owned by a family friend, using her home as collateral. Though the bank owner had been a groomsman in Charles and Idalia's wedding, he refused to forgive the loan when she became delinquent after the stock market crashed. Idalia lost the home she and her husband had built and where they had raised their family.

For the next two decades, Idalia lived with her children, traveling back and forth across the continent, moving from family to family. Also, in this letter, was one of very few times that Elsie praised Barbara, who, at thirteen years old, must have been near the top of her class academically, to be tapped for "A.T.C."

After Idalia died in 1954, Elsie brought her old letters home and reflected on them. This note, written by my grandmother, was attached to the preceding letter that she had written to Idalia in 1933. It sounds strange because Elsie addressed the note to her dead mother.

Elsie wrote:

This is the year [1934] before Barbara became ill. I think you knew she was ill when you left for Seattle. Only of course then so little was known about psychological illness. I believe that if she could have been sent away to school, her chronic maladjustment with its tragic results with all her children might have been averted. But there was no one to know that then. How great was our loss but it is most difficult to foresee the future when it is an uncharted course? Those who come later have the advantage of experience.

In 1907, Elsie, fourteen years old, lived in Everett, Washington. Her parents enrolled her at Miss Harker's School in California—prep school before Vassar. Elsie thrived at Miss Harker's School and graduated from Vassar in 1915. Elsie must have thought sending Barbara away to school would be a positive experience for her daughter, too.

Other questions arise from the original letter: My grandmother loved her brother Nick, so why did she say, "Henry and Nick have been together far too much for far too long"? In Barbara's diary, she often alludes to herself and Polly "wrestling" with Nick's sons. Was there a sexual connotation? My older brother Chris believes Barbara was molested when she was a child.

Just how old was Barbara when she began distancing herself from her mother, staying overnight with friends to avoid Elsie? Another borderline personality disorder symptom that began to reveal itself as Barbara moved into adolescence was black and white thinking. Her acquaintances were either friend or enemy.

I didn't find many letters or pictures in the chickenhouse from 1934 and 1935. I imagine, as with millions of others during the Great Depression, the Philips family was struggling to survive, though with less pain than many.

I did rescue a 1933 edition of Dale Carnegie's *Public Speaking and Influencing Men in Business.* I imagine my grandmother purchased the book for my grandfather. He was a gentle soul and a deep thinker; I believe that the only reason he went into the business world was because of his father's insistence. Hundreds of pages of Henry's letters illuminate his philosophical mindset and his trust in the Lord. He was very active in his Episcopalian Church. After WWII, he became chaplain of the New York Chapter of "Retreads," a veteran organization for men who served in both world wars. In reading hundreds of pages of my grandfather's writing, I've come to believe that he would have been a great minister or educator.

1936

Barbara was fifteen years old in the winter of 1936, and her borderline personality disorder signs began to manifest themselves, particularly her fear of abandonment. In the chickenhouse, I discovered a series of letters, quite repetitious, dated January-April 1936, written by Barbara to her parents, who spent the late winter enjoying the social scene in New York while living at Hotel Vanderbilt and campaigning for Alfred Landon, the Republican presidential candidate who opposed Franklin Delano Roosevelt. The country was in the seventh year of the Great Depression.

Did Henry and Elsie's four-month absence exacerbate Barbara's sense of abandonment? Manic behavior and promiscuity are two common ways for people to act out. The 1936 letters all have the same hypomanic—elevated—tone. Boys were prominent in Barbara's life. What happened between January and April 1936?

While Henry and Elsie were in New York, Polly remained in the Philips family home with her grandmother Idalia and Barbara lived with Dr. Slaughter, a widower and family friend who had a young son, Miles, and a daughter, Miriam "Mimi," who was Barbara's age.

When I discovered the letters, they were rubber-banded together in a plastic envelope, and I realized that Elsie must have placed some significance to them. Here are three of the letters to show Barbara's frame of mind.

Jan 28, 1936

Dear sweet Mom and Dad, I just adored seeing you both Sat. and gee Mommie dear you looked so beautiful darling in that dress and shoes and hat!!!! And Dad dear you were so cute and handsome standing there telling us about putting soda in cider!!! I love you both so much!!! Did you drive back that night late? I went down to St. Lukes with Bruce and had a swell time there were lots of boys there and I really had a neat evening. Scott Goddard brought us back here to Mimi's and we stayed here until Mrs. Mims came for Bruce which wasn't very long. Then Sunday Bruce came down and we did Latin and French together! Today we had a big Math exam. I passed the one we had Friday. And I stayed after school to play basketball and another boy named Charles Leach (a senior about the nicest boy in school, doctor Slaughter thinks a lot of him) brought me home, Fri too! He asked me if I was allowed to go out at nights, but I said no Dr. Slaughter didn't let me. Another older boy asked me to go out with him tonight, Sat; but I said the same thing! I didn't want to especially!!! Pol is fine. Love to you both. BAP (Barbara Ann Philips) xxxooo

P.S. I'm still remembering your adorable preach Dad dear!!!!!

Letter #2:

March 23, 1936 Saturday morning.

Dearest Mom and Dad, I can just see you dear ones in the apartment together! Did you go to meet Mom at the station Dad dear? Didn't she look adorable walking into Grand Central all by her little self? Have you been putting your dear heads together and figuring? That's what Mom dear said you were going to do. Write and tell me all your decisions – I know you'll probably change them a million times but I'd like to know them all and give my opinions when you ask us what we think!!! I like the little white house and our going to Low Heywood?? Very much or I think it would be lovely to stay in New York City winters.

I don't care in the least. "Ain't it a problem folks!!!"

Today is the usual Saturday morning. I'm planning to wash some socks and then write my diary! We didn't wake up till 10:30! What are you going to get for darling little T much okie's [Polly] birthday? It comes on Saturday doesn't it? I'll have to get her something with you when I get in there! The dear little thing is so sweet! She'll be fourteen!! I love you both very much.

XXXXXXX OOO BAP

Letter #3

April 6, 1936 Monday night

Darlingest Mommy and Daddy, Really dearest ones it makes a big lump come into my throat to think how thoughtful and lovely and wonderful you were to us last weekend! It's really impossible to tell you how thinking back over our time together I realize that you two are just about perfect parents. And I mean it sweeties!! No imbiegelling!! That's just a new word I've heard I have no idea how to spell it or anything (maybe it said W instead of up B!) Dear Dad don't throw away that peanut!! I just thought I want it for my scrapbook! But I suppose you've eaten dear Dad because of your resemblance to Jumbo?? Or is it the peanut?? (Sweetie please don't go on that diet) I adore to set the table and simply stack bread on your plate XXX!! I still have that dear Gardenia on my dresser. I'm never going to throw it away! It's still just as white almost as ever and it makes my whole room smell divine!! Idiots Delight was so exciting wasn't it –? Pol and I went to our music lesson. She'll probably tell you about the exciting things she got so I won't ruin it. We had a grand long "lecon" Miss Parker the French teacher took me down and Pol went on the bus a bit before. We had a "coc" and got the bus. Now I'm studying hard! I can't ever tell you or even express how sweet you both are and how much I love you.

XXXXXXXXXXXXX BAP [Barbara Ann Philips]

From the letters we can see that Barbara and Polly often spent the weekends with their parents—the girls were not abandoned, but something traumatic happened to Barbara that winter of 1936. She met and fell in love with a schoolmate, Bruce Mims, despite Elsie's disapproval. Twenty years later Elsie wrote about Bruce as "...a maladjusted adolescent boy."

From other documents, I know that Barbara was involved with Bruce or an older man. Is it possible she got pregnant? An unwed daughter with a child would have been detrimental to Elsie's social aspirations. Dr. Slaughter certainly had the contacts and expertise to take care of the problem.

Eight years later, Barbara wrote a letter to her grandfather Calvin, recounting that winter of 1936. An excerpt:

March 20, 1944,

Grandfather... I can never remember my Mother as Mother. Why, when I was 15... she went off and left me in the home of two mentally deficients whose Father was a doctor never at home.

At some point that spring of 1936, Barbara and Bruce Mims broke up and Barbara blamed her mother. A typical response of a heart-broken teenager dealing with borderline personality disorder might be for her to spiral down into depression—it's not unusual for suicidal ideation to present, or in extreme, to attempt suicide. As borderline personality disorder signs began to impact Barbara's performance, her parents and the mental health field were unprepared to deal with her.

BARBARA'S PROSE AND POETRY

I n the chickenhouse I discovered a waxed manila folder in excellent condition. On the outside, Elsie had written "Priceless Barbara 1936." It was a collection of short stories and poetry. Barbara was sixteen that autumn and early winter. Idalia, Barbara's grandmother, had attended college in Paris, France, in the 1890s and had instilled a love of European culture in her granddaughters. In the chickenhouse I discovered *THE ABBE CONSTANTIN* (1882) by Ludovic Halevy. Inside was written "E. N. Ouimette," Barbara's great-grandfather. As I read the little stained book, I was struck by how much Barbara's writing was influenced by it—the European syntax, motifs, and French language.

These two short stories from Barbara reveal her mindset toward men; her grandfather Calvin Philips was a stern Quaker. The em dashes (—) are a stylistic tool Barbara used.

"For the Love of Flax"

My candle burns at both ends; it will not
last the night;
But ah my foes, and oh my friends, it gives
a lovely light!

—*From "First Fig" by Edna St. Vincent Millay*

The trees, like ancient majestic Druids withstood the strong over-powering wind as it chanted a stern deep hymn. Down along rutty road frequently illuminated by flashes of lightning a small figure could be seen. Like a leaf blowing hither and yon this atom of humanity was almost overpowered by the furies of nature and her uncurbed elements. But as the anger of a mighty man arises almost to insanity and then suddenly quiets to a clear serenity so with this storm. The rain suddenly diminished to a refreshing patter against the leaves, the wind gave way to a melodious breeze, and as if touched by magic the moon slowly, lazily began her climb up her ladder of sky.

Elizabeth was too exhausted at the moment to realize—but she was just passing the little old church with the broken steeple and cobblestone steps. She wanted to go in and say a prayer by the little white candle on the organ and play Liszt's Liebestraum but the old door would not open and she knew the key hung by old Adam's front door. Her heart sank – she would not go to him—yet. He—with his stern Quaker ways and his belief that any worldly music was sin. Once she had been married to him—she still was—but the years had cruelly twisted and broken her strong will and at last she had left him for good! For good? Then why was she back tonight—through all this terrible storm? She had often wondered of human bondage. She loved the laughter and gaiety of the world—the little things—dancing, drink, pretty clothes, friends—yet she had come back to him again and again—only for a little while and then the "song of temptation" had called her back and she had gone.

As Elizabeth walked down the road the rain was softly soothing to the earth that she had so mercilessly hurt. Only the sound of the croaking frogs harmonized with patter. Elizabeth felt more gentle now—she knew she could acquiesce to old Adam's ways now—the rain had changed her. It was too beautiful, too strong to feel small or worldly. She smiled a half bitter half musing little twist—she could see him now just as she had seen him also many times before! He would be sitting—staring into the fire—with an eternally unread book upon his lap. How could he think of her so often? How was it humanly possible for one man to have only one thought? Yet she knew it was true and she shrugged her shoulders and sighed. But she mustn't be foolishly inclined now. She had reached the little white picket fence; quietly she unlatched the gate—how familiar it seemed! And the little gravel walk! She tiptoed up to the covered latticed doorway—there hanging on its little hook she felt for the key—he would be inside here—warm and dry—she shivered a little —yet she was scarcely aware of her wet clothing and numbness as she looked through the little window and saw old Adam sitting there —she hurried back to the church—she must play something before she returned to him.

Just as time had changed Elizabeth—old Adam too was transformed. She saw him sitting staring—staring into the fire—she knew he was thinking of her, yet she had never truly penetrated that Puritan mask. His hair was pure white now and his fine straight shoulders slumped a little. He had built that little house for them— with his strong back he had felled trees and hewn the logs and made tables of pine and maple—she had always wanted him to buy her a little melodium—but that was so long ago—and now she knew she would always go and play the organ in the little church and be kind and gentle and patient with him.

Even as Elizabeth thought of all this, she unlocked the old creaking door and felt for a lantern along the wall. She lit it—the old church smelled damp and musty, but the rain sounded cozy pattering on the vaulted ceiling and she walked reverently up to the simple altar with two candles on it and one beside the organ. She lit these and set the lantern down in one of the choir stalls. She took off the heavy wet mantle hanging from her thin shoulders and undid the knot at the back of her head like two moon beams in the candlelight—her braids gleamed as they fell—she pushed them back—these shining braids that dropped below her waist. They were her pride and joy—since she had been a little girl they had been her crown.

She knelt devoutly at one of the stone steps of the little altar. A long time she knelt there quietly—in that peaceful place—and it seemed as if the flickering candles shone upon her very soul and lifted it right out of her. She slowly got up and moved to the organ.

Suddenly Elizabeth was weeping, sobbing as she made the organ wail in beautiful pathetic strains. She played her Liebestraum and as she played the strains of the inspiring melody the beauty of the song filled the church and when at last it was finished and the last sweet notes had died away in the still night she lifted her eyes to the altar and arose. She blew out the waning candles—melted almost to their ends, perhaps her life was that way—but she had burned her lovely candle at both ends and fully taken of the joy and beauty—all that there was of each. She whispered, "good night little church, thank you dear," and closed the door.

The darkness once more enwrapping her in its soft quietness the moon behind a great cloud—all that there was of the beauty of life she loved, yet she was returning she knew now, forever. He would love and cherish her. She would treat him kindly, and her happiness would come from within.

She rapped at the door. "Adam, oh Adam." It was still now. No sound came from within or without—the kind of stillness that whispers the secrets of the night held the little house in suspense and Elizabeth rapped again this time a little impatiently, "Adam." She turned the handle and there he sat—relaxed, the fallen book—he's asleep thought Elizabeth and over in the corner she saw a little harmonium, carved gracefully and perfectly and ivory keys shown in the soft light. Elizabeth caught a sob in her throat, her eyes filled with tears, she tiptoed over to him and said softly, "Adam dear, it's I, Elizabeth come back to you. Speak to me dear one." Two glistening tears fell down her cheek as her voice broke. She sat on his lap and began to stroke his snow white hair. "Oh my husband—hear me, I've come back to you. I always shall be dear, forever." She laid her golden head upon his shoulder. "Oh Adam can you hear me?" Softly, then more firmly, "Adam!" She shook him—a burning log snapped sending a shower of sparks over the hearth and the pieces burned on, glowing. Suddenly Elizabeth was on her knees sobbing hysterically.

Thus she knelt all night long, utterly fatigued and numb, her fatal flax spread upon his knee. And only the wind and the rain and the glowing log knew that in a beautiful dream the knock of a door and his love for flaxen haired Elizabeth had given him eternal peace.

BA Philips

This next story, laced with French language, illuminates Barbara's gift for languages, but also a troubling side. Twenty years in the future she will treat her last husband, Herman, much as Marguerite treats Felix.

Only a Puppet!

Felix held the bottle of ink up to the window—there were four flies in it. Four little black flies and tomorrow there would be five and the next day six and then he would be able to go fishing! Each day Felix had put the half-filled bottle up on the sunny windowsill knowing that one fly would fall into his trap!

"Felix – *venez-ici a' votre diner immediatement!*"

"*Oui-je viens* Marguerite"-

"*Immediatement-stupide-ja'I dit!*"

Poor Felix—he was so henpecked! Tomorrow he would bring Marguerite a bottle of that "*Tre's cher*" Burgundy—that would console her—yes, tomorrow! It would be the last day before he went to Paris! Ah—Paris, with its noise and laughter and gaiety! He could sit on the magnificent stone bridge high—high above the swirling, gushing Seine. How exhilarating Felix felt! Suddenly his little black eyes twinkled. "Marguerite does not even know that I am going—*eh bien*—I shall not tell her! For once I shall be free." Poor Felix, such a puppet in the hands of fate!

"Felix"!

"Je *viens*- Marguerite."

"Oh no you don't—*grote be'te*. I have waited long enough! No dinner you get today"!

"But Marguerite, I was only---"

"It is plenty! I make your dinner, I tell you it is ready, do you come? No! No! No!!" She screamed and slammed the door. She opened it again—her widespread apron encircling her pillowy figure entirely filled the doorway. She held Felix's dinner in one hand and a knife and fork and spoon in the other. With an angry toss of her cabbage head she snorted, "Here is your dinner *Monsieur*," and with all her might Marguerite threw the plate of food at Felix. Nimble little Felix jumped aside and the plate sailed through the window, crashing window and plate into a thousand tiny pieces. But this was not all for when Marguerite saw she had missed her mark she lifted on high her other great arm and ringing through the mountain air ran sound of knife and fork and spoon hitting the bottle of ink and sending it far, far below. Felix watched his little blue bottle roll down, down the mountain. Two big tears rolled down, down his cheek and on the windowsill round and dark was a puddle of ink with one fly in it.

"Au Marguerite" said Felix quietly, "I am going to milk the goat."

"*Au revoir* Felix. I shall wash the dishes, and Felix" –

"*Oui?*"

"Madame Crosier said she saw you renting a bicycle this morning—you did not tell me—what was it for, pray"?

"Hm-m-m---"

"Come—come you are not planning a trip to Paris, pray"? said Marguerite sarcastically. "You cannot go Felix. You are a bad man—no, I will not let you go!"

"Marguerite, I go to milk the goat." Quietly, prolonging each guttural sound of "goodbye" Felix left and his wife stared after him in wide-eyed astonishment, mumbling to herself, "My thees ees diff' erent Felix!"

Felix had walked down—down through the pretty little village of "Chambourg in the Alps"—now he passed a gushing bubbling little mountain stream with a wild deer timidly nibbling the dewy grass. Dainty orange and yellow Edelweiss covered the mountainside and all the turquoise sky met the snowy peaks like great opals in the sunlight.

Felix thought: This is my home. I love this castle high above, but I shall go to Paris for a little while—just a little while.

Now he was at the foot of the mountain, at the tiny "ville" of Roquebain. "For how many francs can I rent this byc, Jean?" Felix asked.

"Oh *c'est dix francs pour uous mon ami*," answered the old byc shopkeeper with a grin.

"*Merci–merci* Jean *mais—*"

"Are you going to Paris, Felix?"

"*Oui, maintenant.*"

"But *pourquoi*, Felix—Marguerite has not sent you away with her frying pan?" Jean said with a prying grin.

"*Non*–oh *non*" said Felix. "I am going fishing on the bridge of Avignon!" And he started hopping about and singing the reel that all the French peasants know. "*Sur le pont d'Avignon, oui* Jean, all my life I wish to go there and today is the perfect one—tomorrow—no, no, this is it Jean!"

"But Felix, you have no line, no pole."

"It matters not – I am gone aurevoir Jean, demain, I bring back your byc—yes?

"*Bon jour-mon pauvre* Felix you will not return—*jamais, jamais*— no Felix, you are too stupid, *mais mon Dieu. Quelle imagination* !!" Jean muttered to himself.

Felix was far, far out of sight, around the curve of the mountain, down to the cruel Seine with her magenta stick watchtowers and "*le pont d' Avignon*"!

"Gringot, Gringot, where is your master? Did he not milk you this morning? How could it be! *Grosse bete.*"

"Felix, *ou est-il,* Felix!!!" Marguerite called in her most vociferous voice to the shaggy black goat. But Gringot only bleated and ran far away into the daisies and wildflowers.

"Felix, Felix," called Marguerite.

"Felix, Felix" faintly echoed from the mountains and Marguerite went slowly into the cottage on the side of the hill sadly shaking her head and wiping a tear away with the corner of her apron.

Felix had ridden many miles since he bade farewell to Jean and he was very tired when he finally reached "Paris" one evening when all the lights were just beginning to twinkle and the million stars above him were reflecting those little lights in the greatest city in the world that little Felix with such a wooden head had wanted to see all his life. He wandered down the magnificent avenues with trees on either side and many times was almost hit by a cabby in his dazed wonderment.

"Get out of the way you fool!!!" Yelled one young rascal and Felix not saying a word turned slowly to the sidewalk. A policeman bellowed at him, "No bicycles there dumbbell," and like a little mouse crawling into his hole he hurriedly went to the side of the street, in the gutters.

Finally, he crossed the Seine and peering far down into the black cavernous, swirling waters he was overcome almost to the point of losing his balance! "Felix, Felix, go down into that emptiness it is beautiful—it makes you forget—there is no Marguerite there. Go Felix quickly. Go!" a voice spoke to Felix, he jumped and peered about but saw only the big streetlamps and a few passersby. He hopped on his bicycle and in a minute was on the other side of Paris. The bad, gay, noisy side of Paris. Laughter and drink filled the streets. People were out in open cabarets sitting at little tables—sipping wine, smiling eyes. Felix did not care for this. He shunned it and quickly passed into a section along the riverbank of millions of little book stalls. He got off his bicycle and slowly walked past these little marketplaces full of musty old books. He nodded to one little wizened up old shopkeeper and took the courage to ask, *"bon soir Monsieur* – could you tell me where *isle pont d'Avignon"*?

Felix was on the bridge of Avignon. All his life he had seen himself sitting on it, pictured it—dreamed of it. Seen old-fashioned peasant folk dancing on it, singing *"sur le pont d'Avignon."*

This was an old bridge—all the columns crumbling away like castles built upon sand—almost too frail to step on, this skeleton structure. Felix stood triumphant, perched precariously on the edge in the center of the great bridge.

"Look Felix, down there the great rushing river—you are dizzy, do not fall yet—yet—a while, awh!

The great cavernous torrent swept onward—a little fly in a bottle of ink—swept seaward and on the bridge stood hundreds of gay peasants singing "sur le pont." Forevermore!

"Dix francs, children, *dix francs,"* shouted the fat little man ringing a bell. *"Le theatre des puppets est fini, dix fancs, dix francs."*
Barbara Ann Philips

There is a third story—quite a lengthy one. I share an excerpt:

The Millstream

... He had always been making trips to distant places she dreamed of that he called the West Indies and China and the Orient. He always brought her fascinating things. Little ivory carvings and mysterious smelling little bottles and shawls that he laughingly told her she must wear when she was grown to a young woman and must look as beautiful as her Mother (for her Mother had died when she was too young to remember.)

Then one day Daddy had stooped to kiss her goodbye and he had told her that he was going farther than he had been before and so would take a little longer. But he had told Anne not to worry for he wouldn't be so very much longer and if it was too long than she must wait and see him in a distant land where they would both be just as happy as they were now. Then he had tried to smile his carefree smile and he had rumpled her curly golden locks the same color as his—but there were tears in his eyes when he kissed her goodbye.

Anne had waited so long for her Daddy that one day when the river told her that she must wait a little and then she would see both Daddy and Grandfather she cried her little heart out. For suddenly she understood all the deep assuring song that the river was singing her and she knew that she was all alone in the world.

In all three stories the man—an older man—dies. There is no mother figure in two of the stories and in the third, she is dead. Was Barbara struggling unconsciously with memories of a molester from her childhood? Poetry is a window into our soul— our unconscious. I selected this poem from several Barbara wrote the autumn of her senior year. I think it best reveals the angst she was living with.

Somber Dreaminess

If our dreams could remain
As reflections still and
Calm—
We would then be as a lake,
Filled with dewdrops
after rain.
But a life with naught amiss,
Never comes but far
Away—
Seeing beyond ever-changing
Horizons,
Other worlds than this.
As a great Aurora, flaming
in the East,
Our lives, our deaths, all
our very breaths
As sparks fly upward—forevermore

Barbara's borderline personality disorder signs grew, and her academic performance suffered. Old documents indicate that she transferred back and forth between two high schools her senior year: Darien High School, Thomas School, and in the spring of 1937, back to Darien High. The only window into Barbara's life during this time was through Elsie's diary. Elsie's writings also show how the Philips family lived during the latter part of the Great Depression.

Elsie wrote, on the cover page of her 1937 diary, *With a song in her heart and a lantern in her hand*—perhaps a line from a Bess Streeter Aldrich novel. As I previously mentioned, Idalia, Elsie's mother, moved from home to home to live with each of her five children. At the beginning of the year, the Philips family was in Darien, Connecticut, and Idalia joined them for a time.

From Elsie's diary:

Friday, January 1: *A rather quiet New Year's Day we all accomplished much in a.m. Went for long walk, Henry, Gram, and I, warm and balmy. To New Canaan with Polly to visit.*

Saturday, January 2: *I went early in the a.m. to see Martel Thomas [Thomas School headmistress]—very strange after so long a time, rather depressing. But I think she'll take Barbara back. We spent a miserable afternoon in Stamford in the rain shopping while Barbara took her music lesson. In the evening we all went to "Come and Get It."*

Monday, January 4: *Barbara started back to Thomas: after nearly 3 years away. Beautiful morning – I think she's very glad to go. She bumped into Jeannie and Muffy right away and felt at home. It's going to be very hard for us to swing it, but worthwhile, I think. In the evening we dismantled the Christmas tree, etc. another year begins we're full of high hopes.*

Tuesday, January 5: *Wrote out checks to pay bills— wonderful feeling first time long time. I've been able to. Gram is going to help me pay Barbara's tuition. I had to dash to bring Barbara from Thomas. She's not so happy about it tonight. Mimi came to cheer her up.*

Thursday, January 14: *We are so worried about Barb. She is overworked and depressed. Change to Thomas hasn't done her a bit of good and seems to be only harm.*

Friday, January 15: *A very rainy day. Gram in bed trying to avoid a cold. Read "Gone with the Wind." Sewed my skirt and late in the day went to see Miss Thomas. Barb's schedule is too heavy. She thinks she has to make up too much and wants to go back to the Darien High. We had a two-hour session, but Mabel tried to hang on to us. Barb went to Mimi's for the night.*

Sunday, January 17: *A wonderfully fine weekend. Henry and I took Gram to church. Pol couldn't go because Ruthie was coming over and Barb had to study. Thomas doesn't seem to be working out. Too much studying to do. After dinner Barb and I hurried to Stamford for the Joseph Leirime Concert, our first together. He was superb. We had fine seats and only paid one dollar. The five of us had a nice little Sunday night supper before the fire and Gram goes to Nick's tomorrow.*

Monday, January 18: I went to Euthenics class. It does me much good. After luncheon I helped Gram pack to get off for Dottie's and Nick's. Back to argue with Miss Thomas again about Barb transferring schools. It's such a problem.

Tuesday, January 19: Ironed in a.m. Barb at home. Too tired to go to school.

Wednesday, January 20: I sewed madly getting Barb's green dress finished to wear to New York on the 11:40. I drove her to Stamford—Eugenie met her there and they went off beaming. We listened to Roosevelt's second inauguration and we returned in a blinding snowstorm. Tutored the boys then home with the snow very deep. Barb came out with Henry. She reported a thrilling time. She loved the Opera. Her first – Tristan and Isolde Flagstad and Melchior. All her Thomas school friends called her and begged her to stay at Thomas but I'm afraid she can't. It's too hard for her and she can't sacrifice her music.

Friday, January 22: Barb started back to Darien High today. Such a time as she has had making up her mind. Poor child, she is certainly going through mental throes—pretty brave to go back and face the music. Polly, the dear thing went to the Hop with Skip and I guess they had a good time. Life is so full of problems for the young. Barb went to the last dancing lesson. I made cocoa for them when they came home, and they played ping-pong until 1:30 AM.

Tuesday, January 26: Took Barb and Pol and Mimi to "Garden of Allah" in Technicolor, fairly well-done. Barb very cross in the evening. She is having a struggle. I think she'll have to work it out herself.

Thursday, January 28: Barb had a tantrum for no good

*reason. I was awfully upset. Pol and I went to Francie's for
tea. Then met Henry and went to Ostrander's for dinner
home and to bed, exhausted.*

Thirty years later, Barbara recounted her childhood with a
different perspective. In this letter, written just before Christmas
1968 while I was in Great Lakes Naval Hospital, Barbara
attempted to manipulate her mother through childhood
memories.

Saturday, December 7, 1968 Today is Pearl Harbor Day
    Dearest Mother, I am writing to you on the children's
school paper because I want you to think of me as a little
girl and how kind and good and thoughtful, I was to you. No
child could have been sweeter nor more pleasing to her
mother. My, how proud you were to show me off to your
friends! And how you loved to listen to me, your oldest
daughter, play your favorite Chopin pieces on the piano! I
do not believe any of this has changed; and I hope you still
remember all our happy times together—during this Holiday
season.
    I am asking your forgiveness for not having written to
you more often during this past year. As you forgive me, the
Lord will bless you. I think I can explain and analyze why
you have not received more letters from me.
    We all read the headlines from the president on down
that the casualties in Vietnam are serious. With Wendell in
the Navy, I am very sure that you understand how worried I
was about him. Even when he was in training for the River
Assault Squadron. I had never had a son in battle before, I
am sure these times worried me. The battle that Wendell
was in was really fierce.
    Did you mail Wendell a Money Order that was returned

to you? How wonderful it would be if you could turn this Money Order over to me today....

When I was wounded in Vietnam in August 1968, I was shipped to an army hospital in Japan and I called Elsie to let her know I was not critically injured. I contacted her because there was no phone at the farm in Minnesota for me to reach home. Elsie sent me a money order which I never received. How Barbara learned about it is a mystery, but that letter reveals an interesting layer of Barbara's illness; her created memories of a fond childhood and her ability to leverage my injuries into asking Elsie for money.

Back to Elsie's 1937 diary:

Friday, January 29: *Beautiful warm winter day. I made the rounds of 12 poor families and home by 3:30. Pol, Henry, and I went to Nick and Dot's for dinner. Barb stayed home alone—such a phase as she's going through!*

Saturday, January 30; *I finished my baby calls, then to Marie's and Ralph's for cocktails. Henry and I had dinner at the Warner's then to the train to meet Barb and Pol and home for coffee and a little contract. We stayed up too late getting involved with Barb, who slept with me all night—we both felt better.*

Thursday, February 11: *Took Barb, Pol, and Mimi to "Lloyd's of London" in Stamford. Wonderful film. They all loved it.*

Friday, February 12: *Lincoln's birthday. Nice to have Henry home for the day. Took Barb to Mimi's for the night. Then Pol and I knitted by the fire while Henry read us "Kipling's School Days," charming evening.*

Mimi and Barbara were inseparable at the time, yet seven years later, Barbara will refer to Mimi as, "...that good for nothing Slaughter woman." Barbara's polarized opinions of people were an example of black and white thinking, sometimes referred to as "splitting."

Saturday, February 13: *Took Barb to Stamford for her music lesson and shopped for Valentines.*

Sunday, February 14: *We all gave each other valentines Henry brought us three big red hearts of candy. I brought up breakfast at 10. Then, Henry, Pol, and I went to church in Norwalk. Sat with Gram. Skip carried the cross. Barb and Pol had eight for supper for St. Valentine's Day. Delicious little supper. They set the table to look so pretty. Henry and I went to the movies so they could have more fun.*

Tuesday, February 16: *Preparations for going to town to stay in the Bishop's apartment for a few days – Barb and Pol want to stay by themselves. Though we hate to think we will risk letting them. The girls went with me after school to take some clothes to the needy.*

Saturday, February 20: *We got off nearly an hour late for the city again—Henry, Pol, Barb, Mimi, and I stopped at the apartment, left things there—took girls to shopping district. Pol and I bought a new purple sweater. Then to the Music Box. Pol and Mimi to see "Stage Door" picked up Barb and took her to Carnegie to Myra Hess Concert. Henry and I went to [the movie] Dodsworth. Too realistic—we didn't like it. Then went to the Bartizon Plaza for cocktails. Delicious, felt better all went to "Bird in Hand" for dinner delicious chicken, then took Barb and Mimi to Metropolitan Opera "Rheingold." Saw Barb and Mimi off at midnight for Darien. Dr. Slaughter to meet them.*

Sunday, February 21: *Awakened at 10:30, dashed, dressed, breakfast, and reach St. Bartholomew's in time to hear Paul Sargent roast Roosevelt about trying to make New Deal Supreme Court. Back to apartment, cleaned and packed and were off for the country by 8:30. We had a very bad session with Barb when we got home. She is such a problem. If we could only find the solution!*

Monday, February 22: *Washington birthday. Set out with picnic lunch at 1 o'clock for Greens Farms by the sea. Henry built a fire to keep us warm. I sketched a bit. Barb and Pol read a mystery story—Henry and I walked up and down the beach. All wrote and read after dinner – truly a lovely day one of those almost perfect days!*

Tuesday, February 23: *Took Polly and went to visit Gram at Dottie's for tea. In evening we had another session with Barb – she went to Mimi's and wouldn't come home. Henry and I are so worried about her.*

Friday, February 26: *I picked up Barb and Pol at Darien High and took Barb to Dr. Faucet. He says she's very run down—must take tonic. Very sleepy, snoozed before the fire in the evening.*

Saturday, February 27: *Took Barb to Stamford for music. Quiet evening at home—just the family. Bishop Robert offered us his box at Town Hall Monday night. Philharmonic Symphony—we're all very thrilled.*

Monday, March 1: *Took Barb and Pol to school. We dressed in evening gowns, had dinner, picked up Mimi, and drove into Town Hall. Box for Philharmonic—Yella Pessl played Bach on the harpsichord and it was beautiful—St. Thomas choir sang.*

Tuesday, March 2: *Barb should be away at school—she would accomplish so much more. I took Gram's tray up and we visited until noon.*

As I mentioned earlier, Elsie had spent much of her childhood away from home, in private schools, so apparently assumed that was the most productive avenue to education for children. Interesting bit of history: In 1938 Yella Pessl accompanied the von Trapp Family Singers, the family made famous in the time-less classic *Sound of Music* (1965).

Saturday, March 6: *Barb went to Mimi's for the night and Henry and I went to the Warner's and had our usual very jolly evening and I discussed social problems.*

Sunday, March 28: *Dearest Pol's birthday. Easter Sunday —a lovely family day. Gram in her zenith because she had all her family with her—a cold day but we all wore our new Easter things. Polly's sweetness kept us all warm. We were late to church and sat in the front pew. All the Fratts came to dinner. Barb went to Jean Rarick's for tea looking very gorgeous in her new green Easter outfit—she missed Easter dinner with us because of her music lesson.*

Tuesday, March 30: *Barb took Henry to the train— everybody fights to drive the new convertible Ford. Barb practices on the piano incessantly.*

Sunday, April 4: *We moved the piano to the next floor down and so we spent the day making a studio out of the room for Barb. She worked on her concert for 10 hours.*

Thursday, April 8: *We four wanted to go out to dinner together but Barb was mean about it. She never has time to do anything with the family, even eat. she spoiled it for me.*

Tuesday, April 13: *Barb still at the piano at midnight.*

I discovered this note draft Elsie wrote to Barbara's piano teacher:

Dear Mrs. Hedner, We are having difficulty to keep Barbara from practicing from three in the afternoon until twelve midnight on school nights and in order to settle the matter will you kindly settle the matter ...stating how many hours daily she should practice before starting her schoolwork.

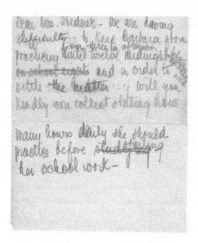

Wednesday, April 21: *We drove to town early in the morning and spent the entire day shopping for Barb's debut Musicale frock and also for her high school graduation. Gram loved it and gave Barb her dress.*

Saturday, May 1: *Barb's day!!! Everything went quite smoothly. I took Henry to the 8:38 Stamford and got all of my shopping done by 11. Felt fresh and found everything I wanted—finished getting things ready for the guests. Barb got off nicely to have dinner with Lois Hedner and then to dress together. Sixteen guests came here to dinner. Dear Barb played beautifully. She really made quite a triumph and looked adorable in the dress Gram gave her. Later she played accompaniments for Mr. Murray's singing—it was a very pretty reception.*

Monday, May 3: *Gram and I had luncheon outside. We had to take Barb to Stamford at four to play for some Women's Club, we went on down, saw the beautiful Japanese Cherries. In evening Barb and I went to see a tutor for Barb to go to "V. C." [Vassar College].*

Barbara Philips piano recital. Darien, Connecticut. (1937)

A tutor? How much had Barbara slipped since she was nominated for the "Academically Talented Class" honor program at Thomas School a few years earlier? Moving from one school to another and then back was a lot for a teenager to handle. Did she find an escape in her music and ignore homework, as Elsie had written to Barbara's piano instructor?

From Elsie's diary, we see that Barbara and Polly attending Vassar College was a foregone conclusion—for their mother.

May 7: *Vassar College. Lovely bright day. Gram, Barb, Polly, and I drove to Vassar. Lunched at Carey's then were conducted about Skinner Music Hall and met Miss Thomson in admissions at exactly 3:30. She was very charming and encouraging. Barb had a grand visit with her and was so enthused. Then we went about campus a bit. Visited the wonderful new gym—put the convertible top*

down—it wouldn't go all the way and we looked so funny.
Barb drove most of the way home. Had dinner at a nice inn
on the way. Got home about nine after a very successful
day. All the greens just budding out were so lovely.

 Saturday, May 8: Barb worked on College Boards and
went to Greenwich with Mimi. Barb brought Mimi back for
the night.

 Thursday, June 17: Barb graduates from High School—
she isn't a bit happy about it.

Why was Barbara not happy about graduating? More than
eighty years later, I watched my granddaughter Kadance—
Barbara's great granddaughter—prepare for her senior year and
how excited she was. Why was Barbara upset? Did she not
achieve her high school goals? Was she battling depression from
her break-up with Bruce? Concerned about the impending life
changes? Why weren't there any entries about graduation festivi-
ties? Was Barbara overwhelmed with her Vassar College
entrance exams? Or was it a combination of several things going
on in her life?

 Friday, June 25: Dear Barb finished her last college board.
Pol and I shopped for her, got her a new hat and swimsuit.
By 12:30 she was off for Jean Ruggles in Rye looking as
though she had just stepped out of a band box—pretty as a
picture. Excellent for her if she can stand it.

When Barbara received a rejection letter from Vassar
College, Elsie must have been stunned. In hindsight, it should
not have been a surprise, considering how Barbara bounced back
and forth between schools her senior year as she struggled academically. Elsie no doubt lashed out at Barbara, at her daughter's
failure, reinforcing Barbara's sense of abandonment.

34. Indicate below for each daughter who has completed high school, whether she has gone to Vassar, other college, or did not go to college.

	Oldest	Second	Third
Vassar	☐ 1	☐ 1	☐ 1
Other girls' college...	☑ 2	☑ 2	☐ 2
Co-ed college	☐ 3	☐ 3	☐ 3
Vassar and other undergraduate college.	☐ 4	☐ 4	☐ 4
Did not go to college.	☐ 5	☐ 5	☐ 5

35. IF NOT VASSAR, why not? *Barbara Ann. tried to enter too young—16. Should have been discouraged by Joe Gleason—was brilliant student. music also.*

* Opinion question. Use appended sheets for your comments.

Katharine chose to specialize.

(33-41)

Thirty-seven years later, on September 17, 1973, Vassar sent out a biographical update to the Class of 1915. In response to question 35, asking why Elsie's daughters didn't attend Vassar, Elsie wrote, "Barbara Ann tried to enter too young—16. Should have been discouraged by Joe Gleason. [Barbara] was a brilliant student—music also. [Vassar rejection] Ruined her life."

Thursday, July 15: *Polly, Barb, and I went to Dottie's to luncheon. Farewell for Gram; she leaves for Seattle [Washington]. The first time Barb has been out in months. She is so eccentric. What a problem!*

It was the summer Amelia Earhart disappeared in the mid-Pacific while attempting to circumnavigate the globe. That historical event wasn't mentioned in Elsie's 1937 diary—she had greater worries. The July 15 notation was the final entry. The chickenhouse documents held few clues as to what happened that summer. As I mentioned earlier, Elsie revisited her old letters decades after she had written them. I found this note attached to a letter Elsie had written to her mother in 1937:

When you [Idalia/Gram] went west [July 1937] I would much rather have had you stay here. I knew I needed you badly because you yourself knew that Barbara had already become ill. It was just a few weeks after you left that she tried suicide. But I couldn't beg you to stay.

That was Barbara's first documented suicide attempt. Did the Vassar College rejection drive her over the edge, or was it a culmination of failures, including the break-up with Bruce? As I searched for answers, I came across this next note. On October 22, 1956, Elsie wrote in her Mental Health Diary:

Barbara, it is now 20 years (1936-37) since you threw away your attractive personality because of a maladjusted adolescent boy who had a chip on his shoulder because his father went off and left his mother destitute with two little boys to bring up. You withdrew from people and you changed your whole personality from loving people to hating people when you were just sixteen—just three years older than Chris [Barbara's oldest son] is now. Hating people has never done anybody any good but most especially it hurts the person who hates.

Elsie blamed others for Barbara's problems: Joe Gleason at Vassar, Idalia for leaving, and Barbara, but Elsie never reflected on her own possible shortcomings.

1937-09-24 EUROPEAN SOJOURN

Six weeks after Barbara's suicide attempt, Elsie and her two daughters set sail for Europe. On September 16, 1937, Robert Lewis Paddock, the Episcopalian Bishop, wrote:

> Dear Elsie, I'm glad to hear that my letter to Barb helped a little. Enclosed find a check of $200 for Barb's schooling. It's a gift. I never make a loan. I hope you three have a wonderful trip. I'll try to see Henry once in a while and comfort him in his loneliness. God bless you all. Your Devoted Uncle Robert

In the chickenhouse, folded in half, tucked inside a scrapbook, I discovered this photo of a seventeen-year-old girl. Lifeboat resting in the davits behind her, she stands on the weather deck of the SS *American Farmer* in New York Harbor. The photo is stamped PROOF, NEWS EVENTS PHOTO SERVICE, PULITZER BUILDING, and dated September 24, 1937. I studied her face for the longest time, trying to imagine what was going through her mind.

Barbara Philips, on board the ship, SS *American Farmer*, in New York Harbor (September 24, 1937)

She was four months beyond high school graduation and less than two months past her suicide attempt. Note the trappings of affluence: Barbara's chin is tucked into the fur collar of a calf-length suede coat. Her almond eyes hint coyness highlighted by a tiny smirk dimpling her full cheeks. A Marlene Dietrich stovepipe tilt-style hat perches at a saucy angle. Black netting halos a fresh perm. She has a light fur, fox perhaps, draped over her left arm with a folded lap-robe beneath. A small clutch is tucked snugly under her right arm. It may be a chilly afternoon because her folded, gloved hands hug her stomach.

Elsie started a new diary. [For the complete European narrative, including diaries, scrapbooks, and pictures, you can Google

"Wattpad," *Chickenhouse Chronicles, European Sojourn.*] Some excerpts in this narrative illustrate Barbara's frame of mind and her relationship with her mother.

Friday, Sept. 24: New York City SS *American Farmer*

We left the dear little home on Five Mile River [Darien, Connecticut] exactly at noon without too much trouble getting off. Henry has been wonderful; all the help he has given us when he hates so to see us go. Barb has been almost better than I had hoped for—at least not baling too much or being too unpleasant, and dear Pol has been perfect—working like a Trojan and so happy and excited about going. We picked up Mimi and reached New York to have luncheon with the Bishop, who has been so marvelous about assisting us to get off, at one thirty. At two-thirty we started for the boat and got awfully nervous trying to get through the bad mid-afternoon traffic to the pier.

We were finally on board at about three thirty, with more baggage than ten people should have. Many friends came to the boat, beside many telegrams and packages— everyone had to leave long before the boat sailed—We were three hours late in sailing. We steamed out of New York Harbor by twilight and could see hardly anything—missed

*the Statue of Liberty so I haven't yet seen it. We are invited
to sit at the Captain's table— (Uncle Horace Philips) no
doubt.*

*Sat, Sept 25, 1937: Second Day. Barb is very seasick.
The stewardess is taking care of her.*

*Mon, Sept 27, 1937: Fourth day out. A perfectly
beautiful day–warm and sunny. The Gulf Stream. We got
Barb out for the first time. She simply reclined in her chair all
day while everyone else played games and had a gay time.*

The three women spent a few days in London with Henry's
cousin Eloise Garstin and then crossed the English Channel and
visited Paris before traveling to Brussels where they were going
to live. Barbara began to distance herself from Elsie and Polly.

*Sun, Oct 10, 1937: Bruxelles [Brussels]! Barb went skating
by herself. Mary Ann, Polly, & I walked to the Port Louise
and had chocolate at a darling little place. The pastry is
marvelous but quite expensive. Dinner in the Pension—very
nice. It's really a lovely place. Barb ordered breakfast for 7
a.m. so that she could go to Mary Ann's to practice [piano].*

*Tue, Oct 12, 1937: Pension a` Bruxelles Barb had
breakfast brought in at 7 o'clock as usual. Then set out for
Mary Ann's Aunt's to practice. Dear Polly went with me and
we walked all day looking for an apartment. We covered the
whole town. We saw one darling belonging to a Baron
which we would like to take, $35 a month and it's a Baronial
palace. Barb is very ugly and disagreeable. She has started
to study with Monsieur Bosquet, one of the heads of the
Conservatory, and it seems to upset her.*

*Tue, Oct 19, 1937: Barb is working too hard on her
music. Three people arrived at dinner time to complain.
Barb was very insolent to them and we had a most
unpleasant evening. She first quarreled badly with Polly and*

then with me, then slept, cried herself to sleep & slept 14 hours.

Sat, Oct 23, 1937: *We begged Barb to come to the opera with us, but she was only ugly and slapped and kicked me and made me feel terribly for the afternoon. I can't stand much more of it. It's worse than I expected. Polly and I tried to do things downtown, but I felt too terribly. Barb certainly has something terribly vital the matter with her.*

Tue, Oct 26, 1937: *Barb started at 8 a.m. When she's up so late I don't see how she does. I did housework all day long. There's much work to taking care of and keeping house for my two darlings. Only one a darling. The other a constant worry.*

Barbara's mood swings are interesting—also the intense schedule she keeps, constantly on the run. Studies show a correlation between borderline personality disorder and sleep problems. Was that one of Barbara's issues—sleep deprivation?

Personality disorders, mood disorders, and thought disorders have many overlapping signs. Today, mental health professionals acknowledge that there is a lack of scientific data to support many theories about mental illness. In 1937, the world's lack of knowledge was staggering.

For example, in 1941, Rosemary Kennedy, John F. Kennedy's sister, had a lobotomy to correct her violent mood swings and seizures. The operation damaged her brain, and she was institutionalized for life. (She died in 2005.) In the 1930s, other options were institutional commitment, insulin shock therapy, and electroshock therapy.

Wed, Oct 27, 1937: *Walked to Polly's school to pay a thousand francs on her tuition. Stayed and had tea with Mr. & Mrs. Scovell. They are both charming. Polly loves the school. I'm so glad for her. Barb goes out every night and stays out so late. I suppose she goes to concerts, but I wish I knew where. Oh! When will she come out of this!*

Wed, Nov 3, 1937: *We now have dinner at noon so as to get some into Barb. It seems to work very well. These days are too divine—warm and sunny.*

Sat, Nov 6, 1937: *Barb brought breakfast to Mary Ann, Polly, and me. The first time she has. I asked her to—but she didn't eat with us. Polly and Mary Ann went skating in the A.M. When Polly came back, we went marketing together then had a late dinner. Barb didn't eat with us.*

Elsie's observation of Barbara's eating habits brings up another manifestation of borderline personality disorder. Did Barbara struggle with bulimia nervosa and binge eating?

Sun, Nov 28, 1937: *In the evening we had a terrible struggle with Barb. She was her very worst. Too tired—she had worked too hard.*

Mon, Nov 29, 1937: *Such an interesting day. Barb invited a French opera singer to luncheon. We had such a jolly time with her. She sings and laughs all the time. Barb traded all her clothes and jewelry with her.*

Tue, Nov 30, 1937: *Barb thinks the French lady stole fifty francs from her. We decided not to accuse her but when she comes this eve to go to the opera with Barb, Barb is going to try to sell her an old green dress for fifty francs. It worked.*

Barbara's accusation of the French lady stealing fifty francs is the first recorded incident that will repeat itself in the future. Impulsive spending is a feature of borderline personality disorder, as is deception. Did Barbara spend the money and then blame her friend for the theft?

December 1, 1937: *Such a day with Barb. She does not seem to improve. Whatever shall I do with her? She sets upon Polly and me whenever she feels like it for no good reason. Mary Louise de Groote went with me, and we discussed the best thing to do with her with M. B. [Mansour Bosquet, Barbara's instructor at the Conservatoire.] He didn't seem to have a very good solution except that he is going to do his best to make her cut down her hours of work, eat more regularly, change occupations, and sleep more. After French class I went for coffee with a girl from Baltimore. She has been to Johns Hopkins and has the university here. I'm going to try for it for Barb.*

The December 1 entry is very revealing of how Elsie records several issues that are plaguing Barbara: Rage, work—practicing piano too many hours per day, lack of sleep, possible eating disorder. Barbara struggled with her weight and fluctuated from being very slim to very "weighty" as Elsie described her in 1939. The second sentence, "She does not seem to improve" suggests ongoing violent behavior.

Thur, Dec 2, 1937: *I mustn't take coffee any more at night because I am not sleeping so well—worry over Barb, I guess. We seem to be making no progress with her happiness. She has everything she wants in the way of music and yet she is not happy.*

Sat, Dec 4, 1937: *Barb asked for beef steak, so I got her some in spite of turkey dinner tonight. Shopped in afternoon mostly for Barb—bought her a Brussels lace collar for her black velvet dress. She played the piano late, so we taxied to the Meyers for dinner.*

Tue, Dec 7, 1937: *Uncle Horace is better. Barb is not. She wouldn't write a Christmas note to her father. I'm beside myself to know what to do to cure her of her mental unhappiness. Met dear Polly and her friends downtown and it cheered me a lot.*

Sun, Dec 12, 1937: *Barb asked me to go to Philharmonic, Jacques Thibaud, guest artist—so I went and enjoyed it very much. Then we came home to a delicious chicken dinner. Barb didn't eat hers until it was cold—then asked Polly to go to Fedora with her.*

Fri, Dec 17, 1937: *Barb troubles me again today—I never cease worry about her. I think I'll see the Minister next.*

Sun, Dec 19, 1937: *Barb walked out just as we sat down [to dinner]. Wouldn't eat any & went to concert. I followed but didn't go in because they wanted 30 francs for standing room—far too much. Then went to "Captains Courageous" & it had gone so went back to Palais de Beaux Arts & went to Drole de Drame. Not so funny to me. Polly & I had a cute little supper. I'm going to look for a student pension [boarding house] for Barb.*

Sun, Dec 26, 1937: *Barb was so villainous that I decided not to come home all day. Went to the Anglican Church we were supposed to go to Xmas eve. Returned home at eight on the bus.*

Thur, Dec 30, 1937: *Barb so disagreeable again. I stayed "en ville" [in the city] in the pouring rain until I was put out of everywhere. Went to the English Tea room—very expensive. Bought material for Polly's dress. Home wet and discouraged about eight o'clock. Felt better when I was warmed up. Had a little Medoc wine.*

Fri, Dec 31, 1937: *I went en ville & got tickets for us for "Tovaritch" this New Years' Eve. It was superb, and I was so overjoyed to be able to get Barb to go. The first thing non-musical since she's been here. The grand Salle was beautiful, everyone very dressy. The play superbly acted by the best Parisian Actor and Actress. We laughed and laughed.*

1938

January 1, 1938: *"Another New Year is dawning."* Barb has been on the piano every moment of this long holiday season.

Tue, Jan 4, 1938: *Barb doesn't go out so much these cold nights. I'm glad she hasn't had a tantrum in ages. I think she's slightly better. Barb plays divinely. I listened most of the afternoon. Polly came home from Mary Ann's about seven and we had a feast. It snows all the time now and is nasty. I read L'Abby Constentine almost all night.*

Sat, Jan 8, 1938: *A very pleasant evening. Barb went out just before we had supper.*

Sun, Jan 9. 1938: *Barb and I went to see again Stokowski who is so wonderful. I treated to hot dogs.*

Tue, Jan 11, 1938: *These winter days are not pleasant, and Barb is more disagreeable than ever. She's nearly killing herself working. She went to Antwerp today for a concert and said nothing to us about it.*

Thur, Jan 13, 1938: *Made plans to move and now Barb doesn't want to.*

Fri, Jan 14, 1938: *Barb is worse every day. Today had 100 franc book sent up C.O.D. from music store. I had to pay it with my milk money—said nothing. Cried a bit at which she threw my purse at me, metal handle hit me in the eye almost put it out. I have a nice black eye to go to Mrs. Gross's to Tea.*

Sat, Jan 15, 1938: *So discouraged over Barb. She won't let us give up the apartment and yet she doesn't want to stay here.*

Sun, Jan 16, 1938: *Such a thrilling day. After being so discouraged the silver lining came out. After church, the Kusenkmyers, friends of Polly's from Washington Hall, told us about a lovely boarding school in a grand location. Polly and I went right over, and she is going to take Barb for $40 a month with piano included. It's a grand school with about twenty boarder girls from all over Europe. It will be a wonderful experience for Barb, girls from all over, only French is spoken.*

Thur, Jan 20, 1938: *This time dear Polly got out on the wrong side of bed. I had had enough with Barb and when Polly wouldn't go back to school because she would be late, I left and stayed all afternoon. Went to Grace Moore and "When You're in Love," very well done. Felt better when I returned but not much.*

Elsie's coping mechanism when dealing with her daughters was to escape—leave the apartment for hours on end. Quite often over the years, Elsie would go to the theater and escape her realities in the latest movie. Is this what she did when Barbara was a child? 1920s letters hint at Elsie and Henry leaving their daughters with caregivers quite often. A sense of abandonment during childhood is cited as a primary developmental characteristic of borderline personality disorder.

Some readers may question the veracity of my transcriptions because of Barbara's ongoing bad behavior. I've been asked why I didn't just publish the original documents. Most readers will quickly understand why when they begin to read this sample. I spent hundreds of hours deciphering thousands of pages; these pages are actually more legible than many. (B.A. is Barbara Ann.)

Elsie Philips' diary. (January 24, 1938)

Mon, Jan 24, 1938: *Just when I thought Barbara Ann was better, she becomes the worst. Didn't like the fit of a Brussels lace collar I tried all afternoon to make look right on her black velvet—cursed me as she went out. I asked her to be pleasant with such a lovely week of music coming up. She set upon me and would have pounded me to pieces only Polly threw a large pan of dish water upon her. She was dressed to go to the Corbort Concert on which she had spent 150 francs—Corbort's interpretation of Chopin. Then she took the rest of the dish pan and dumped it on Polly. Fled the kitchen and broke some dishes. Never have you seen such a mess. After, she went to the concert one hour late.*

Tues, Jan 25, 1938: *I felt so badly I couldn't cook dinner so we all went to the Family Pension where go all the Persian students from the University. I can't stand these violent attacks by Barb. It doesn't seem as though I should have to but that's the artist and Philips temperament. In the afternoon I went down and bought concert tickets for the Menuens in late April then bought Barb another lace collar.*

Why did Elsie reward Barbara's violent behavior with concert tickets and a new lace collar? Elsie mentioned the "Philips temperament" and was closer than she realized—today we know that genetic vulnerability to mental disease is passed from generation to generation. Research shows there are several gene-environment factors that can create psychosocial stressors that might amplify that vulnerability.

Sun, Jan 30, 1938: *I slept late. I got front row seats for Barb and me for Deleiber Philharmonic with Christmas money. Barb wouldn't tell me when it began and so I missed the first of it—spoiled the great treat. Music lovely. I walked over half the way home.*

Wed, Feb 2, 1938: *Sewed hard putting Barb's clothes in order for her to go to the Boarding School.*

Thurs, Feb 3, 1938: *Lovely day. I stayed at home and enjoyed our lovely apartment for one of the few times when Barb was out.*

Sun, Feb 6, 1938: *Another perfect day. I brought Polly a late breakfast in bed. We went walking about one—had a bite at a delicious pastry shop on Avenue Louise. Then home to enjoy our beautiful room for one of the last times while Barb went to a concert.*

Sat, Feb 11, 1938: *I paid M. Gerard for a month so that now nothing can take away Barb having had a month of French Boarding School. I hope she makes a good go of it. It should be fine for her. Then Polly spent the day in preparation for her Valentine Dinner Dance at school. She and Gerta frosted the cake and made sandwiches. At the last minute Barb nearly ruined it by saying Polly couldn't wear her white dress. Polly stormed and eventually Barb weakened. I told her no more concert tickets if she didn't. So she fixed up Polly and Polly went off happy. Then Barb asked me to take her to "Saratoga" which we did and in between had a bite to eat.*

Mon, Feb 13, 1938: *Did final shopping for Barb to take with her to Droissard Institute.*

Tue, Feb 14, 1938: *Barb got off for Droissard Institute shortly after 11 without the least hitch. I do hope so much it's going to be just the right thing for her and she finds herself there. We are not to see her.*

Tue, Mar 1, 1938: *I took Barb her allowance. I think she is much better. She is beginning to think of someone besides herself. She asked about Polly's birthday.*

Thurs, Mar 31, 1938: *In the evening I went to hear Eduardo del Pueyo play Beethoven's Sonatas. Saw Barb — she looked away, and it made me feel very badly. I wonder how much longer she is going to keep it up. It almost makes me hate music.*

Fri, Apr 15, 1938: *Got Barb's Easter box ready & took it to her, talked with Mme. Gerard. I'm discouraged. I don't think she is much better. Mme. Gerard is going to talk with M. Bosquet.*

Mme. Gerard was the housemother of the girls' boarding-house in Brussels where Barbara lived. After Elsie returned to New York the two women exchanged letters about Barbara.

Sun, Apr 17, 1938: *Easter Day! I was awakened by the arrival of such a beautiful bright red azalea plant from Barb I was overcome with happiness because of her thoughtfulness. Then to brunch with the Lippens. After, George told me about the reading of all the crests [coat of arms] and then back for dinner with them. Later, I took George & his wife to Diana Durbin. I enjoyed it almost more the second time. Then they took me to an ancient tavern— such a curiosity from Knights of old. We had Cherry Beer with a raw egg beaten in it—Lambert's beer. I also saw a wonderful underground parking system for autos—New York should have it.*

Wed, Apr 20, 1938: *Dearest Polly has talked me into going to Paris for four days.*

Twenty-four years after Europe, on April 5, 1962, Barbara wrote this letter [excerpt] to her mother. Did Barbara forget what happened or did she create this memory of abandonment? Elsie's diary has the azalea plant delivered on Easter morning, three days before she and Polly left for Paris. Barbara did not deliver it because Elsie spent the whole day with her friends—no mention of Barbara.

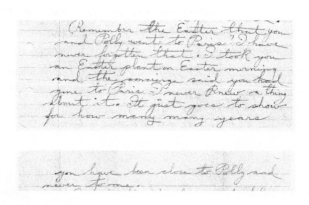

...Remember the Easter that you and Polly went to Paris? I have never forgotten that. I took you an Easter plant on Easter morning and the concierge said you had gone to Paris. I never knew a thing about it. It just goes to show for how many many years you have been close to Polly and never to me.

Barbara's sense of abandonment haunted her more than two decades later.

Sun, May 1, 1938: *May Day. Polly & I had bruncheon about noon, studied and worked and in late afternoon went to Institut Droissard to take Barb her allowance. She was playing when we came in and never have I heard such beautiful music. So finished so advanced. Polly thinks she's much better and enjoying the school a lot.*

Wed, May 11: *Paid $100 to Scovell [for Polly's school]. Pol certainly has enjoyed school here. She will always remember it as a marvelous year. Took clothes to Barb. The Turkish woman advises me not to leave her here at the Conservatoire. Then Barb and I went to have tea with Emile Bosquet. Very pleasant. He talked to her about getting out more and doing more outside things—He may not give her so many lessons. She and I talked afterward but not very satisfactorily.*

Sat, May 14, 1938: *Our last day in Brussels.*

No mention of Barbara—no farewell other than the short visit to her school a few days earlier. For the rest of 1938 and the first half of 1939, I found no correspondence between Barbara and her parents. There must have been some communication because they had to pay tuition, living expenses, and an allowance. I wonder if Barbara just immersed herself in her music?

1939

I n the early spring, the world was drawn to the brink of war as Germany, Italy, and Japan annexed and invaded their neighbors.

This letter, written to Elsie from the boarding house director Mme. Gerard where Barbara was staying, reveals insights to Barbara's state of mind—also how two times, Barbara's possessions disappeared, but were later found. The letter was translated from French so the syntax may be a bit confusing. The envelope has a French postmark on it from 262 Avenue Messidor, Uccle, Brussels, addressed to Mrs. Elsie Philips, 5 Prospect Pl., New York.

Feb 18,1939

Dear Mrs. Philips, you know undoubtedly from Barbara that I have been seriously ill for six weeks and that I have had to come to the country to recover. During this time, I have had good news of Barbara. She was eating very well and was in a good place from the point of view of sociability. Something occurred that spoiled everything. Barbara lost a small object which she was very fond of and which came, I think, from her grandmother—sort of a brooch or small button. She is convinced that someone took it from her and told my friend Mrs. Delchevalerie, who is taking my place that she was going to leave the house, not wanting to stay where people steal. I wrote her a letter to calm her down and told her that I had complete confidence in the three servants that I have at the moment —and that I can't believe that it was theft. She said to us that "if the object is not found in three or four days, she will leave the boardinghouse." This would be from every point of view regrettable. First of all, for Barbara herself, that is, necessary to recognize, you know, I don't know where she would go, in an area that neither you nor I know?

Everyone there thinks well of her, and even though the basis is very good with her, one needs psychology and patience to get along well with her, and that she be happy.

Secondly, it is also too bad for me, as you know. I have always done my best. I have kept in mind her welfare and followed your ideas. I had Barbara during the long vacation (she would always talk about leaving but never left). I kept the house open for her, the housekeeping and servants which was a large source of expenditure for me. Now I am having the greatest of difficulties; I have too few foreign students and each day that passes I lose money.

Wouldn't it be too bad and unfair if she deprived me of yet another boarding student and in such an offensive way? When I was already ill, but still at the school, there's something similar occurred. I heard her say very loudly in the house that someone had taken her cross—she said it to everyone, and the cross was found again some hours later in the cloak room or the bathroom. I will do everything possible to keep Barbara from leaving before she has heard from you. Try to get her to stay until the end of March

(Easter vacation). If she stays a little while, her first reaction will pass, and everything will be all right.

I will wait to hear news from you and send you, dear Mdm., my very cordial regards and my belated though sincere wishes. L. Gerard

Barbara sent Polly a card while on Easter break,

April 17, 1939:

This is the Alps. There is snow every-where but it is not cold. We went to Grasse —the perfume is very nice. You will see (if I get by the Customs today!!!!) There are skiers on all the mountains where it's not melted. Love Barbara

Elsie wrote this next letter to Barbara:

Monday, May 15, 1939

Barb Dear, A year ago today Polly and I left Brussels. It seems so long ago and so very long since we have seen you. I am commencing to worry about your clothes. Have you bought anything that you need at all? I am thinking that your other clothes must be pretty worn out by now. Have you bought any shoes? Have you had any trouble with your teeth? I fear it would cost quite a lot to really put your mouth in good order, but you should have your teeth cleaned anyway and perhaps have some of the most needy work done.

I got Polly a little dark blue and white dotted summer dress in cotton with dark blue jacket to match and she liked it so well I ordered one like it for you. They hadn't another in stock, but it seemed to take you so long to get packages from here I suppose it will be the middle of the summer before it arrives. Gabby Midler expects to go over this summer to see her mother. I will send some things by her so do tell me what you would like and what you need. What size do you wear now? Mlle. Gerard wrote you were dieting —I wonder if you vary as much as Polly—she seems to vary as much as three sizes when she is dieting she was very bad about it this fall and the principal of her school made me take her to a doctor who fortunately prescribed the right thing and she picked up right away. But she dropped down from 18 to 22nd in her class of 32 which made the principal very mad since she was on a very special scholarship supposedly for ability. She is picking up again but will never make good enough marks for college much to the school's grief.

If you plan to study with M Bosquet again next year what do you plan to do this summer? It does not seem as though it is good for you to stay in the school all summer. Do try to answer as many of these questions as you can as soon as you receive this.

We went out to the school to a musical a week ago given by the head of music at the school who is the German Refugee and plays Magnificently.

I think it wonderful you are getting on so well with M Bosquet. Always our deepest love to you, Mother.

JUNE 1939

L ooking back, the warnings Hitler gave the world with his constant lies—beginning with the German military buildup six years earlier—should have prompted leaders to unite against him much sooner. By summer 1939 it was too late. Germany was fully rearmed with a well-trained Wehrmacht (army).

Barbara (left) and Marcel, near Ypres, Belgium. Spring break from school in Brussels. (Spring 1939)

In retrospect, it's easy to ask why Elsie didn't demand that Barbara come home. The armies of Germany and Italy were on the move, yet I wonder if denial or disbelief of impending war is universal. During the summer of 1939, even heads of state did not believe Hitler planned to invade and conquer Europe.

Elsie wrote in her diary:

Monday, June 5, 1939: Queen Mary in. Card from Barb where three girls went. Stayed at the seaside for 13 francs. Took their provisions and stayed near the King's seaside home. Bicycle to Yepres.

JULY 1939

Barbara could not have known, but she was about to embark on an adventure that would have life-long ramifications. She wrote to her mother:

July 6, 1939,

Dear Mother, I hope you will have a very happy birthday. I received your letter yesterday, saying you expected when it arrived, that I would have made plans. I leave tomorrow morning at half past six and neither an answer to my letter relating the projects nor the package of clothing nor the American Express money have arrived. Perhaps you do not want me to go on this voyage [travel through Europe].

I wasted a whole morning going to see Mr. Broy and being sent to talk to the Secretary at the [American] Embassy. They don't know anything more than anyone else, but I assure you Hitler is afraid of the Allies.

The American Express didn't telephone me, but I went down ten minutes before closing time and the forty dollars had come. Naturally Mademoiselle D Decker had offered to lend me as much as I like but I wouldn't have wanted that.

Today I went with them [Mr. and Mrs. Broy] to the French Embassy for the National Fête. They know the Ambassador and Ambassadress very well. It was she who gave me a prize at this Distribution der Prix. If we went to Rome, they would give us a letter to the Pope. We [Barb, Eva, Helena] each bought 10 German Marks (49 francs), 300 Italian Liras (306 francs), 1000 French francs, and about 30 Belgian francs—does that make $40 to you? I also took out the ten dollars that you left there.

The address [where we will be staying] in Poland is Eva Barbacka, NOWY SACZ, CHELMIEC (Pologue) I hope you have a happy birthday, Love, Barbara

Elsie wrote in her diary:

Tuesday, July 11, 1939: *A great red-letter day—I felt fine. Pol and I went to Orchard Beach for the day. Had a wonderful sunning and grand swimming. Henry made a sale to Yale the first in a long time and we had a long letter from Barb telling about her [plans for a] wonderful trip, all over Europe, encircling it for the summer. We answered air mail "Dixie Clipper." One of the first trans-Atlantic crossings.*

In the letter Barbara wrote to her mother, she said, "…I assure you, Hitler is afraid of the Allies." That mindset came directly from the American Embassy in Brussels where Barbara had recently visited. The world was in denial that Hitler planned to regain what had been lost in World War I and to expand his empire.

As a result of Germany's WWI defeat in 1918, Germany had lost Danzig per the Versailles Treaty. By summer 1939, Hitler's Nazi party had infiltrated Danzig's governing body to the point that the German army was in control of the city and surrounding countryside.

After the September 1938 Munich agreement, which forced Czechoslovakia to cede a part of their country along with Sudetenland, which Germany had also lost as a result of their defeat in WWI, Hitler moved forward with his program of aggression. On March 15, 1939, he annexed the remainder of Czechoslovakia, which included Skoda Ironworks, a large weapons manufacturer.

Czechoslovakia shared a border with southern Poland. Hitler was now free to move the German army up to the Polish border from the north, west, and south. Barbara and her friends were about to enter a simmering political cauldron. Elsie mentioned war news a few times in her diary, but the United States was far removed. She saw no risk in Barbara's traveling across Europe. I reconstructed Barbara's travels that summer from chickenhouse documents and interviews I did with Barbara.

Spain — July 15, 1939: The three girls left Paris and traveled by bus to Biarritz, on Spain's border, where they stayed overnight on an Atlantic beach. Barbara said that the Spanish Civil War had just ended, leaving the rebel leader Franco as victor. Hitler had assisted Franco, Barbara recalled. The girls bussed down into Spain. They must have spent a few days at a lodge because Barbara recalled riding on a mule or donkey up into the Pyrenees Mountains.

Marseille — July 18, 1939: Barbara, Eva, and Helena arrived in Marseille, where they stayed for three days and visited many cathedrals. Barbara told me that Marseille had been a famous Mediterranean seaport in early days. The girls visited Nice, walked through acres of flowers, and visited perfume manufacturers. She said they gambled while in Nice, but it was probably at their next stop, Monaco, where they visited a gated castle, and Monte Carlo.

Rome — July 22, 1939: While visiting Vatican City the girls saw Pope Pius XII on the balcony. Barbara recalled that Eva and Helena knelt. The girls visited the Sistine Chapel. Seventy years later, Barbara spoke almost reverently about the Michelangelo art and in Milne, the famous Last Supper painting by Leonardo De Vinci.

Venice — July 26, 1939: In Venice, Barbara recalled the canals in which they rode gondolas. The girls had their picture taken in front of St. Mark's Basilica. This was the end of the bus tour, and Helena left the group and returned to her family in France.

Printed as a postcard, the snapshot is dated,

(26 Juillet [July] 1939)

From left to right: Barbara Philips, Eva Barbacka, Helena Janowski in front of St. Mark's Basilica.

Czechoslovakia — July 28, 1939: Eva and Barbara traveled by train through Austria to Czechoslovakia. Barbara recalled the Nazi guards at the border—how they were very strict. Hitler had annexed Czechoslovakia in March 1939. Barbara recalled that guards traveled on the train with the passengers through Czechoslovakia to the Polish border. The girls changed trains and traveled on to Eva's home, to the town of Nowy Sacz.

AUGUST 1939

Nowy Sacz, the village near where Barbara lived on the Barbacka farm was in southern Poland, not far from the Czechoslovakian border. Located in the Western Carpathian Mountain range, the village was founded by King Wenceslaus II in 1292. It was on an early trade route between the Mediterranean and the Baltic. For centuries, the village seesawed between political and religious factions. Today the area has many historic sites and is a destination spot for tourists, hikers, and skiers. Mountain resorts and a national park border Jezioro Reznowskie, (Lake Roznow), a twenty-mile-long reservoir. In August 1939, Hitler's army was massed at that southern border of Poland.

It was a pivotal month in Barbara's life. Europe was poised on the brink of war and she was at the epicenter. In 2009, Barbara told me that she stayed at Eva Barbacka's family home for three weeks. She recalled that the children were very religious and knelt at bedtime for prayer. Barbara said a maid brought bedpots around in the evening after prayers. The girls went to Warsaw for a few days and visited Eva's school friends who couldn't speak French.

Eva and Barbara spent about two weeks at the Barbacka dacha—a mountain estate that Eva's family owned. In this mountain paradise, Barbara met a Polish engineer, Konopka Kristaw, who proposed, and she accepted.

The following original documents, discovered in the chickenhouse, reveal the fantasy world in which Barbara lived. Kristaw was a business owner who worked in Krakow [Cracow]. He must have been very concerned about how he could protect his assets with the impending German invasion. In this first letter, written soon after Barbara and Kristaw met, we glimpse the world Barbara had stepped into. Note that Barbara was fluent in French, Latin, English, and had a working knowledge of German and Spanish.

My very dear Berbi, (Barbara)

You know well, what I gave you in the forgotten French language. I better speak and write in Latin. Therefore, forgive me and please do not be irritated if I made errors. You must—and I ask you for it—write to me in French, because you know this language well. Write me, in which language you want me to write. Now you do not understand me, and you are afraid to write in Latin. You anyway should answer in French. Believe me, that only the wishes for your happiness and for your good luck are in my heart.

Take my sincere greetings. I hope to come in the next days.

Barbara's nineteenth birthday was August 11, 1939. The romance blossomed. She had known this man for less than two weeks. Kristaw sent a second letter on August 12, apologizing for not being with Barbara on her birthday—business delays.

Along with the letter, he sent a marriage proposal that he asked Barbara to rewrite and send to her parents.

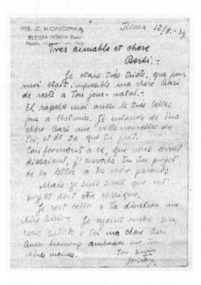

A few days later Barbara sent the following letter to New York.

My very dear parents: As you know, I live on a farm of a friend's parents. I am very happy here. They are very friendly people. I've met a young Polish engineer, Mr. Konopka Kristaw, who owns in the vicinity of Cracow a farm and oil fields. He is very nice, well raised and mannered. He doesn't smoke, drink, or play cards, very religious. Two of his brothers are Jesuits and he has a sister who is a nun at the convent of St. Claire. I like him a lot and he is charmed by my music. He wants to marry me, if you, my dear parents would give me your permission and blessing. For my part, I would like to stay and live in Poland that I like a lot.

I love the Poles; they are very decent and friendly. If I marry, I will live in the south of Poland around Cracow. I am alone in Europe; I want to have the support of a husband and I want my choice to be good.

Kristaw was not a "young Polish engineer" as Barbara had told her mother. He was a forty-six-year-old widower—Barbara was eighteen when she met him.

Barbara's parents in New York were completely unaware of her situation, but Elsie was focused on world events. More than eighty years later, I share a few headlines that she saved in her voluminous *War Scrapbook*.

Elsie's diary casts light on Barbara's adventure and reinforces the mindset of people in the United States. Even as newspapers headlined the impending war threat, New Yorkers flocked to the beaches, theaters, and parties.

Wed, August 2: *A hot fussy day. Polly and I went shopping. At just 4 Gerta, Greta Cahn, and Herbert came for tea. The first time Polly had seen Gerta since Brussels.*

Friday, August 4: *Gerta came in early; she and Polly went to the Statue of Liberty then home. I got them a nice little lunch. Then they went to Heifetz in "They Shall Have Music" Polly's treat.*

Friday, August 11, 1939: *Dear Barb's birthday and a nice letter from her this a.m. first from Poland. Fascinating description of mountain estate of Eva's where she is visiting. In evening a package of candied fruits came from her from Nice.*

Monday, August 21, 1939: *The war jitters over Poland are now the worst yet. Briton has ordered all Britons to leave Poland; Warsaw especially. We wonder whether Barb has left yet or not. I suppose we will know in a few days. The suspense is getting worse.*

Tuesday, August 22, 1939: *Thank goodness word from Barb from Poland written on the 8ᵗʰ. She talks about German maneuvers across the border in Czechoslovakia in September no more. She is having a wonderful time visiting Aka [Eva Barbacka] in a fashionable resort swimming, mountain climbing, dancing, tennis, and Bridge. The headlines blaze war talk. Germany and Russia have signed a pact. The Cahn's cousin, Walter, Pol, and I went swimming at Orchard Beach—pleasant but far too many people there. We took a picnic lunch.*

Wednesday, August 23, 1939: *Germany's demand for Poland has reached tremendous headlines and extras. We are awfully nervous for Barb—What a life! to have to be constantly in a state of extreme anxiety. Kay, Polly, and I took a picnic to South Beach Staten Island, all very pleasant. Almost alone on beach. Tide and swimming just right. Very thrilling to watch the Queen Mary go out with capacity in spite of war clouds.*

Thursday, August 24, 1939: *The Communists have joined hands with the Nazis—but just what you would expect Hitler and Stalin to do.*

Hitler and Stalin signed a non-aggression pact on August 23, 1939. Hitler had secured his west flank. Less than two years later, on June 22, 1941, Hitler violated that pact and invaded Russia.

Saturday, August 26, 1939: *!!!X!!! A frightful shock this a.m. in the air mail, mailed by Barb from Poland enclosing a letter from a young Polish Engineer asking us for permission to marry Barb—apparently immediately. We are simply stunned. We don't know what to do—of course our inclination would be to cable to wait until xmas. Think of her beautiful talent being stored away in Poland, the tension spot of the world and apparently, he owns the very oil fields Hitler wants. We three, Henry, Polly, and I went to "The Little Foxes" Tallulah Bankhead—very cynical but gorgeous acting.*

On August 26, 1939, Eva's father warned Barbara that she must flee Poland. He put her on a train in Nowy Sacz. She must have been frantic with worry about Eva and Kristaw. There is no record of her saying goodbye to Kristaw. Nowy Sacz was less than one hundred miles from where the opening shots of WWII were fired one week later, on the night of August 31, 1939.

The proposal letter was probably the last time Barbara heard from her fiancé. My researcher discovered that Kristaw's two brothers and sister mentioned in the 1939 letter, "...two brothers who were Jesuits, sister who was nun at convent of St. Claire Jesuits"—died in Nazi captivity.

Elsie's diary continues:

Sunday, August 27, 1939: *All we did was listen to and read war news and worry over Barb and wonder what to do. I have the worst splitting headache all the time. My news clipping book is up to date. Polly went to Gerta's for the day. At 6 Polly and Henry played tennis for 2 hours to stop thinking—I certainly don't like that stupid game. Henry and I went to Kay and Warings for Chinese checkers to stop listening to the news.*

Monday, August 28, 1939: *We can't sleep or anything*

the war news is so bad. The [passenger ship] Normandie crossed "blacked out" in a zigzag crossing. Polly and I worked until three then went to Kay's for lemonade, marketed then home for a late Bridge with Henry. I'm so worried about Barb and her war danger and her marriage that I can't see straight or think. I feel suffocated all of the time.

Elsie was worried "...about Barbara and her war danger and her marriage." Had Barbara in fact, gotten married? In her 1960 psychiatric evaluation, after she was committed to Fergus Falls State Hospital, she alluded to a fourth husband—he would have been Konopka Kristaw. In this next diary entry, Elsie asked Barbara to wait. With Barbara's impulsiveness and the atmosphere of war hysteria in Poland, is it possible she was already married?

Tuesday, August 29, 1939: The radios are booming hourly war news from all the great European Capitols—War itself could only be some degrees worse. A letter from Poland from Mme Barbacka, Barb's hostess this morning saying they are not so terrified of war, but it was mailed twelve days ago. I sent an air mail to Barb asking her not to think of marrying the Polish man until xmas.

Wednesday, August 30, 1939: German-Russian Pact signed. Everybody amazed at such double-crossing. The good out of the evil means out the window go all the "isms" that have been cursing this country. Polly's cold and throat are bad. She does not feel well. In the evening we doctored her with everything known to man fearing a bad illness.

Thursday, August 31, 1939: Polly woke up all well— miraculous. The war tension is very bad. We are nearly crazy worried about Barb. I worked until about 4—napped because I can't sleep at all—too many worries. Haven't been sleepy at all in four days—Barb's safety, Polly's school, our place to live. Henry is holding up well under the strain.

SEPTEMBER 1939: ESCAPE FROM POLAND

Over the course of eighteen months, Hitler had schemed to flank Poland from the north and the south. Those "Heavy Troop Movements" west of Krakow and along the "Mountain Passes" in the Carpathian Mountains were exactly where Barbara was—where Eva Barbacka and Kristaw lived.

As I studied this old clipping (next page), I was again amazed that it had survived for more than eighty years; note the mouse-nibbled edge from lying in the chickenhouse for the previous twenty-four years.

Elsie's diary continues:

Friday, September 1, 1939: !!!! *Barb has arrived safely in* Brussels! *At six a.m. Germany marched on Poland. Bombed the very spots where Barb was only a few days before.* (In the opening hours of Hitler's attack on Poland, his Luftwaffe bombed Warsaw.) *Never have we ever had such a thrilling airmail written Tuesday evening in Brussels the minute she arrived after the most miraculous escape. With barely enough money she started at 9 a.m. Sat. [August 26] having been warned by Eva's papa to flee the moment the German-*

...OR, FRIDAY, SEPTEMBER 1, 1939

Arrows on map of turbulent Europe indicate latest German activities and the area which seems likely to be the first theatre of the next war. It is the Polish-Slovak border in the Carpathian Mountains, where Hitler has placed an estimated 700,000 men and Poland an equal number.

Russian Pact was signed. She spent last Sunday in Warsaw — people were gaily digging trenches and singing. As she was leaving, the microphone announced, "no more trains across the border." She was let out at 5 a.m. in a Polish frontier [border] village. A tall Polish American Jew saved her. Talked the authorities into letting her across and made arrangements for her in Berlin. She had the same luck in Aachen, Belgian Border—never were we so thankful. Kay took me out to lunch and then I went to St. Barts and said prayer.

"Eva's papa" as Elsie mentioned, no doubt carried vivid

memories of World War I and the carnage that had been inflicted on civilians in total war. He recognized the imminent threat of Hitler's army. Elsie also mentioned Warsaw where "people were gaily digging trenches and singing." The German army captured Warsaw in September 1939, within three weeks of Barbara's passing through. The city began a five-year nightmare of Nazi rule. During that period, an estimated 100,000 died from starvation and Nazi murdering of Jews confined in the "Warsaw Ghetto." In 1942, more than 250,000 were shipped to extermination camps.

Poland had an active underground resistance. When Russian forces approached Warsaw in August 1944, the infamous "Warsaw Uprising" occurred. The Polish underground Home Army battled the German army but could not win. Russia could have helped, but stood back watching and allowed the German army to eliminate what Stalin considered a future threat of Poland's ability to self-govern in the post-war world. From August 1 to October 2, 1944, German soldiers burned Warsaw and killed thousands of Polish men, women, and children. After the October 2, 1944, surrender, more than 700,000 were shipped to concentration camps and slave labor camps. This was the slaughter Eva's papa had visualized six years earlier. How many of those "people [who] were gaily digging trenches and singing" five years earlier in Warsaw survived the war?

Elsie's diary continues:

Saturday, September 2, 1939: !!! *Another air mail from Barb from Poland written on August 23, mailed on the 24th. She planned then to leave on Sept 1—no war fear. Hitler is continuing to bomb Poland where Barb was. Henry, Polly, and I went to Radio, "Fifth Avenue Girl" excellent picture— propaganda against all the troubles in this country.*

Sunday, September 3, 1939: !!!! *England and France declared war on Germany this morning! It doesn't seem as tho it could really be true! They will immediately go to the aid of Poland. We went to St. Bartholomew's to say prayers for Barb's safe return to Brussels. In the afternoon we walked up to 130 Fifth Ave WQXR to see the war news broadcast by Edwin Howard [Armstrong]. At six Henry and Polly played tennis, I watched. Polly plays a pretty game. We hear nothing but war news all day long.*

Monday, September 4, 1939: *A day full of horrible feelings as the Second Great War goes into murderous action. We are relieved to know that Barb has made her miraculous escape from Poland, but she is not in complete safety in Brussels. We hope that we hear that she will start home soon. We went to some little light thing at the Normandie to distract us. It was impossible to be gay— there are too many momentous events to go thru this month.*

Saturday, September 9, 1939: *Wonder of wonders a cable early this morning from Barb asking for money which means that she is about to leave for home. They are not allowed to cable sailing dates and names of steamers. All must be kept in secrecy because of the German U-boats sinking so many steamers. Athenia with 1500 passengers the first day—almost all lives saved.*

There is no record of what Barbara did those first days back in Brussels. Had she returned to Institute Droissard? Was she frantically trying to contact Eva and Kristaw back in Poland?

THE COMPANY WILL APPRECIATE SUGGESTIONS FROM ITS PATRONS CONCERNING ITS SERVICE

WESTERN UNION
CABLEGRAM (15)

CLASS OF SERVICE

This is a full-rate Cablegram unless its deferred character is indicated by a suitable symbol preceding the address.

SYMBOLS

LC   Deferred Cablegram
NLT   Cable Night Letter
Ship Radiogram

Received at 376 LEXINGTON AVE., N. Y.

NBD18 13 CABLE=BRUSSELS 9 1245

LC PHILIPS=

5 PROSPECT PLACE NYK CITY=

CABLE 40 DOLLARS AMEXCO BRUSSELS

=BARBARA.

Barbara wired her parents for money. "LC" is telegram
jargon for "Elsie." (September 9, 1939)

SEPTEMBER 12, 1939

Two weeks after Barbara fled Poland, she wrote the following essay while enroute home from Europe on the steamer *American Farmer,* by coincidence the same ship she had steamed to Europe on two years earlier. The essay is one of the writings I rescued from the chickenhouse from a packet Elsie had labeled "Barbara, Priceless!!" This piece best illustrates Barbara's time in Europe and the angst she lived with. Just nineteen, she wrote with a gloom beyond her years. Note the borderline personality disorder signs Barbara revealed through her essay—concern about her weight, abnormal relationship to food, feelings of low self-esteem, and sense of abandonment, to name a few.

MEMOIRS '38-'39

E va Barbacka was a typical Slavic type—a very pale complexion, a round sweet face, large grayish blue eyes and a head of reddish-brown waving hair.

To tell the truth I had always been a little afraid of her. At that time, I did not know that the Slavic race had an exceptional gift for foreign languages. It seemed to me that Eva spoke French amazingly well. At Institut Droissard she spoke better than any other foreign girl and in her Secretarial School it was known that she made brilliant success of her examinations.

The first year we were there we hardly spoke to each other. She had loads of Polish and Belgian friends and I was too wrapped up in my studies to pay attention to anyone.

September [1938] was nearly at an end. Each day had monotonously followed the next all thru the vacation months. There had been a bit of war scare, but aside from that, nothing had interrupted my routine preparation for entering the Conservatory.

One night as I lay in bed thinking over endless thoughts the doorbell rang way downstairs. Mlle del Chevalrie was an exceedingly cautious old lady of eighty-four. She was very pious and devoted to Mlle Gerard, the Directrice of our pensionat. The latter had enjoyed a great deal of success formerly. Droissard was the oldest and finest finishing school in Brussels. She had adopted a niece of Mlle Chevalrie and in this way as the niece grew older and married, her interest in the school had dwindled to nothing.

The old lady Laure (Laura) was always here to put on her bedroom slippers and count out the linen and answer the door-bell. She hoped to live to be one hundred and counted her eighty-four years as nothing at all, only taking the precaution of going up and down stairs one at a time.

Naturally it is a Belgian precaution against burglars and air drafts to inquire thru the keyhole before opening the door.

From my open window the answer came clearly resounding thru the silent rue de Florence. Eva Barbacka had returned from Poland.

It is an extremely tiring journey. She had not even woken up the next morning when Mlle Pre'vot, a typical little Belgian teacher, took her a tray.

Eva said there had been hardly any noise of war near her home in the Carpathian Mountains. According to her, the govt. had taken all the precautions of avoiding a panic, even mobilizing the soldiers at night. It seemed to me she always looked down on the Belgians and never told them anything of her private life.

In the evenings she would come up to my room or I would stop at hers. She always did most of the talking, telling of all the sufferings of her people. Poland has always been under the tyranny of Austria or Germany or Russia. She adored the Emperor Napoleon but said he had always deceived the Polish soldiers, making promises of their liberty which he had never been able to fulfill. She had an enormous will and flair for political argument.

There were very few pensionnaires there that year. Josette Clarenes and Jenny Maris from Diest, the Flemish part of Belgium. I never had any trust in Josette. She was secretly jealous of me and at the same time proud of her blond coiffeur and slimness. She knew that was my Achilles Heel and was always harping on it in a sly way. If I went without eating, she went without, too. If I left the table before dessert, she did likewise. During the months I went without a bite of supper, she never failed to bring me up a plate. It was a perverted manner of preventing my attempts to diet. However, it does not matter now as no one essay [effort] I've ever made has been—the least lasting or successful.

As I look out to sea from this writing-table, I ask myself what I am doing—on my way home. Few of us are extremely far-sighted. When we three left Brussels the fifteenth of July [1939], I had entirely planned to stay in Poland for the war and a long time. Diaries are stupid things. As Andre' Maurois says, we all go through Climates. I have not kept a diary for three years. The very fact that I relate these events shows a revolution. We all have burdens and scars and roads that we might have taken—but one must never regret. It is necessary to believe that the Climate surrounding one at a given time was the unchangeable part of the planned (or unplanned) chain of destiny. Of course, this theory does away with all initiative. I have many and bitter reasons for feeling that way. They say that in this world some are born weak and some are born strong and that each should accept his place.

The novel *Climates* is a twisted story of love, the psychology behind love, unfulfilled love, and betrayed love. Barbara apparently saw realistic life-lessons in the novel's plot. It was a hazardous mindset for a young woman just ripped away from her fiancé—or was it her first husband?

BOMBING OF GERMAN SUBMARINE U-53
AND KAFIRISTAN SURVIVORS

On September 17, while Barbara was writing about her European experiences, German submarine *U-53* and several other U-boats—known as a wolfpack—were on patrol searching for a British convoy of merchant ships that had been reported to German Naval Command in Berlin.

International News Photo Slug
Lifeboat Crews Rescue.

In the late afternoon, *U-53* torpedoed a British steam merchant ship, the *Kafiristan,* 350 miles west of Cape Clear, Ireland. The *Kafiristan* had been enroute from Cuba to Liverpool with a cargo of 8,870 tons of sugar.

The doomed ship sank slowly, and thirty-five surviving British merchant sailors escaped in lifeboats. *U-53* surfaced and took the British lifeboats in tow, toward the Irish coast. Two hours later, *U-53* Captain Ernst-Gunter Heinicke hailed the *American Farmer* and ordered them to take the British survivors aboard. The

following original documents are a first-hand witness account of
the rescue.

Boarding the American Farmer after "Humane"
torpedoing.

*Off the European Coast...Two members of the crew of the
British freighter "Kafiristan" are shown being helped aboard the
SS American Farmer by a ship's officer and one of his men after
the lifeboat from the "Kafiristan" was raised to deck level. The
picture was made at sea, Sept. 17, last, after "Kafiristan" had
been sunk by a German submarine 400 miles off the Scilly
Islands. Capt. H. A. Pedersen of the American Farmer told of
humane actions of the U-boat commander who ordered his vessel
to remain on the surface until all crew members of the British
freighter were picked up safely. Then the sub was chased to the
bottom by an airplane that opened an aerial attack on the
submersible. Six members of the crew of the "Kafiristan" lost
their lives when the lifeboat which they were in was partially
submerged. The American Farmer rescued the 29 others.*

.   .   .

Barbara loved retelling this story throughout her life, and during one of our last interviews, I heard it again. Barbara, along with other passengers, no doubt stood on the *American Farmer's* deck, perhaps leaning against the rail, listening as the U-boat captain issued orders through his megaphone. Memory is an interesting thing and not to be trusted—especially about traumatic events. According to Barbara, the *American Farmer* lowered her lifeboats, rowed to *U-53*, and loaded the *Kafiristan* crewmen. The loaded lifeboats were midway back when several British Swordfish airplanes swooped down and strafed *U-53*. Barbara said the planes circled, came in low, and dropped a bomb on the U-boat's conning tower. She said it sank with all hands. I think that violent confrontation became a flashbulb memory, always near the surface of her mind.

As the *American Farmer* steamed west across the Atlantic, passengers must have listened to radio broadcasts in an effort to stay abreast of the fast-developing German invasion of Poland. September 17 had been a busy day. British aircraft carrier HMS *Courageous*, home to the Swordfish aircraft that had attacked *U-53*, was torpedoed and sunk by *U-29*, another member of the German wolfpack.

On that same day, the Soviet Russian army invaded Poland from the west. The German army was bombing Warsaw, where Barbara had been only three weeks earlier. The German army captured 400,000 Polish troops. Barbara's world was collapsing. Eva and Kristaw were in the heart of Poland's destruction.

Elsie's diary continues:

Sunday, September 24, 1939: <u>Barb arrives</u> 2 years today. We arose and dashed thru breakfast to reach the pier in time. The Farmer (Barb's ship) came in at eleven thirty and there was Barb, the fifth off the steamer. She was certainly lucky to make the first steamer she tried. She'd hadn't a cent of money. There was Captain Pederson on the Bridge.

*They did have the exciting voyage and rescued the crew of
a British freighter and saw the British plane sink the German
submarine right before them. Barb isn't well—we brought
her mammoth trunk up in the taxi and then took her to
Childs in the Plaza for dinner.*

Monday, September 25, 1939: *Polly commences St.
Agatha's. Barb and I set out early to see about school for
her. She wanted to try Brearley [School] so we went there;
very nearby but there were no ways of making the
curriculum fit her past work. Then to Juilliard [School of
Music] and after to Bernard [College]. Juilliard seems to be
the only possibility. Poor Barb feels like a lost soul.*

Thursday, September 28, 1939: *Barb and I went to the
New York Hospital Clinic. I think it best for her to have a
general overhaul as she doesn't feel at all well. We had to
wait and wait and then only given an appointment for
tomorrow.*

Friday, September 29, 1939: *Barb and I arrived at New
York Hospital promptly at one. We were told it would take all
afternoon.*

What happened beyond the diary entries after Eva Barbacka's father put Barbara on the train in Nowy Sacz, Poland, on
August 26? Rail distance from Nowy Sacz to Brussels, Belgium,
via Warsaw and Berlin is approximately one thousand miles.
Today it is a leisurely two-day trip. But by August 26, 1939,
many of the rail systems in Europe had been commandeered by
the military.

During one of my last interviews with Barbara in 2009, she
recalled the German army troops controlling the rail stations.
"Arrogant strutting Nazis," she called them. She spoke of the
Jews in Berlin with yellow stars stitched to their coats. She told
me that she saw trainloads of German troops traveling east,
toward Poland. And now, after reading Elsie's diary account, I

wonder just how this young woman negotiated her way across those borders.

Did Barbara complete her "Memoirs '38-'39" after the U-boat encounter? I imagine her sitting in a deck chair, lap robe keeping the sea breeze at bay, dark curls tumbling around her face. There is no mention of the U-boat encounter, but with this fatalistic last sentence of her essay, *They say that in this world some are born weak and some are born strong and that each should accept his place,* perhaps she was trying to make sense of the violence she had witnessed.

U-53 did not sink. When the British Swordfish strafed and bombed the submarine, the boat crash-dived, leaving some gunners topside. They were killed. Five months later, on February 23, 1940, *U-53* was sunk in the North Sea by British destroyer HMS *Gurkha.* All hands perished. Captain Ernst-Gunter Heinicke had been transferred earlier so he was not on board. His act of chivalry, rescuing the twenty-nine British sailors on September 17, 1939, was lost in the fog of war, except for that aged ticker tape.

The *American Farmer* was torpedoed and sunk by *U-52* while in a convoy east of Greenland in April 1941.

OCTOBER 1939: BARBARA, HOME TO NEW YORK CITY

Life in New York was seemingly unaffected; a few weeks earlier, while Barbara was trying to grasp the reality of the combat she had witnessed, Elsie, Henry, and Polly were having cocktails and looking at pianos. That was the world Barbara returned to. Her mother could have no idea of the traumas her daughter had endured and the memories she carried. Barbara's father had served in World War I and was recalled during World War II. He understood.

Four years later, in 1943, as Barbara's life spiraled out of control, Henry wrote to Elsie from Camp Maxey, Texas: "I've prayed so much that her [Barbara's] life would straighten out—the more I think of it the more I feel it is possible her war experience, unconsciously to her, was eating at her vitals—how tragic life is for the world." Henry, alluding to Barbara's witnessing the U-Boat strafing, bombing, and the death of the sailors, recognized post-traumatic stress disorder (PTSD) four decades before the medical world put a name to it.

Elsie's diary continues:

Sunday, October 1, 1939: *A very rainy Sunday and not very pleasant. We all went to St. Bartholomew. Dr. Sargent was marvelous as usual. I find such peace there with such beautiful music. Barb made a Frenchie little luncheon—then after an argument about a lace hank,y she and Polly went to Gerta's to Tea. Barb had a wonderful time playing their Steinway which they sold this afternoon.*

Monday, October 2, 1939: *Barb walked all the way from Juilliard. Her piano didn't come. We are furious with them. In the afternoon we went to the YWCA to see about reducing exercises for Barb. She is very unhappy about being weighty.*

Thursday, October 5, 1939: *Barb commences Juilliard. I fear she won't like it as much as Conservatorie under Emile Bosquet. He was a great teacher. It will be hard for her to make the adjustment. I hope she won't forget her French soon. In the evening Barb and I went to National Music Week at Carnegie.*

Friday, October 6, 1939: *Barb and Polly went to Swing at Carnegie but was so crowded they couldn't get in—didn't have money enough for movies.*

Monday, October 16, 1939: *I cleaned the whole house and did a big washing. Then to the New York Hospital to see Dr. Russell. He thinks Barb is definitely a psychiatric case. She is to see Dr. Henry next week. I hope they get at it.*

There is no doubt that Barbara was physically and mentally exhausted after her ordeal. Why didn't Elsie encourage Barbara to rest—take a short break to assimilate before returning to school? Or were they both so committed to Barbara's future as a pianist? Recall two years earlier, Elsie had written, "... she can't sacrifice her music."

Wednesday, October 18, 1939: *Barb went riding in Central Park, beautiful morning. I got a nice luncheon for her which she ate. Then went shopping for books for her. Went to Barnes and Noble—18ᵗʰ and Fifth and sold some music books for her and bought some. Barb went to the "6" exercise group at 4:30. Polly went to Marion Setting's from Brussels then met Barb at St. Bartholomew for choir.*

Barbara, home in New York, from Europe. Note the round
face and baggy coat. (autumn 1939)

Wednesday, October 25: *Such a rush day. Went to the hospital with Barb took all a.m. on her diet. This time she is going to try to stick to it. After getting her luncheon at home I went to the Vassar Club.*

Pictures from the 1920s-1930s document Henry Philips and C.D. Fratt as being quite heavy, so Barbara may have been genetically predisposed to obesity from her father and grandfather on her mother's side. Through the decades, pictures show Barbara fluctuating from approximately 115-160 pounds. Today we recognize the impact of genetic and environmental influences on our health. How did her eating habits compound that problem? What role did food have in Barbara's psychological world? Did she struggle with bulimia nervosa? I remember, as a child on the farm in Minnesota, how more than once I went upstairs and discovered Barbara eating food that she had stashed.

Doug, one of my mental health resources, opined, "…Barb's eating and weight gain and loss seem to me to be in the normal range. One hundred sixty pounds, I don't think, is obese. The fluctuation might have been an attempt to gain some control in her very stressful life. As far as the hoarding and then eating, that could be indicative of trying to deal with unmet emotional needs, or simply just trying to respond to a need for some simple pleasures in a household that demanded resources be shuttled to the rest of the family."

NOVEMBER 1939, ANGST

I try to imagine the stress levels in the Philips' apartment. Henry was earning a mediocre salary as a bond salesman on Wall Street. He had a high maintenance wife and two daughters, one attending a private high school and the other, an expensive music college.

Again, Elsie's diary is the best window into the Philips' family dynamics.

Wednesday, November 1: *Went to the hospital at nine with Barb. Waited until 11:30 to see Dr. Russell then had only brief talk with him. He was still busy with Barb. I wonder if he will prove to be any good.*

Friday, November 3: *Finished Barb's things and took her bags to meet her at 125th St station to go to Stamford to meet Dr. Slaughter to drive her to Ithaca to spend weekend with Dr. Slaughter and go to Cornell-Columbia game.*

Sunday, November 5: *Such a pouring, rainy Sunday. Barb did not return from Ithaca.*

Monday, November 6: *Barb returned. Was snowbound in Ithaca.*

Dr. Slaughter was the widower with whom Barbara had lived the winter of 1936 while Elsie and Henry spent several months at Hotel Vanderbilt in New York City. What was his relationship with Barbara, that three years later, when she was of age, they traveled to Ithaca for the weekend, apparently alone? Elsie didn't mention him one time after they left Darien in 1937. Barbara must have reconnected with him upon her return to the U.S.

Elsie's diary continues:

Friday, November 10: *Margaret Brown came to tea and B.A. [Barbara Ann] came home early. I was as charmed with her as ever. Henry is cheered about the business aspects. He went out with the boys later.*

Saturday, November 11: *Armistice Day. How ridiculous to celebrate the quiet guns this year when they are booming away harder than ever. At 1 Barb and I went to Stouffer's for luncheon on Park Avenue then to see "Tobacco Road" [the play] before it went off after its six-year run. Such a horrible grubby thing. It depresses one. Then we went to Maxwell House for coffee.*

Sunday, November 12: *Beautiful day. We went to St. Bartholomew's. Barb and Polly always go to the 9 o'clock and sing in the choir. Barb plays for the 11 o'clock Junior Choir. Henry and I had a beautiful walk home up dressy Park Avenue in the noon day sun. Barb and Polly went to a French concert. A girl asked Barb to go to concert at Town Hall.*

Tuesday, November 14: *I had to go to the hospital with Barb—a headache. After, we went to a terribly realistic French movie, "That They May Live." The Dead of Verdun 1918 come to life in 1939. Barb enjoyed speaking French with Gabby.*

It must have been a severe headache to go to the hospital—

how could going to war movie soothe her throbbing temples? As a child on the farm, I remember Barbara's getting the most splitting headaches, which she attributed to her glasses being out of focus. But I wonder, if the tremendous stress she was under, living with her parents in 1939, and twenty-five year later, isolated on the farm with a husband she despised, factored into her headaches. I remember her on the farm, drinking extra strong coffee to alleviate her pain.

> Thursday, November 16: *Gala week! Old home week for the Vassar girls. Miriam here from Washington. Uppie also had a very attractive girl from Mansfield. After, we walked up Madison and came here for "High Tea." Had a good visit— Barb played beautifully. All very charmed with Barb; Henry came home in time to see them.*

On November 18, 1939, Barbara received a letter from Helena "Ann" Janowski, one of the girls she had attended school with in Brussels. Here is the first page—full transcribed text follows.

[Controle Postal Militaire censor stamp on envelope].
(Autumn 1939)

Dear Barbara, I was delighted to get your letter last week. I wrote to you at Brussels some time ago—I imagined you would have left but hoped it would be forwarded. We are staying here as I should think it will be pretty safe. My father is back in his old Regiment, The Royal Engineers, but fortunately he is staying here although he has to go up the line a lot. I went with him last Friday, I enjoyed it awfully it was great fun, but I'm afraid I couldn't let you know anything about it.

I wrote to Aka [Eva Barbacka] just before the war broke out, but I've heard nothing at all from her. Poor thing I wonder what has happened to her. You must have had an interesting crossing, weren't you terrified. I should have been. I'd give anything to be in New York, it's always been my dream to go to the States. Perhaps one day I shall get there but after this war I shouldn't think anyone will have any money to do anything with.

I myself think the war will last about 3 years, a grim thought—I hope I'm wrong. I read last night the White Paper issued about Nazi cruelty in the concentration camps. It made me feel quite ill. If they treat their own nationals [Jews] like that, what will they do to the prisoners of war? The sooner the Nazi element is wiped out the better for everyone.

Do write again soon, my dear I shall be interested in how long this takes to reach you. About three weeks I imagine. Lots of Love, Ann

Ann alluded to the "White Paper" detailing Nazi cruelty the autumn of 1939. It took the United States over two years and Pearl Harbor before intervening. This letter must have terrified Barbara, not to know the fate of Kristaw or Eva.

Elsie's diary continues:

Wednesday, November 22: *Spent all a.m. in the hospital with Barb. I like the new Dr. Brown on the case very much. Hope she will get somewhere. After three years Barb seems not the least bit better to me. Yes. I suppose she is some in some ways. No violent scenes now. Just silence. Dr. Brown has her on nine pills per day. Henry bought a beautiful turkey*

I've known Vietnam veterans struggling with PTSD who have been medicated and behave like zombies. In the infancy of psychotropic medications, how did those "nine pills per day" impact Barbara's personality and her ability to succeed at Juilliard? The November 22 entry suggests that Barbara did throw "violent scenes" three years earlier.

Elsie's diary continues:

Thursday, November 23: *"Thanksgiving." Will we ever be through with this man [President Roosevelt] and his mad cheating the people? His egoism and selfish ideals to gain more power. The whole world is wrecked by the four of them – Roosevelt, Stalin, Hitler, and Mussolini. Connecticut didn't celebrate today. Henry bought a huge turkey and we had a delicious meal and a very good time. Dottie asked Barb to play for her which she did very beautifully but didn't feel well; couldn't eat her dinner.*

DECEMBER 1939

As WWII raged across the globe, movie goers in the United States stood in line for the premier of *Gone with the Wind* with an all-star cast including Vivien Leigh, Clark Gable, Leslie Howard and Olivia de Havilland. The country was quietly ramping up for war. On December 29, a B-24 heavy bomber made its first flight in San Diego, California, but for most Americans, life moved on with no war-time shortages or concerns.

I've come to realize that as we age, we try to make sense of our past, to find peace with it. When Barbara returned from Europe, she was obviously dealing with several issues—psychiatric and physical. I know the disconnect she must have felt. In 1968, I remember as I recuperated, my first weekend passes from the hospital at Great Lakes Naval Base. I recall how, at family gatherings, as people joked about sports, fishing, partying, I listened silently and felt completely alienated. Don't they understand, I thought, that people are dying in the jungles and on the rivers while you stand joking and guzzling cold beer? I recall the terrible guilt, believing that I should be back with my riverboat crew. Barbara had reentered a similar world—a world an ocean away from the killing, a world that hadn't been touched yet by war.

Playing endless mind games, re-playing events, fantasizing an outcome where nobody dies—these things continue more than fifty years later. That is the nature of post-traumatic stress disorder. I remember the emptiness, the desire for solitude, the melancholy—all beneath a blanket of silence. It took thirty years for me to visit a VA Hospital where I was diagnosed with PTSD. So, I empathize with Barbara—her rages, her constant need to escape.

In a 2011 interview with Karel Knutson, a WWII veteran who lived not far from our farm in Nebish, Minnesota, he told me that in 1950 he and my stepfather Herman had driven into Bemidji together to attend agriculture classes. One evening, not long after Herman and Barbara were married, Herman told Karel that Barbara had sat up in bed during the night and pointed out toward the moonlit lake beyond the field and said, "Look, in the lake, a submarine. My lover is coming to rescue me." Herman had confided to Karel, "There's something wrong with Barbara." I imagine she had awakened from a nightmare, disoriented and terrified, and flashed back to *U-53* and the terror it re-awakened.

People with borderline personality disorder often have a co-diagnosis of PTSD, higher than the general population. If Barbara did suffer with borderline personality disorder, she was more vulnerable to PTSD. In retrospect, I now wonder if, when she was acting out, she was having a flashback. As I mentioned earlier, Barbara's 1960 court commitment strongly hints that she did, in fact, marry Kristaw Konopka in 1939—that he was, in fact, her first husband.

An excerpt from Barbara's 1960 psychiatric exam when she was committed:

13. Prior to patient's present mental disorder there were no peculiarities of personality reactions except ....
Insidious onset of symptoms. Patient has fared poorly in selection of her three (perhaps four) husbands. One was unable to hold a job more than a day or two. Another actually carried a gun and was brutal in his treatment of his previous wife

Between 1942 and 1951 Barbara married three different men, yet her 1960 evaluation suggests "(perhaps four)." Was Kristaw Konopka that fourth husband, the "lover in the submarine," coming to rescue her?

By late winter 1939-40, Barbara was undergoing therapy from mental health professionals at New York Hospital. They prescribed medication and she enrolled in a weight-loss program. In trying to understand the New York social climate into which my mother was trying to reintegrate, I searched for era narratives. I discovered that they were almost nonexistent.

I did find one very insightful book, *Where Do People Take Their Troubles?* (1945) by Lee R. Steiner, a member of the American Association of Orthopsychiatry. From the back cover: *...she [Steiner] presents here an endless pageant of emotionally troubled people who, in their search for solace, become followers of self-appointed "consultants" who invade the unlicensed field of psychological practice: radio performers, religious healers, spiritualists, astrologers, numerologists, and other purveyors of cunningly conceived concoctions.*

In the then unlicensed field of mental health, these "psychoanalysts," as they presented themselves, were free to prey on a vulnerable public. Even the educated were duped. We know from my grandmother's diaries that Barbara was overweight and lonely. Her friends had been sucked into the maelstrom of WWII. She must have felt isolated. How early did she turn to hucksters who—for a price—offered to solve her problems? "Inferiority Complex" was a keyword "consultants" used to shame the vulnerable who were already struggling with depression.

Elsie studied many mental health books including *War*

Elsie's Mental Health note folder.

Department Technical Manual 8-325, OUTLINE OF NEUROPSYCHIATRY IN AVIATION MEDICINE, which she must have obtained from her husband while he was training at Fort Oglethorpe after he was recalled to active duty. On page 20, she noted this section that discussed the Freudian hypotheses about how sexuality influenced mental health: *"...the compelling primary instinct of sex is repressed more than any other and its frank discussion absolutely taboo in modern society, and partly because the opposition pushed Freud and his followers to the extreme of explaining practically every phase of human feeling and activity on a sexual basis. It would seem wisest, with unbiased mind, to adopt a compromise viewpoint and deny the sexual instinct primacy in causing mental illness, while conceding it due importance as a causative factor."*

During my interviews with Barbara, she told me that Juilliard had accepted her as a graduate school assistant and that she graduated from Juilliard. After her death I contacted Juilliard and received her transcripts. Barbara's grades were mediocre and reminded me of when I attended Marquette University in the early 1970s and dropped out after a few semesters. Barbara had registered on October 5, 1939, and completed winter quarter 1939 and spring quarter 1940.

Barbara carried a huge load—an invisible load. The "nine pills per day" must have affected her ability to study. I think she became overwhelmed with the pressure of Juilliard, the ghosts she was living with, and her mother. So began a decade of running from problems—a common borderline personality disorder defensive mechanism.

My oldest brother Chris retains memory fragments from the 1940s, but eighty years later, they are fuzzy. Barbara refused to talk about her life during the decade; even in end-of-life interviews I did with her, she remained silent. As I have said, I will be forever grateful that my grandmother saved so many primary source documents—and that Barbara did not destroy them after she inherited the treasure. Today I believe she secretly wanted her story told but had no idea of the detailed documents in the chickenhouse.

INSTITUTE OF MUSICAL ART OF THE JUILLIARD SCHOOL OF MUSIC, NEW YORK

Record of BARBARA PHILLIPS   Entered October 5, 1939

Program   Dip. Piano

Graduated

t.S. Units from arien, Conn. 6/37	1939–40		Hrs. per wk.	Winter		Spring		Summer	
				Gr.	Pt.	Gr.	Pt.	Gr.	Pt.
	Piano	Gordon Stanley	1	B#	3		3		
		Instructor's rating		B		B			
	Th 12-21	Elem.; adv. harm; ctpt; anal.	2	C	2	B-	2		
	SS 12-21	Elem.; inter. sight-singing	1	B+	1	B+	1		
	Dic 12-21	Elem.; inter. dictation	1	D	1	B-	1		
	KH 11-12	Elem. keyboard harmony	1	B	2	B	2		
	Chorus		1	H	½	H	½		
	Music history		2	A-	2	A-	2		
	Ensemble	Piano	1			B+	1		

Deficiencies

Graduate Candidacy
Prev. ed. and degrees

Matric. pending

Matric. completed

Thesis title

Committee action
Entrance exam credit
Th 11   2
ET 11   2

EXPLANATION OF SYMBOLS

Passing { A Excellent / B Good / C Fair }

Not passing { D Privilege of re-examination / F Failure / X Absent from examination / WD Withdrew from course }

O Entrance deficiency
P Passed
H Credit for attendance only
* Jury examination

A point represents one semester hour
A semester consists of fifteen weeks

NOTE: While point value is indicated for private instrumental and vocal study, credit is not acceptable toward the degree or diploma until student has passed the final graduation examination.

Not valid without impression seal and actual signature

Certified as a Correct Copy   APR 1 5 2019

Date   Registrar

PART II

LETTERS FROM THE LOST
YEARS

1940

The decade was defined by World War II. When Barbara fled Europe in 1939, she had witnessed the opening days of the global conflict as Hitler's Wehrmacht invaded Poland. Forty-four months after the Japanese Imperial Navy bombed Pearl Harbor, six days after the United States dropped the second atomic bomb, Japan surrendered on August 15, 1945. More than eighty million people across the world died.

The daily European war news was a constant reminder for Barbara of her lost friends in Poland. At the end of the 1940 spring semester, she left Juilliard and traveled to Seattle, the city of her birth, and stayed with her grandfather Calvin Philips. Apparently, the visit was short-lived, and Barbara returned to New York City mid-May 1940 and wrote this letter to her grandfather.

May 18, 1940. Central Branch—YWCA 610 Lexington Ave., New York

Dear Grandfather, I arrived in New York safely and have

a permanent position earning so that I will be able to put myself through Summer School of the Juilliard Musical Art Institute. This semester commences about the middle of June. I would be most grateful to you if you could send all my music and clothes and things to arrive as soon as possible as I must start preparing already for my piano entrance examinations. If you would be so kind as to send a letter to arrive at the Y.W.C.A. on the twenty-sixth. Just say when the two locker trunks are arriving, and I can get them at whatever depot they arrive. I hope everything will be in the trunks so that you won't have any more trouble with me. In the trunk I found some linen belonging to you. If you want it just say and I'll send it back. I have no permanent address as yet and will probably be moving around 'til I find something I like—a studio type of room. Just send the letter [to the above address]. Barbara

The letter raises several questions. As Barbara would often do in the future, she ran from her problems. Why was she living at the YWCA on Lexington Avenue upon her return to New York? Had her violent streak resurfaced, and she was not welcome at home? I suspect she was struggling, trying to keep a grasp on her life.

When Barbara moved to Seattle, she must have planned to stay out West. Why had she left so abruptly, leaving the things she valued most? She alludes to trouble she and her grandfather had and speaks of linen found in her trunk. Throughout her life, Barbara had a habit of keeping things that struck her fancy even though they didn't belong to her. She offered to return her grandfather's linen, acknowledging that she had done wrong. Apparently, it was quite a troubled stay. A few months after the May 18th letter arrived, Barbara moved to Los Angeles, California, where the Philips family had relatives.

In reconstructing Barbara's past, here is the best information I found that revealed where she met her future husband, John Curry. In 1950, Elsie wrote to Eleanor Roosevelt:

> ... Disconsolate over her [Barbara's] music career being ruined by Hitler she went to work in an airplane factory [in 1940] and married the man who worked next to her in the factory.

I wonder if they both worked at Lockheed Aircraft Corp in Burbank, California. By 1941, the U.S. was gearing up war manufacturing and hiring thousands of new workers, including women, to work on the production line. Barbara wasn't capable of holding long-term employment. The "man who worked next to her in the factory" must have been John Curry. By the winter of 1941, Barbara and John had left the aircraft factory and traveled the West, eventually to John's home in Las Cruces, New Mexico, where Barbara wrote this next letter.

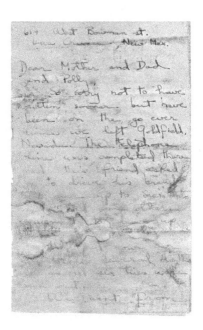

When I salvaged this letter from the chickenhouse, it was terribly damaged from water and mouse urine. There are a few full sentences. Here is the first page. Under a bright light and microscope, I transcribed the complete letter:

> 619 West Bowman St. Las Cruces, New Mexico
>   Dear Mother and Dad and Polly,
>   So sorry not to have written sooner but have been on the go ever since we left Goldfield, Nevada. The telephone line was completed there, and this friend asked me to drive his brand-new car up to Sacramento. From Sacramento we traveled to Everett and I stayed with grandmother a couple of days as she has probably written you. We stayed with Aunt Katherine and Uncle Nubs a couple of days in Seattle. (The rest of page 2 is too water damaged to transcribe.) The climate here is very warm and sunny; flowers are blossoming.

(The rest of this page is impossible to decipher.)

Barbara must have felt a lost soul as she drifted across the country during 1941. She flitted from Seattle, to New York, to Nevada; from Sacramento, California, back up to Everett and Seattle. The last sentence of the letter sounds like winter in southern California. On December 7, 1941, the Japanese bombed Pearl Harbor. The U.S. declared war on Japan.

Over the next few weeks, the West Coast was in a frenzy. Blackouts were ordered. Phantom aircraft were reported up and down the California coast. Spooked gunners fired thousands of rounds into the night skies. The Coast Guard rented machine guns from Hollywood. The New Year's Day Rose Bowl in Pasadena was cancelled. I imagine that seeing the panicked crowds flashed Barbara back to Warsaw, Berlin, and Brussels, as Hitler's war machine had invaded Poland fifteen months earlier. Barbara and John Curry fled California to John's parents' home in Las Cruces, New Mexico.

1942

Six months after Japan bombed Pearl Harbor, the Battle of Midway took place. From June 4-7, 1942, the U.S. Navy turned the tide of war in the Pacific when it sank four Japanese aircraft carriers and one heavy cruiser.

This next letter was badly water damaged. I extrapolated words that could not be recognized. I think the letter was written early winter 1942 because Barbara married John Curry soon after.

614 West Bowman St., Las Cruces, NM

Dear Mother, I received the package the day after your letter. Thank you so much for the white linen dress and the housecoat, they are both very pretty, especially the material on the white dress. It must be hand woven and hand embroidered. Did you get it from the museum? I can easily turn that cuff that is darned. It fits all right and the length is good. Grandfather wrote me from Philadelphia saying he had seen you all and wanted to know if we would be in Los Angeles around or after the tenth. He said to write a letter there to the Biltmore and mark it "hold." I have done that, telling him I am not sure whether we will be there or not but will let him know if we are. I hope Gram is all well from her cold now. Yes, it would be nice if we could both come East soon. Love to Pol and Daddy. Affectionately Barbara

This was the most positive letter Barbara wrote during the 1940s. She sounded happy. Barbara and John Curry were in Los Angeles on February 2, 1942, at The Patio (Outdoor Waiting Room), Union Station, Los Angeles. Elsie's mother sent the following note:

Dear Elsie, A postcard is not enough but better than nothing. First to tell you we are—Johnny [Curry] and I, having a social whirl. Barb and I went down to the seashore for luncheon fried shrimp! Francis Floyd gave a big luncheon for me today at the Ambassador. Love to all, Mother [Idalia]

On March 1, 1942, Barbara and John Curry were married in Yuma, Arizona. Why Yuma rather than Las Cruces? John's was an old family. His grandfather, George Curry, had served with Theodore Roosevelt in the Philippine Islands during the Spanish American War. George Curry went on to serve as Governor of New Mexico Territory. John, Barbara's new husband, was named after his uncle who had been gunned down in an 1885 frontier lynch mob shootout.

A few weeks after the wedding Barbara wrote to her family:

April 10, 1942 224 S. Olive St., Apt. 14 Los Angeles California

Dearest Mother and Daddy and Polly, We are back in Los Angeles now. We came here in quite a hurry as I had a bad attack of appendicitis in Las Cruces but did not wish to be operated on there. There was only one private hospital there and the fees are extremely high. When we arrived here, all the hospitals were all filled up but the attack subsided so will await the next emergency. The weather here is very hot -- one would think it were July or August. The birds are singing and big poinsettia bushes and other flowers bloom outside the window. I caught a terrible cold Sunday as we went to see my sister-in-law and her brand-new home. Although it was warm outside it was very cold inside as they hadn't turned on the heat yet. The marketing situation is pretty bad here as you can't get butter, eggs, meat, canned milk etc. How is it in New York? Write soon, Love Barbara

Another symptom of borderline personality disorder when in a stressful situation or anxiety kicks in, is co-occurring somatic illnesses. I believe Barbara's "bad attack of appendicitis" was an early indicator that she did not want to live in Las Cruces and used it as an excuse to get out. Barbara was twenty-two when she wrote that letter. For the next sixty-seven years, she never complained about her appendix.

For the Philips family, 1942 was a pivotal year. Henry was recalled to active duty with the army. Barbara was married and Polly met her future husband. This next letter from Barbara to her mother shows Barbara happy and stable except she and John don't have a permanent address.

December 24, 1942 Mrs. John C Curry. Los Angeles, California.

Dearest Mother and Polly,

Just received your long letter today and have written to Dad at Maxey (army training base in northeast Texas). I do not know what towns that are near but suppose it will get there as the Post office is no distance from it with all the camps and forts. I sent you all small presents but do not know if they will arrive by Christmas. You were too kind and generous to send us gift as I understand you were not receiving regular finances due to Army red tape. However perhaps things are regulated by now. Received letters from Gram and Grandfather also. Grandfather sent the usual calendar. Gram said she had sent money and a card to Las Cruces also and Katherine had sent one there. Gram sent me Nick Fratt the III address in San Antonio and wrote that he is engaged to a girl in Washington DC. He said his mother had given him a huge diamond ring—he wrote Gram that they didn't get enough food.

Polly sounds like she has a nice Defense job—perhaps it is out in New Jersey. I heard there were a lot of shipyards out that way. Too bad Dad's orders were so mixed. I told him John's father was about the same station he was during the last war and was already on a boat out of San Francisco harbor when Armistice was declared so they had to turn back. Wishing you both a Merry Christmas and good luck in the coming New Year. Love Barbara

1943

A t the beginning of 1943, Barbara was five months pregnant. She and John lived in Los Angeles. Barbara wrote two thank you letters to her mother for Christmas gifts. She sounded in good spirits. Her father Henry was a prolific writer. His letters offer an insight to our country and how WWII affected families at the most personal level. Over the next three years, his letters were laced with concerns about Barbara—they are perhaps the best window into her life. Henry and Elsie learned of Barbara's pregnancy from someone other than Barbara. Elsie often read and reread correspondences multiple times—and no doubt tucked some of the letters in wrong envelopes—so to make sense of this narrative, I sorted them chronologically.

This first letter is from Henry in Camp Maxey, Texas, to his wife Elsie in New York in its entirety so the reader might get a sense of his philosophical mindset.

22 January 1943, Friday evening.

Dearest Mum [Elsie]—I thought before piling into the hay I would scratch off a note to you. Our first week is nearly at a close and a busy week it was, it's left me pretty tired but satisfied. I had the best day of all today as the big rush in drawing equipment is about over and I was out in the open with the company practically all day. The weather is warm again, I'm down to a field jacket now but I still wear the slip on under my shirt. I'm so happy to have it, it's so cozy and warm and I love to wear it and think of your dear hands that knitted it. Such a sweet letter from you today, you are darling to write so frequently, and I love you for it when they mean so much to me away down here. Nothing but dirt and drilling and instructing; I like the life though and if you were only nearer it would be so much nicer. I'm feeling good again and out in the open all day with no money earning worries, I've gotten quite relaxed mentally, at least my worries are on a different line. I'm so anxious to do this job right all these fine men in the Army eager to learn everything and so dependent on the officers and noncoms to give them the education they need or may need should they ever get in a pinch. It worries me greatly that I may fall short of giving them the utmost. But I love that responsibility and feel so happy that I have my dear wife thinking of me and wishing too, that all goes well. Am glad you're going to get a suit; get something good, you always look swell in a suit, your dear figure seems just right for one. And get a good genteel hat. If you will wait a little bit I think I'll get my longevity soon and I'll send you some extra money – you know I don't need any of the $190 and when (note the when) I get my move up we will be in fair shape. I'm feeling comfortable that you have a savings account for we will need it afterwards and you've always been a beaver at putting money away whenever it came in regularly. I hope we never see those bitter days ever again. So pleased you heard again from Barb. It seems sometimes as if all I've saved out of this world's woes is the steadfastness of our life together which I never want to lose. I love you and I want to keep it that way. I'll be so glad when we're together again even if for a short time. This brief month in a new environment has brought to me in a strong way the realization that our life together through thick and thin ups and downs has been one of wonderful and understanding companionship. I want nothing more than its continuance. Well Dearest Heart good night – hope you are okay and taking good care of yourself for our future life together. Give sweet Polly my love. I hope the dear girl that we love so much is not over doing. Tell her I think of her a lot and I worry about her well-being Henry

Henry learns that Barbara is pregnant:

Feb 6, 1943. Dear Mum—What news! I suppose we could have expected it sooner or later but now that the news is here it is indeed a surprise. I hope and pray she gets along okay and will write soon. Well we knew someday we would be old and grandparents after all these years together, and I'm so glad we've stuck it, but I don't feel a bit older and here you are buying spring clothes. Love, Henry.

Sunday, February 7, 1943. Dear Mum, after I wrote you last evening, I hit the hay and had a grand sleep; up for 8 o'clock breakfast and what a glorious day it has been. This morning I went for an 8-mile walk, by myself, way out in the woods and I was amazed to see this lovely little violet. I so wished you had been right there to pick it and pin it on you. It would seem almost as if the back of winter is broken after a day like this and finding that violet—well after lunch I took a nap and decided to go for another walk, only about 3 miles this time in a different direction. So I really did have a good day.

Now in addition to a bit of worrying about dear Polly's health and such and wondrous lack of sleep, I've started to worry about Barb. Let me know when you write her, do you think she would be pleased if you made it very evident you would love to have her come home if John were called up? You would know best about this. I remember what a trying period of time you went through just before she was born and then later with Polly. Just thinking how many years ago and how upset the world was then. The dear girls have had such hectic years. I hope they feel there have been happy years too and we pray that when they are our ages the world will have righted itself and there will be some bit of common sense and serenity. Those will be, we hope, our "Years of Grace." Always My Heart To You Dear Wife – H.

Brown tobacco-like flakes tumbled out of the envelope when I first opened it—no doubt the violet Henry had sent. A sentence jumped out at me. "I remember what a trying period of time you went through just before she [Barbara] was born and then later with Polly." Today we know that a mother's stress during pregnancy can impact fetal development.

What stressors might Elsie have been dealing with in 1920, the year Barbara was born? Beyond normal stressors, pockets from the 1918 Spanish Flu Epidemic were still popping up. WWI had ended but Henry was still on active duty with the army. Elsie, all her life, was politically active. One week after Barbara was born, on August 18, 1920, the 19th Amendment was ratified. I'm sure that Elsie, throughout her pregnancy, was actively involved in campaigning for women's right to vote and worried it would fail.

Henry wrote to Elsie,

February 9, 1943. We seem to be thinking alike about Barb which is natural after all these years. Do write her. I think she'd welcome the knowledge you are apprised that she will soon be a mother. What do you think of writing her directly to the point and urge her to let you know what you can possibly make or do for her to help out. Ask how she is and if any complications etc. and make it all very evident you stand ready to pitch for her.

Barbara hadn't told her parents that she was pregnant, apparently unaware that they knew. This was the first hint that she would restrict my grandparents' access to us children in the future. In this next letter, Barbara and John have moved again.

March 25, 1943, Mrs. John C Curry, 944 ¼ S. Breed St., Los Angeles, California

Dearest Polly and Mother, This is to wish you a very happy birthday and thank you for your letters and the paper doilies and money order. As you can see we have moved again. It is practically impossible to bring oneself to find a place to live in this city now. The housing situation is so difficult. There are so many demands for homes and apartments that it is lucky the government made that law about raising rent. There is a banana tree and kumquat tree outside here. The latter are yellow plums but the bananas are green and they say that they never get ripe here. Thank you again for your letters and everything and many happy returns of the day to you. Hope you keep well, Love, Barbara

John Curry and his son, Christopher—Barbara wrote on
the back, "Taken in Beverly Hills, Cal. "Toto" and Pop
(August 1943)

Barbara and John's first son was born one month later. After
Barbara's March letter, I found no more from her for the rest of
1943.

In this next letter, John had moved to Las Vegas, Nevada, for
work. The U.S. had been at war for two years and there was a
manpower shortage in aircraft manufacturing plants. If,
according to Barbara's letter, she and John were working at
Sperry in San Pedro, why did he leave?

John wrote the following letter to Elsie.

October 12, 1943. Basic Magnesium Inc., Anderson's
Camp, Las Vegas, Nevada

Dear Mom: here I am working near Las Vegas, Nevada,
at a very important war industry still in the experimental
stage. I know you have heard of magnesium and the part it
will play in the future. I have always been interested in
metals of all kinds especially when there is still something to
learn of a new one. This is the largest plant of its kind in the
world. Barbara is in Los Angeles. At the present I am
making arrangements for FHA housing here, it will take at

least a month or so. The baby is looking very well. I wish you could see him. He is such a good looking boy. Haven't much more to say. Love to all also to Pop – Johnny

In a Christmas letter to Elsie, Polly wrote,

I got a nice letter from Barbara yesterday she said she was so far away from everything she didn't get a chance to do any shopping. Have you got her new address, 118 Copper St., Henderson, Nev.

By the end of 1943, Barbara had moved to Nevada and was living in company housing, surrounded by sand and sage brush, with John at work all day. Over the course of the next year, a series of letters reveals just how troubled Barbara was.

It was not only Barbara that Henry and Elsie stressed about. In 1942, while working at a USO canteen serving soldiers, sailors, Marines, and airmen, Polly met a soldier, Daniel Batten. Early in 1943, Polly eloped with Daniel when he was transferred to Madison, Wisconsin. Unaware to anyone, Polly's schizophrenia symptoms began to manifest. On April 10, 1943, Elsie received this letter from Polly—an excerpt:

Dear Mother—Guess what! Big excitement. Danny and I are getting married Tuesday at 11:30 in the morning. Everything is all set now. We have the witnesses and everything. I do hope you like the idea because you'll know how much I care and want to marry him. I thought I would send a wire to dad Monday when we are more sure of it as Dan might not get his day off Tuesday. I wish like hell you two could be here, but such is life.

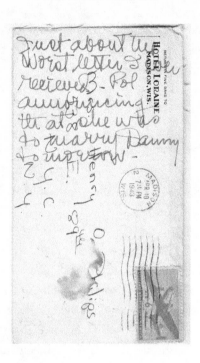

Postmarked April 10, 1943, Elsie wrote on the front of the envelope: *Just about the worst letter I ever received. Pol announcing that she was to marry Danny tomorrow.*

A few years in the future, after her divorce, Polly disappeared for six months. I have dozens of letters Polly wrote and countless entries in Elsie's diaries and mental health journals about Polly. Hers is a sad story, another story to be told one day, documenting a beautiful young girl's spiral into schizophrenia.

1944

By early 1944, Henry was stationed at Camp Shanks, New York, approximately fifty miles north of New York City. Barbara lived in Nevada, and Polly was in Florida with her new husband, Private Daniel Batten. Elsie, living in New York, received a constant flow of mail, but she was lonely. With the huge war build-up in the New York area, there was a critical housing shortage, so Elsie decided to rent her apartment on a short-term basis. She planned to travel west and visit Barbara and other relatives she hadn't seen in many years.

Barbara was not, at first, aware of the plan—she seldom communicated with her mother, but wrote long rambling letters to her grandfather Calvin. Just as we, today, forward emails and retweet, Calvin sent the letters on to his daughter-in-law Elsie. Thank goodness she saved the letters so almost eighty years later, a detailed, accurate window into my mother's troubled psyche is preserved. Elsie struggled to understand her daughter's behavior. She could not comprehend Barbara's rejection and silence.

On Feb 3, 1944, Barbara sent a letter to Elsie from Henderson, Nevada. The "busybody" that Barbara refers to is either her paternal grandfather Calvin or maternal grandmother Idalia.

Dear folks: Thank you for the two dollars and the stamps, also for the $10 bill. I haven't much to say—just mind your own business and go about your own plans as if that old busybody in Seattle hadn't stirred up a tempest. Kindly leave me alone. From now on any letters you find it necessary to write may be addressed to General Delivery here. If I am not here they will be forwarded to me. I may go to Los Angeles. My husband has been reclassified and is working in defense until such time as he is called. Thank you for the money. The kindest thing you can do is to go about your own business entirely as before. I never informed you of anything except what letters you have of mine. Sincerely, Barbara Curry

A second letter in the same envelope sounded as if Elsie had sent Barbara a care package. As future documents reveal, John and Barbara were having marital problems. John left soon after this letter was written. Barbara mentioned radio tubes—she always loved listening to classical music. In the 1940s radio programs for the lonesome and the lovelorn filled the airwaves. I wonder if Barbara listened to *Good Will Court, Voice of Experience, Court of Human Relations,* or any of the hundreds of other radio programs that were yesterday's version of *Dr. Phil?*

Back to the second letter Barbara wrote to her mother:

Dear Mother, The package arrived this morning with the four radio tubes, camera and film and crochet hooks. Since your letter just came yesterday telling about the tubes, I didn't expect the package for several weeks, so was very surprised that it arrived so soon. I received both your letters telling about the colored film. The film you sent with the camera says panchromatic on it. I'll find out for sure if that means it's a colored film and be very careful with it. The radio tubes work all right although nobody, no matter how expensive the radio set, can get anything here during the day, just at night sometimes. However, it's better than nothing.

The writing paper would be all right but I'd rather have blocks—all sizes with letters or numbers etc. wooden blocks if they make them anymore. Large ones and small ones but the paint on them must not be lead as that is poisonous to eat. You can find out from psychology books what other toys a 1 ½-year-old child can understand but I think it's mainly blocks, perhaps a few wagons or trucks but nothing that comes loose and can be swallowed.

That's all I can think of. Blocks, beads (large) and spools. If you have any empty spools you can send them as I haven't hardly any. I ordered some blocks at Christmas time and when they arrived the whole box full was so tiny they could have all been swallowed. I sent them back. But I hope you will be able to find some great big ones. Be sure to tell me how much money to send for the radio tubes, camera etc. I expected the radio tubes might break but that paper was good. We had a terrible windstorm here and all

the power went off. Well, Thank You for everything, love
Barbara

In a letter that Polly sent to her mother, she mentioned that
Barbara was inquiring about her old beau Bruce Mims. Polly
commented that Bruce had gotten married. Barbara must have
been angry at John, for her to inquire about Bruce. Another
symptom of borderline personality disorder—splitting. At the
beginning of the relationship, Barbara placed John on a pedestal
as the perfect mate. But no one can live up to that ideal. Barbara,
over a period of two years, went from admiring John to despising
and wanting to be rid of him. Did she get violent with him, as
she had done with others in the past?

This next letter was written by John Curry to Elsie:

Feb 8, 1944 118 Copper St., Henderson, Nev.

Dear Mom: Barbara and I have been very unhappy for
the past few weeks. I am not very certain that we can live
together very much longer in these conditions. We have
discussed that I should join some branch of the service until
this war and turmoil is over with. Then things may be better
later. I have advised her to go home to you or my parents so
that she may have a good rest to settle her nerves. She has
been very nervous lately. Our small income has gone each
week to pay for furniture, food, and rent. The furniture is all
paid for now. Please write to her very soon and give her
some good motherly advice. If you know Barbara as well as
I do, I am sure she will do the right thing while I am gone.
The allotments from the government will take about 90 days
to come through. In the meantime, she must have a place
to stay for the sake of our child. We have definitely made up
our minds that I leave to the induction station in Los
Angeles tomorrow. There isn't very much more to say –

Lots of Love to You and Pop, As Ever Johnny

In this next letter Barbara wrote to her grandfather Calvin Philips in Seattle, she sounds as if she is losing touch with reality. She accuses her husband of asking Calvin for money. However, as a future letter will confirm, Barbara herself asked for it, but was ashamed because of past transgressions.

118 Copper Street
Henderson, Nevada.

Dear Grandfather,

I was very surprised to receive the fifty dollars from you. Naturally we are destitute week after week. Most of the time we live on a sack of potatoes with just a dollar left over to buy milk for the baby. But this doesn't mean I would ever think of asking you for money. Gambling is legal up here and my husband has the gambling disease. Every week he loses his $60.00 pay check. I never see the money. We've been up here six months. I hope you will keep this matter confidential and not tell the rest of the family. Still I would never think of asking you for any cent of money again. I realize you wished to "wash your hands of me" long ago. And you bear me an unfriendly grudge for some reason. Therefore, there is always some strange Welfare Organization or the Red Cross to help me out. As an innocent child of one year must not be made to suffer for such crimes.

The letter continues:

I did not send you that telegram. How can I possibly pay you back when we are destitute week after week. When your money order arrived I didn't even tell my husband, but decided to hide it for a real emergency for the baby. He has no right to lay his filthy gambling hands on your money. Finally he asked me if I'd had any money from you. I then learned that under the influence of liquor he had dared to send you a telegram. I don't even know what he said.

I then learned we had exactly $.50 in the house to last the whole week. No matter he shall not touch your money. That is enough to buy milk for the baby for a week and we shall live on a sack of potatoes as we have done many times before. I know all this doesn't influence you in the least. Excuse me I mean interest you. I know you wished to have nothing more to do with me long ago. But my child shall not be made to suffer. A thing like this can be brought before the Child Welfare Board and that's exactly what I'm planning to do.

If you want your money back you may have it. I put it aside for a real emergency for the child which is likely to happen any time.

Just because I have a rich grandfather doesn't mean he [my baby] has any right to your money. I realize you wish to have nothing to do with us. As I say there is always some Welfare Society or the Red Cross which is glad to help me.

I realize you live in a peaceful and prosperous life in Seattle and we have no right to interrupt it. As I say you may have your money back if you want it. I'd rather accept charity from strangers than from my Grandfather who seems to bear an unfriendly grudge against me. Please keep this matter confidential and don't tell the rest of the family of my unfortunate circumstances.

Love, Barbara

This next letter Barbara sent, in the same envelope, was long and troubling. She rambled back into her childhood with accusations against her mother and created an elaborate ruse about John. Barbara apparently didn't know that four weeks earlier, John had informed the family that, "… I leave to the induction station in Los Angeles tomorrow." Barbara's sense of abandonment by her mother and her husband was amplified.

Tuesday, March 14, 1944

Dear Grandfather: You ask that I inform you by return mail whether John has been called into service. Since you know all the facts so far, I might as well tell you the whole truth up to date. John has completely deserted me and my two children, Yes, I am going to have another child in a few months. Now, as we both know, he has committed two penitentiary offenses. The first was obtaining money under false pretenses, the second desertion.

He left here at 6 o'clock last Wednesday morning, March 8, saying he was going to work as usual. At 9:30 the same morning the government man came to the door saying they wanted the house back as my husband had terminated. He had hidden a suitcase outside the door with just a few clothes and so when the government man came at 9:30 and said he had terminated, it's the first I knew. Quickly I went to the Welfare Board and told them he had left me without a single cent of money. They went directly to the War Manpower Commission in Las Vegas knowing he would have to clear through there before he can get a job anywhere.

It seems that John had just left the War Manpower Commission a few minutes before the Welfare Chairman arrived. He found out that John did not get a clearance release. John asked for a release because he said he was going in the Service. The W.M.P.C. said he could not have a release until he showed proof that he was going in the Service. This he did not have. Therefore he will not be able to get a job anywhere. Unless, as the Red Cross says, a black market operator or farmer takes him on. Also, he might escape across the border into Mexico and work there. Therefore, I do not know at present, if the district attorney or the Red Cross or anyone will ever be able to locate him. If a man deserts the Army or his family there are many ways for him to disappear, I guess. I told the Red Cross I don't care if they arrest him, but they seem to think the wiser thing to do is try to locate him and bring him back without arresting. We had been talking about trying to get him into some branch of the Service for quite some time as he is 4-F on account of his eye. Although the Red Cross says they would accept him on limited service.

So after he committed his offense to you, I wrote a letter to his draft board and asked them to please examine him again and take him into some branch of the Service if possible. He saw me write that letter and apparently underneath he was really scared to go in the Army, for fear of being killed. Because it was the very next morning that he deserted me without a penny. I don't know what he expected me to do.

The Red Cross is helping me right now, so the baby won't starve and so we'll have this roof over our heads. They would've thrown us out of this house immediately were not for the Red Cross. As these homes are only for B.M.I. plant workers.

But as the Red Cross says, they can only help out for so long. Then what? You can imagine how such a frightful shock has affected my nerves. It is a terrible awful thing that has happened to my brain and I might even fear a nervous breakdown the way I have felt so weak and shaky the last few days. But Grandfather there is no use communicating these circumstances to my Mother. I would like to send you the letter I received from her last Saturday after you had informed her that my husband had gone into the Service. She said I could stay in this house until convenient as they could not evict me. She said I should go to the Red Cross for help. She said she was very tired and was going to rent her apartment for a very high price and go away for a year or so maybe. Imagine, my own Mother. I'm sure if I had a child I'd tell her to come home at once and be happy to make a home where my children could always come. I know you said once that my Mother always tried to live above my Father's income. This is very true. Therefore you must not judge me too harshly, Grandfather. If you read your psychology books you will find that in the old days the parents had the power of life and death over their children.

It is still the same today. If the child grows up unhappy and a misfit in society you must not blame the child it is the fault of the parents.

I can never remember my Mother as Mother. She was always more interested in Social activities and running the town and taking care of Nicholas's three children for years. You have your proof today. She is more interested in running off and visiting relatives and friends for a year and renting her apartment at a high price, than she is in having her destitute daughter come home. Therefore please do not inform her of my circumstances. She has already rented her apartment and it is no use. Therefore please do not judge me too harshly, Grandfather dear, if I was a misfit in your home. It goes back much farther than that. Why when I was 15, the most important year of my life when I should've been studiously preparing for college she went off and left me in the home of two mentally deficients whose Father was a doctor never at home. You remember that winter. She sojourned in New York at the Vanderbilt Hotel—most swanky in New York. But could not afford to send us to private school in the city. So left my sister in an already overcrowded home and me in an abandoned home with no supervision. Now that I look back on it I don't see how Mother could do this, then to leave me alone in Europe in that unhealthy atmosphere when I should've been at home enjoying the youthful years of American womanhood. It is too late now to repair those years but I hope you see my point if I made you unhappy in my visit to you. I never told you this but the night I was to leave your home in Seattle—remember—I received a telegram from my Mother. In it she asked me to please not come home. That's why I didn't show it to you. It was too late to turn back and I said, to myself – all right if she doesn't want me home I won't go there.

When I was a very small girl in California I remember having two very beautiful China dolls and a brand-new red child's bicycle. In a temper one day my Mother threw both my dolls to the floor and they broke to bits. Another time she ran over my new bicycle purposely, it seems. Both disasters broke my child's heart at the time. These two events seem symbolic of my later life. It seems like she is still breaking or wrecking my life. The most important partnership in life is marriage. I only hope that I prepare my children to choose a wise mate with whom they may lead a happy life. Entirely opposite from my life.

What does the future hold for me? Right now, less than nothing. I can only live from day to day and wonder what bitter blow tomorrow will bring. Of course you are entitled to a peaceful life Grandfather, that's what I meant when I said it was a shame to bother you with my troubles.

Please don't tell any of the family on either side, of my circumstances. I would rather starve then have them laugh behind my back. Don't even tell Grandmother Fratt as she would only say "I told you so." She met John and didn't like him. You may tell them he went in the Army if you wish. I will inform you if the Red Cross locates him. Although I doubt if they will. If a man deserts his family, I think there are plenty of ways to disappear. I'm truly sorry Grandfather, that I disappointed you so. I hope you think better of me now. And don't think that I don't appreciate greatly what you've done for me. Love, Barbara

What wasn't in the letter? Barbara had set herself up as the proverbial "damsel in distress" for emotional and economic gain from her family. Future documents reveal that she knew exactly where John was from the moment he walked out the door.

Calvin wrote to Henry and replied to Barbara. Calvin's statement in the letter to Henry, "Something should be done before she commits some act," articulates the unspoken fear of Barbara attempting suicide again, this time, placing Christopher and the unborn child at risk.

Friday, March 17, 1944

Dear Henry, your airmail letter of the 13th has just come. The same mail brings a distressing letter from Barbara. She suggests me to not inform the family of its contents. Privacy will not help solve this problem. Truth in the open with family is better. I am therefore enclosing a copy of her letter dated March 14 and copy of my reply. I do not know what to do. You and Elsie may have some thoughts on the subject. Something should be done before she commits some act. Let me hear from you on the subject.

Affectionately, Father PS. Since writing the above I concluded to wire you.

Calvin's reply to Barbara:

March 17, 1944

Dear Barbara, Your letter of the 14th has just come. The information you give me pictures a very distressing situation and frankly at the present time I do not know what to suggest. Keep me posted of any change of address that I may contact you when I have something to say. I think you are entirely wrong in not wishing to have your parents know of this situation. If there have been family disagreements in the past, it should be possible for all concerned to overlook them and come to a harmonious agreement, particularly in an effort to solve your problems. It is your duty to inform your Father and your Mother of your situation.

Affectionately, your Grandfather

Calvin had five sons, but no daughters and must have been at a loss dealing with Barbara. The following day he sent her a second letter.

March 18, 1944

Dear Barbara: Here is a money order for $50, which I have concluded to send to help out with your expenses until your problem has been solved. I have given a lot of thought to the problem these last few hours, and my earnest conclusion is that it is one for you and your Mother to solve. Your Mother has an object lesson in the sacrifices by your Grandmother Fratt in caring for Dee's baby for several years. Dee is your Grandmother's daughter. You are your Mother's daughter. I think you should, at once, write your Father and Mother, and tell them truthfully the whole story. They are the proper ones for you to turn to under conditions that have developed. Forget the quarrels that may have taken place in early years. Both you and your mother have added years to your ages since those quarrels took place and have acquired a different and broader viewpoint of life, and it should be possible for both of you to make a new and fresh start and be helpful to each other. I see no other solution to the problem.

Do not withhold anything in your letter telling your parents of the situation. At this point I am going to remind you that in the past, your statements have not always balanced. By this I mean they have not always agreed. You may not intentionally have misrepresented, but when statements by the same person differ there is naturally doubt as what to believe. The best approach to the subject, therefore, is a complete and truthful statement of your present situation that your parents may be better able to decide upon a course.

Let me know whether you will adopt this suggestion.

Affectionately, your Grandfather

Dear Henry: above is a copy of a letter I have just written to Barbara, which speaks for itself. I concluded she must have some money relief and therefore sent her this additional $50. I hope you and Elsie will be able to solve the problem to the satisfaction of all concerned. Affectionately, Your Father

Each time I worked with these letters I was again reminded how thankful I was that Calvin, Idalia, Henry, and Elsie forwarded and shared all correspondence, and that Elsie preserved them for so many decades. Without the letters, there would be little record of how very troubled my mother was.

Barbara, two months pregnant with her second child, replied to her grandfather:

March 18, 1944

Dear Grandfather: Mother just called me from New York. She said that you had said I should go there. Please, Grandfather Dear, I don't want to go to New York. I have two babies now and a New York apartment wouldn't be at all suitable for them. I don't care if I live in a shack. Just so it's a house of my own where each child has his own sleeping room. That is essential. Then I must be able to have them out in the sun the greater part of the day. That is essential. Then I must be able to do their daily wash while still watching them. Don't you understand Grandfather dear? I must have a little cottage for the sake of the babies. A New York apartment wouldn't do at all. I told mother that. I told her to please tell you that I wanted to go to you. You said in your letter to me that before you had been willing to pay for my music education. Well this is far more important —my two children. Your two great grandchildren. You will live in posterity if you help them. And after all that's what everyone really wants to do isn't it?

You've been in Real Estate business all your life and as I said I don't care if it's just a shack just so it's my own house where the two children live healthfully and peacefully. It doesn't necessarily have to be in Seattle; because I know all the defense workers have taken everything. It would have to be in some town near Seattle where the defense workers aren't located. What about Whidbey Island or someplace like that. Just so I can get milk every day for the children. I don't care where I live.

But don't worry Grandfather I'm not coming until we get this husband business settled right here and now, once and for all. I don't want it to drag on for years. Don't you agree with me? His father is a Justice of The Peace and Desk Sgt. on the Police Force. He is trying to help locate him. If we can locate him and get him on limited service in the Army then I'd get $50 per month plus $30 plus $20 for each child. Then I wouldn't be dependent on you. Many wives live on this salary. If you could just find me a cottage with two bedrooms – one for each child and I could sleep in the living room. I'm sending you a government book on how to bring up your child so you'll know where I'm getting all my essential information. Especially I want this next child to start out right in life by having his own room and his own bed where he can sleep undisturbed. My poor first child didn't have either. And he developed terrible nervous crying habits and all kinds of digestive disorders. I took him to about 30 different doctors and they said he needed his own room and his own bed to start out with the right habits.

Do you think it will be possible to find a cottage on Whidbey or in some remote place? I wouldn't even care if it were in the worst section of Seattle if it was a house. I remember seeing a very poor section below your old house. Please Grandfather dear, I wish you could find it in you to forget your disappointment in me in the past and help me now for the sake of my children. They'll always be grateful to you if you help to bring them up right; as the first six years are the most important in each individual's life. Can't you forgive me now Grandfather and help my children. Maybe you can't and don't want to. In that case I'll just go out and work for their living and stay here. Because this house costs $11 per week and I could work all night and take care of them in the day – maybe. It's a possibility.

You've worked so hard all your life and I should certainly think God would reward you greatly for helping your great grandchildren. It's for their sake. And you just couldn't help loving them once you've seen them. I can't think of anyone else in the family who needs your help at all except me.

You don't know what a feeling of security your character gives me Grandfather. If only you could help me and I could depend on you. You are so trustworthy, if only I could depend on you. I've felt so helpless for such a long time. My own parents are so flighty. They have no future to offer my children. It's the children I'm thinking of, not myself. Whereas you're so steadfast. A person could always depend on you if you were willing to help them.

You remind me of the Grandfather in "Little Lord Fauntleroy," who was so mean to the Mother of the little boy all through the book, but who finally became kind in the end.

If I were a very wealthy woman, I'd buy the best trained nurse in the U.S. to take care of my children. But since I'm not, I only try and be the best trained nurse I know how, for my children. That's why I am adamant in the fact that they must have a quiet babyhood and a peaceful and happy place to live. I just couldn't live in an apartment with them and no air or space or sunshine or washtub or clothesline.

I have confidence in you Grandfather Dear, that you could find me some little place like that without too much trouble. What about all those places where people go in the summer. I remember them. Maybe I could get one of those for the summer and be looking around for a warmer place for the winter.

Above all, it's the Mother's peace of mind that keeps her children well and happy. That's why I must live apart with them with no one to boss me or disturb their naps. When they nap I always keep the house perfectly quiet. And at night if they feel like "crying it out" I let them. And not pick them up and hush them for some neighbor's sake, which spoils them ruinously.

There's an Army Nurse lives next door to me. She's married now and has a baby but she still keeps her name at the hospital if they need her for an emergency. She tells me that she wouldn't go home to her Mother. It would make her too nervous and spoil her peace of mind with the children, besides the fact that there's not enough room. She says she couldn't stand to have her Mother fussing around. I said I felt the same way. She said most girls feel that way. They wouldn't go home to their Mothers. I know it would spoil my calm and peaceful manner with the children. It would make me nervous all the time.

It's early Sunday morning now and I better run up to the post office with this letter before the mail goes out at 8:00 o'clock. I hope you will write me soon, Grandfather dear and God bless you. It was very nice of you to wire my Mother but she doesn't need to give up her trip as I couldn't possibly go there anyway. I hope you understand my point of view after I've thought it all out wisely.

Please try and see my point. And forgive me for the past. I hope one of your friends will know of a vacant cottage in some town up there. I want to be near you so you can see the children often. I told my Mother I'd rather go near you because you have more stability and foresight for the children's future. My own parents have never known their plans from one moment to the next. And I absolutely want my children to grow up in one place and have a feeling of security about their home – rather than be moving around from one moment to the next. Well, I must close now. Please understand me Grandfather dear because I am your own Grandchild. God bless you again on this beautiful Sunday morning. Love, Barbara

Barbara's statement about, "those places where people go in the summer" was prophetic. In 1952, Barbara, with five children by then, ran from her Minnesota husband Herman. We moved into exactly the cottage she visualized in this letter. Ironically, the home was owned by a close friend of Calvin Philips. I'm quite sure Barbara had visited the cabin, located near the north end of Lake Chelan in the Washington Cascades, when she was a child. I wonder if it was the "cottage" Barbara fantasized about when she hinted to her grandfather.

Calvin's reply to Barbara:

March 22, 1944
  Seattle, Washington
  Dear Barbara: I have read and reread your letter of March 18. If the apartment house in New York is not a proper place for you to care for the children, your thoughts should include a plan that will let your Mother help you wherever it seems best for you to live. She is the natural and proper person for you to turn to under present prevailing conditions, and I am sure if you expressed an earnest desire to have her assist, she would recognize it as a duty above the duty that she feels toward the Shipways [wealthy family friends who lived on Long Island, New York]. You cannot live alone and provide for the children. At the present time and until and unless John has been located

and compelled to provide for his family you must be relieved of household duties to do such work as your condition will permit. Your Grandmother Fratt has made a suggestion that is entitled to consideration. She thinks you should come to Seattle and take a house or an apartment where she will live with you and relieve you for some sort of work. She says Norbert's wife, who has some position with one of our daily papers, is desperately in need of assistance for light work—office position, paying in the neighborhood of $100 per month, and that she could probably immediately offer you a position. Grandmother Fratt also suggests your Mother would doubtless come to Seattle and make her home with you and also take a position and help provide the necessary expenses for maintaining the home. A further thought she has is, that when the war is over and your Father has been released he may wish to reestablish himself in business on this coast.

I think one of the first questions to be settled pertains to your marital situation. In your letter of May 18, you said "I am not coming until we get this husband business settled right here and now once and for all. I don't want it to drag on for years." This program seems sensible. Do you mean by this, that you contemplate asking for a divorce? If so how quickly, under the laws of your State can it be had. I would like to be advised regarding this question. I would also like to be advised of the approximate date you expect the second baby will be born.

Your problems, Barbara, are not insurmountable. As I view the situation from the information at hand not only in connection with your marriage but from the contacts with you when you were in Seattle, is that you must adjust yourself to a forgiving attitude toward life. For some reason there has evidently crept into your life a feeling against family and loving ones. There is love in the hearts of your parents. If you have had differences in the past, now in your more mature years these differences must be forgiven and forgotten and you must throw your heart open to receive the love that I know your Father and Mother want you to have for them. They are the natural ones for you to turn to. You must avoid the thought of going through life with adverse feelings. Life has a lot of happiness in store for all of us if we will throw our hearts open to receive and if you will do your part in finding this happiness I know it will come to you. In your letter of March 18, you appear to appeal to me and me only to help you solve your problems. I want to do what is proper in guiding you and helping you, but it is wrong for you to expect me to bear all of the financial responsibility that may develop in getting you readjusted. I think my responses in the past is evidence that I want to do my share, but there are others who will want to join in assisting you, and it is proper that they should be permitted to do so. As I stated in a previous letter you must be open and frank and truthful in all of your statements that we who are willing and trying to help you can do so in a way that will be for you and your children's permanent good.

I think at this time you should let me know and let your parents know just how you are fixed financially. Have there been any obligations or debts incurred that should and must be met. If so what are they and what are the amounts. How are you fixed at this time for ready money. Did you receive the $50 that I wired to you and did your husband get any part of it? I also sent you another $50 by Express Money Order just a few days ago, and a letter from your father says that they have sent you a little money. Let me have this information and also what it is costing you per week and month to live. We must know and we must have such information as that to properly guide us in seeing that you do not suffer from want. It should be possible before very long to decide upon the question of your moving to Seattle. If John is located and is placed in the Army as his Father plans on doing, the allotment from the government will do much toward solving the problem of support. Your parents and your relatives will together find some way to get you reestablished, and in a way that you will not suffer, but you must do your part by cooperating with us and giving us the information we should have to guide us in properly re-locating you. Affectionately, Your Grandfather

It must have been heart-wrenching for Henry and Elsie to watch their daughter flounder, and yet Barbara refused to communicate with them. In the chickenhouse I found two hand-written telegram drafts dated March 11, 1944, that Elsie had written. I imagine she was playing with words, trying to decide which message Barbara might be most receptive to.

One:

Dear Barbara. Have just written you a long letter. Think you should prepare to come East immediately. Will arrange funds. As soon as you get my letter and have made plans send us a night letter collect. Tell what your plans are and how much you need. Love Mother.

Two:

We hope you will come to live with us. We sincerely do. You and the baby and when this turmoil is over you and Johnny can pick up from there. We love you Barb, we've always always loved you. Let mother know when you will leave, and she will send you $100 or if you can't come East let mother know if you will want some money.

After procrastinating for a week, Elsie sent the telegram she had been drafting a week earlier. On March 18, 1944, Barbara sent her mother another postcard, *please write and tell me what prompted you to send the telegram.* Barbara obviously had no idea that her grandfather was sharing her letters.

Barbara sent a letter to her mother:

March 21, 1944 118 Copper St., Henderson, Nev.

Dear mother, I don't know the meaning of the letter you wrote. If my husband wrote you any letters, please forward them to me. No, I have not told grandmother Fratt anything about anything she is too occupied with her relatives in Seattle. No, I do not want her here. Please do not gossip as you have probably already done. However, I hardly think it to your credit that your children grew up to choose the wrong life partners. Perhaps for this reason you will not gossip. Where did you get your information? Since you heard by chance please do not pass it along. What good would it do you to have John's parents address. They are uneducated. They could not write you. I may stay here and work the night shift and have a girl sleep overnight with my children. I must hurry now and get this off on the 4:00 dispatch. Love Barbara

P.S. You don't need to write the Shipway's anything— just go ahead with your travel plans as I would not come East in any event, and don't change your plans. Thanks a lot for the five dollars. I hope I can pay you back someday.

Barbara continued the charade that John had left her. Was it a calculated scheme to gain sympathy—and money—from her family? A letter to her grandfather Calvin:

Monday, March 20, 1944 Barbara Curry, Henderson, Nevada

Dearest Grandfather: I received your 2 letters today with the enclosure of $50. It is good to know that there are still some kind, wonderful, generous people in the world. I have much to tell you.

The Red Cross is paying my rent and they buy my groceries. Just the essentials for the baby; milk, eggs, fruit, vegetables etc. They say they will make my husband responsible for these items when they do catch up with him. The head of the Red Cross here says she can't tell me everything they are doing to try to catch him. But this is as much as I know. I told you they have contacted his father and he is on the police force and they have his cooperation.

Now, please keep this entirely confidential. The head of the Red Cross has many friends. And through political pull, she hopes to get his draft board to draft him within the next few weeks. If this is possible, then the FBI will be on his trail and from what I've heard, they are much stronger and smarter than these grafted police forces. Also, she says the FBI will not treat him as a criminal but as an irresponsible boy. Whereas the police would just beat him up and throw him in jail and she believed this would make a worse character of him—to be among other criminals. Let us pray this plan works out. Then you see, I will not be dependent on you but will have my $80 per month. Also, the Red Cross arranges your hospital fee for the baby wherever you are. So you see, they say, this will take quite a little time, the only thing I am hoping is that you will hear of some little vacant cottage where I can bring up my children. I hope Grandfather that this idea does not anger or contrary you. I wouldn't even think of asking you to find me a house in Seattle, because I know what an impossibility that would be. So all I ask of you is to think of some town which is not near enough for those defense workers to commute; then make inquiries for a small modest cottage with two bedrooms and one bath. I don't care how ugly or dirty it is, as I can clean it; just so there's plenty of sunshine around it.

My goodness, if I am forced to work for a living why spend $120 to travel all the way across the United States? I might just as well go to work on the night shift, in the plant here so I could keep this house and pay someone to stay with my children at night. Of course I will do this only as a last resort if you do not wish me to come near Seattle. Because I know it would be torture to work all night and care for the children all day. I imagine I could get about 6 hours sleep but I would be awfully cross with the children being so tired, I'm afraid. Youngsters of that age keep you on the go every minute.

My next point is, Grandfather; what did you mean about my truth in letters. You said the stories differ sometimes. Please tell me right away, what you meant. I know for a fact that my husband is a terrible liar. The Red Cross called his sister in Los Angeles to find out if she'd seen him. He'd been there for a few minutes but had not told her his address. But he did tell her that I had thrown him out. Can you imagine such a lie? I never did such a thing. At least I know my child and I are dependent on him and I wanted him to work in the plant until he'd saved enough to tide us over until his first allotment came from the Army. He just didn't want her to know he was afraid of being killed. But the FBI will get him I hope, and put him on limited duty. Also I believe he wrote my mother a letter telling her I was the one who was breaking us up. She had the effrontery to write me a letter scolding me for taking his son away from him. Can you imagine—insult upon injury when he has deserted his two children and wife—a criminal offense. Then your letter came telling her the truth. So that's what you must mean by stories that differ. My mother probably had the nerve to write you and tell you of his lies to her. I never heard of such effrontery.

I hope you recognize the truth Grandfather. I think you do. You know the whole story from the beginning. You know he lost the whole $60 paycheck. He got scared and didn't know what to do so he sent you that telegram in my name. Then when I turned against him for the first time and asked him how he dared forge my name to such a request he was surprised. Then when he realized I really meant for him to go in the Army after all his big talk about joining up for two years, he really got scared. He left me one morning at 6 o'clock by hiding his suitcase outside the door (I had helped him pack it because we were planning to get him inducted during that week.) He dared to terminate and draw all his money without telling me a thing about it. He left me destitute and we were both going hungry as I wouldn't touch that money of yours. I had previously borrowed $2 from a clergyman for milk for the baby for that week before your money came. Please tell me if you meant anything else by stories that differ. It makes me wrathful that he should dare write a letter to my mother and tell her lies. You know for a fact that the police have not been able to locate him for two weeks. I only hope the FBI catch him.

I think that's all for now I don't know what else you meant by my stories not resembling each other. Please give examples of my statements not having balanced in the past. I don't know when they have not agreed. Please tell me. When have my statements differed?

I must remind you again that I have to live alone with the children for their own good and no one else's. Today the Red Cross lady came and woke the baby from his nap. He was cross all day and could not go back to sleep. He missed two hours important sleep from his life. I hope you understand my point in this matter. Much love to you and I will hold your gift as an aid to my traveling expense if you will allow me to come near Seattle. Affectionately, Your Granddaughter, Barbara

The phrase "... when I turned against him for the first time..." jumped out at me, as being untrue—otherwise, why would she even mention that fact? Barbara also mentioned the FBI searching for John. I smiled as I transcribed the paragraph in which Barbara accused John, that he "...dared forge my name...." Twenty-three years later when I was in the navy I came home on leave for a month. I had directed the USS *Rogers* payroll officer to send my paycheck to the farm. I told Barbara and Herman to watch for it; the check never arrived so when I returned to the ship, I visited with the payroll officer to stop payment. A few weeks later I was visited by an FBI agent. He showed me the cancelled check, endorsed by Barbara Affield and asked if I wanted to press charges—which, naturally, I did not. When I wrote her a letter asking for my money, she claimed to have no knowledge of the check's existence. Barbara's fiscal duplicity spanned the decades.

The following day, Idalia wrote to Elsie in New York. It's quite revealing of Idalia's Victorian attitude about a single mother and how to protect her reputation, by telling people that "Bar's husband has been drafted."

March 21, 1944 Idalia Fratt, 1102 Harvard No. Seattle, Wash.

My Dearest Elsie, My head is in a buzz. I called Mr. Philips and he came up immediately but not being accustomed to his business way of settling things I didn't tell him half I wanted to, but he seemed to think my idea alright. It was the first thing popped into my head and after calm reflection may see flaws—but my idea is to have Barbara come here to me. Let you continue your plan only coming here to see Barbara and the rest of us instead of going to Las Vegas. All we have to say is that Barbara's husband has been drafted. Hundreds of girls are at home for the same reason.

Mr. Philips relieved me greatly by saying he had sent Barbara a hundred dollars and talked as if he might send her a ticket, but he left before I said half I was going to. I said one thing about bringing Barbara here was the difficulty of finding a place but he thought that could be managed.

Did Barbara tell you about expecting another little one? She wrote that to Mr. Philips. That is too bad, but she still may be able to do some light work of course. I couldn't support a family of three without help even if I get a little dividend out of the Mill, but if Barbara could get a Defense job even for a little while it would make it much easier to get a place to live.

Bushels of Love, Mother

Calvin Philips wrote to his son,

March 23, 1944 Lieut. Henry Philips, PO Box 6545, Philadelphia, Penn.

Dear Henry: Your letter of the 20th has just come. Also I received one yesterday from Elsie. Another letter has been received from Barbara today, dated the 20th. Although she asks that a number of the statements contained therein be treated in confidence, I do not feel that this entire matter can be properly handled unless all of us intimately concerned know what each other knows. I am enclosing a copy of Barbara's letter of the 20th, it need not go beyond you and Elsie, and I think we should all respect Barbara's request that, that portion she wishes treated in confidence be so handled.

It is comforting to know that the Red Cross is giving considerable attention to this matter and affording relief. Apparently, Barbara is not suffering for want at this time, and there is therefore not a need for haste in having her removed.

I do not have the address of Barbara's father-in-law. You will notice that I am asking her in my letter today just where her father-in-law is now located. When I have other information of interest, I will pass it to you.

Affectionately, Calvin Philips your Father

On the same day, Calvin answered Barbara's letter:

March 23, 1944
Dear Barbara, Your letter of the 20th has just come. There is no need to make an effort to find a house here for you until there has been definitely determined that you are to come here and live and if so whether with your Grandmother. And also we should wait until we know when you will be prepared to make the move.

In one of your recent letters you mentioned intending to remain where you are until the husband question is settled. I asked whether that meant you intended to seek a divorce and if so, how much time would be required. I think the house can be found, although it may take a while to obtain just what you want. If you are to live in a small town near Seattle, you would not have the opportunity to carry out the suggestion of your Grandmother that you make yourself available for a position under Ruth.

In one of your recent letters you spoke of the cooperation you are receiving from John's Father in an effort to locate him. You say that John's Father is a Justice Of The Peace and Desk Sergeant on the police force. Is he located in Henderson or elsewhere, and what is his first name? Affectionately, Your Grandfather

Barbara, all her life, was extremely secretive. The fact that her family knew nothing about John Curry's family was typical of Barbara's penchant for secrecy. The next envelope I found in the chickenhouse was from Calvin Philips in Seattle to Elsie in New York City. There were three letters enclosed.

The first one is from Calvin:

Seattle, Washington

Dear Elsie, just after posting my other airmail letter to you of this date I received your long letter of the 22nd with enclosures, which I am returning here with.

Your letter of the 22nd tells of a number of happenings in Barbara's early life that we never knew about. Some of our friends, not related to the family stated at times "isn't it too bad about Barbara," and all we could say was yes, for we were too proud to admit that we the grandparents did not know something that they non-members of the family knew. I am very strongly inclined to the belief that strictly family matters belong to the family and not to outsiders. I am pursuing that policy in connection with Barbara's present difficulty; consequently, if information reaches non-members of the family, it will not be from me. It is this policy of frankness inside the family that has prompted me to send you copies of all of Barbara's letters, even though some of them made charges against you and Henry. There is nothing to do for the present but wait for further word from Barbara. Affectionately, Calvin Philips, Your Father

The second letter in the envelope was written by Barbara to her mother. Barbara still wrote her return address at 118 Copper St., Henderson, Nevada. I've read and transcribed many dozens of letters that Barbara wrote to her mother over seventy years. This is the only one that begins, "Dear Mamma." There were a few other cards and letters in which Barbara wrote to her mother, "I'm still your little girl." As I transcribed this next letter, I thought again about how terrified Barbara was of being alone.

Dear Mamma, although the packages haven't arrived yet thank you in advance. I got your letter yesterday. I think that's a very good idea of yours to go to the country and collect some news. I hope you make the trip soon. If you will do me a favor while you're out there or maybe even in the city, I'll send you all the photos you want and maybe even make a trip East to visit you. But you must do this the way I tell you.

I notice you always kept track of your ex-boyfriends and even went out with them on occasion even though you were married. So, if you don't mind, I wish you would do me the favor of finding out whatever happened to Bruce Mims. I wonder who he married and what he's doing now and where he is. You never mentioned him in any of your letters. I'm sure you could find out, slyly through the different channels, without letting anyone know who wants to know. Above all, if that good for nothing Slaughter woman (Mimi) is in town don't you dare mention the subject to her. She wrecked our happiness once before and she'd do it again if you gave her the chance. Don't dare ask her by any means as she broke us up once and would do it again if she had the chance. Don't even mention the subject to her. You'll have to find out some other way. If you do, I'll send you all the photos you want and maybe I'll even make a trip East to visit you. I hope you can do this without too much trouble. And above all be on your guard not to let anyone know you're more than casually interested. Find out where he is, what he's doing who he married. Be sure to please destroy

this letter as it's confidential. Don't show this letter to a soul
destroy it right now. Love Barbara

Barbara once again reached back to her lost love, Bruce. She
condemned the young woman, Mimi Slaughter, who at one time
was her closest friend. Note how Barbara attempted to blackmail
her mother for information. Mimi didn't marry Bruce—two
years later when Mimi died, she was still using her maiden
name. On December 3, 1946, *The Times Record, Troy, N.Y.*
published the following article:

State Police and Yates County Sheriff's deputies searched the
shores of Keuka Lake yesterday for traces of a brother and sister
reported missing since last Saturday when they apparently set
out to cross the lake in a canoe. Police said Miles Slaughter and
Miriam Slaughter were last heard from.... The brother and sister
are children of the late Dr. and Mrs. W.H. Slaughter of Darien,
Conn.

Dr. Slaughter had died after he and Barbara's weekend trip to
Ithaca. There was no record of his passing in Elsie's or Barbara's
correspondence. There is also no record that Barbara ever
learned of the boating tragedy. As with so many of the letters,
this next envelope again had three letters tucked in it. The first
was from Barbara to her grandfather. Why did she continue the
lie about John? I believe by then she was manipulating her
grandfather for more money.

March 25, 1944 Mrs. John C Curry, Henderson, Nevada.

Dear Grandfather: Thank you for the financial assistance
you have given me. From now on any correspondence you
find it necessary to write me may be addressed to General
Delivery. It will be forwarded to me. I may go to Los
Angeles.

My husband has been reclassified and is working in
defense until such time as he is called. Of course, I do not

expect you to bear all the financial responsibility in getting readjusted. I merely asked you to find me a modest house in some remote town that would be easy since you are in the real estate business. But since this does not suit you it is very well.

I gave you a confidence and you betrayed it to the whole family. Even the Fratts. I hope you realize you have avenged yourself 100 times over and repaid me as much for any little misdemeanor I might have committed in your home in Seattle. You have humiliated me before the entire family.

You expect me to forgive people for ruining the first 25 years of my life, yet you can't forgive me for a few little faults in the past. I knew it wasn't in you to forget my faults since you were giving a dinner party the night I arrived in Seattle to revisit you. You wouldn't admit me to your home at that time nor ever again it seems.

Thank you for what you have done. Sincerely, Barbara

Barbara, all her life was an artist at weaving fact and fiction to fit her reality. Sadly, as children, we learned early not to trust her.

Calvin replied to her letter:

March 28, 1944 Calvin Philips Seattle, Washington

Dear Barbara: No one in good health would write such a letter as I received from you today in an envelope postmarked March 25. I did not tell the Fratts of your condition. They were probably informed by your Mother. I have kept your Father and Mother posted regarding your situation and efforts to help you. They are your parents and you are their daughter and it is proper that each of you should know the others condition and situation financially and otherwise. I do not believe in these family secrets.

I am not going to attempt to reply to the charges in your letter. What I have done for you and what I have recently attempted to do for you speaks for itself. Someday you will regret having written this letter. But I am not going to hold it against you, for it is quite evident you are not well. You have no right to absent yourself from your family, nor to conceal your whereabouts.

In closing I will say to you if and when you are again in need of financial assistance, I hope you will communicate with me affectionately,

Your Grandfather

Included with this third letter, Calvin sent copies of the two prior letters.

March 28, 1944 Calvin Philips Seattle, Washington

Dear Henry: The above is a copy of a letter just received from Barbara. Attached is a copy of my reply. I am sorry for this turn of the situation. It may be, however, that the husband having been located and reclassified will soon be in the service. If so a monthly compensation to Barbara will be provided.

I really think the efforts should be continued to have Barbara located somewhere in this part of the country. Evidently her Grandmother Fratt's offer to keep house with her did not appeal to Barbara. Barbara is probably at the period of her pregnancy when women are deeply despondent. In any event it seems that she is desperately in need now of affectionate assistance and direction. The natural person to give it is the mother. Elsie may feel that her duty is beside Barbara at this time. Someone who can and will sit down and discuss plans with Barbara is what she is most in need of at this time. I probably will not receive any more letters from her. If you learn of anything, I

hope you will communicate with me. Affectionately, Your
Father

This next letter was stained from water and mouse urine and
filthy from the chicken house. There was some rodent gnaw,
representative of many of the documents. Some were in pristine
condition; others I had to piece together and use a magnifying
glass and bright light and then extrapolate the message from
phrases I could read.

27 March 1944 Henry Philips
Dear Mum [Elsie], Renting for a
year seems a good thought. Go
West, and get Barb started. Let her
look after the house and kids and
you can kind of be a guest or
anything you want. But I'm really
very afraid we're going to have to be
the main support for some time, but
I can't see how we can do it otherwise. We've had many happy years
together, will have many more
together but right now with the war
which I think as events are shaping up will last ever so much longer
than we anticipate. Rather my term of service will. I feel Barb's situation is beginning to work out, but I do feel we, you and I, will have
to be the eventual ones in the deal and we must be prepared. Good
night Dearest – it was a sweet weekend – All My Love, H.

The writing in this next letter from Barbara to her mother is
much smaller and clumped together than Barbara's normal handwriting. Was this letter an example of her rage? There is no
greeting or closing. The phrase "all literature that I wrote
myself" is no doubt alluding to Barbara's 1936 writings that I

discovered in the chickenhouse that Elsie had labeled "Priceless Barbara 1936." Again, as I read the letter, I was thankful Elsie did not send "all literature that I wrote myself" because more than eighty years later we can glimpse Barbara's deepest thoughts and fears.

March 28,1944 Barbara Curry General Delivery Henderson, Nev.

Before you rent your apartment, and go away on your trip, I wish you to send me <u>all</u> of my possessions. Grandfather sent you a lot of furniture etc. at a high cost, so I hope it won't be too much trouble to send <u>all</u> of my possessions to <u>General Delivery</u> here. Please do not hold out on me – send C.O.D. (cash on delivery). If you wish but I mean it when I say send <u>everything</u>.

1: <u>All</u> of my music. Literature, text, books, including <u>everything</u>. I don't have many possessions in this world but I consider <u>all</u> of this collection rightfully belongs to me. Heretofore <u>you</u> sent what you thought I might want. But I know what is missing and I wish <u>every bit</u> of it sent here. I don't know what else I can say to impress you but, apparently you probably won't send it.

2: <u>All</u> of my books. French books and my children's books especially. A. A. Milne, Alice in Wonderland, Book House, East of the Sun, Nursery Rhymes, Once Upon a Time Tales, Mother Goose. Including <u>all</u> books that are rightfully mine. These two requests are for <u>business</u> purposes. I may be teaching the younger grades in a town near here so kindly send all music books, literature, and also all literature that I wrote myself.

3: Kindly send me my own silver cup and child's fork and silver spoon that rightfully belong to me. I hope you will not hesitate to do this and do your <u>own</u> selecting of literature etc. Also send any other dishes, bric-a-brac and silverware that belong to me. I can't understand why you haven't sent the cup fork and spoon etc. long ago.

4: Also any small pieces of furniture that belong to me. Bookends, footstool small table and chair etc. paintings, pictures, photos, etc.

It is too bad you were misinformed concerning my status of health. It is absolutely untrue that I am expecting. If I were you, I wouldn't listen to any gossip or rumors until I had been personally informed by the party in question. Any other rumors or gossip you heard were entirely unfounded. Go on about your business and have a nice trip. All I ask is that you send all of my possessions COD. This does seem a small request beside all the things you possessed plus from grandfather at a high cost. Forget all that you heard and have a nice trip. But be sure to send all my possessions COD before you go. I can't think of what excuse you could now give for not sending everything. Right AWAY, please do not hesitate

Barbara and Christopher at Basic Magnesium Inc.,
Anderson's Camp, Nevada (April 1944)

Barbara was, in fact, three months pregnant. I remember
several of those children's books that we had lying around the
house when I was young.

Elsie's reply:

April 4, 1944 Elsie Philips New York, New York
    A normal reaction when all the family have rallied to your
SOS would be a letter of kindness instead of meanness.
You are mistaken if you think it was none of our business. If
all children were as trying as you, most people would be
better off without any. When you called collect, I agree with
you that it's not time to be alone but possibly to enjoy
people.

The United States had been at war for two and a half years.
Early summer of 1944, Elsie rented her New York apartment and
traveled west; first to Martel, Tennessee, where she spent time

with a few Vassar College classmates. These next few entries from Elsie's diary are a glimpse into wartime America and what she experienced traveling across the country by train.

June 6, 1944: *D-Day. Enroute Memphis, Tenn. What excitement when I awakened in the morning to hear first in the ladies dressing room from a "U of J" graduate that the Great Invasion is on. I went right out to the club car and the radio was booming away, telling about it. On the Rocket, Rock Island Express, beautiful train at eight and I listened until bedtime in the Observation Car to the Invasion news over the radio. F.D.R.'s [President Roosevelt's] speech almost spoiled it.*

June 7, 1944: *Oklahoma City, arrived at 6:30 a.m. At noon went on to Amarillo, Texas arriving 10 p.m. Had to wait in station until 2 a.m. for the Santa Fe going west.*

June 8, 1944: *On train—Going through Arizona and New Mexico all day. Very different country—sagebrush but I didn't see many adobes. Had bad reservation experience— 3 conductors held conference and decided I should get off at Needles, California. At 2:30 a.m. for connection for Las Vegas.*

June 9, 1944: *3 a.m. Indians and Mexicans rolled in blankets all over station floor in Needles. A nice MP [military police] let me through a troop train and put me on a terrible coach car on rear of mail train bound for Barstow where the first conductor should have taken me. Reached Barstow about 8 a.m.—had to wait until noon for any train for Las Vegas. Such a hot ride over desert country. Reached Las Vegas at 6 p.m. What a town—just a play town—nothing but drinking and gambling. Quite nice hotels.*

Elsie must have been excited to visit Barbara, whom she hadn't seen for several years, and her first grandchild. This next letter gives some insight into Elsie's first contact with Barbara. Henry's new duty station placed him in the Military Police Detachment on board a troop ship. Between June 1944 and December 1944, he participated in several cross-Atlantic troop convoys as officer in charge of troop discipline on board ship. This was his second crossing.

July 15, 1944 Henry Philips V-Mail (at sea)

Darling, here I am again "somewhere in England." The trip was very smooth but what fog and rains. Quarters are okay and food was good. I was so relieved the very last minute to get your long letter from Las Vegas. What a woeful situation it must be, and dear Barb what a mess she is in. This younger, generation so headstrong, so know-it-allish. I wonder if the war will leaven it all? It looks as if we must dedicate the next phase of our life to her and her problems. I am anxious of course to learn of your continued progress with her. Have a letter for me by about July 25 and I hope to get it soon thereafter. I pray every night all is well with you and that we may have guidance in this problem of Barb's, it sounds as if you have made a good start. All My Love, Henry

Votre tout l'evore

Elsie mailed this sad letter, started on August 23, to Henry. She made no reference to visiting Barbara or seeing her first grandchild, who was sixteen months old, but Elsie did visit Barbara's doctor in Henderson.

September 6, 1944 Elsie Philips Las Vegas, Nevada

Dearest Henry, It's a strange feeling I have when writing to you when you're away, not knowing where you are or whether they'll forward the letters or not. It's much like "I sent a letter into the air, it fell to earth, I know not where." I'll be dying to know whether you are allowed to go to Paris for all the wild celebrating. I can imagine nothing more thrilling than to be there to see it, the joy on the people's faces must be superb.

And if they don't forward letters to you, I will see you before you read this because unless something happens to the country, the way things are now I will be in New York City when you arrive.

I wrote a confidential letter to the doctor in Henderson asking him to help me get Barbara to go to Dr. Wright in Las Vegas and evidently, he is so ignorant or so conceited that he read her the letter which of course put an end to everything. It just made her more anti than ever and since then and it's nearly a month and I haven't heard one sound from her.

I could tell from the moment I saw him that he was a very poor excuse for a doctor. Of course, all the best ones are at the battle front or too old. Well again we have no luck, but we won't give up hope. Barbara has such cunning that she has persuaded them all to her way of thinking which isn't thinking normally at all. Surely the baby has been born by now. I console myself that Barb won't feel at all well for at least six months. If at the end of that time she's not any better there's a possibility of getting her to the right doctor.

Well it all came up because we decided against going in the hole again for her when she wrote that she wanted to come East in March. We have to decide whether the $800 we've saved up this year is worth it or not. I think we'll decide that it is. We once practically went to debtor's prison for her and I don't think that was worth it. Though she was getting much better until the war came and blitzed her out of Europe. She's really a war casualty. We are the first to have one in the family.

Now her neurosis is that the whole family is against her, though all -- your father, my mother, me, and others have sent her money and many presents. It's dreadful that someone down there doesn't send us word. The stupid Doctor writes me that he doesn't understand why she says all her family is against her. If he can't recognize a bad neurosis when he sees one, he shouldn't be a doctor. The baby must have long since been born and perhaps she's been near death's door, but I don't understand how she got John persuaded to silence. Except that he feared I was going to get him into big doctor bills for her and he's had so little education that I suppose he's not really convinced he can't cure her himself and in a way who can blame him when the stupid Doctor is of the same notion and even your father.

I think now that only a very good doctor can cure her. The only danger is that she will persuade John to go and they will disappear again indefinitely until it is too late to cure her. It's a little bit harder to disappear though with two babies. I'm reading a very good book on neurosis written by an eminent New York doctor. I think I'll go to see him when I get back and ask him what he would think of sending it to Barb.

The other day we had a wonderful day in the country. Your father brought your brother, Calvin Jr. He is a real neurotic case—similar in many ways to Barbara. He never spoke unless spoken to and then only answered in monosyllables. He never mingled among the crowd, but wandered off by himself and sat among the bushes. I think I will ask your father if he thinks I could arrange to have dinner with Calvin (I'll probably have to pay for it) but it might give me some clues about Barb.

Since I can do no good by returning to Las Vegas, with Barb having persuaded everyone there that her family are all wrong and she all right, I might as well get right on back to New York. I expect to leave here in about a week. I think I'll make the reservation tomorrow.

I've had a wonderful visit here, that is as much as one could enjoy it with the Barbara mess on my mind. But now I'm getting sick of visiting -- five months of it! Everyone out here has entertained me. While we were in Olympia, Nick got a telegram from the War Department saying that Bill was wounded in Saipan.

How things are tearing ahead in Europe, now the Allies have Brussels and today they are in Antwerp. So thrilling! 100 mile gain without a shot came over the air. Hearts full of love and more when I see you, Elsie

The preceding letter answered the question of why Barbara did not move back to New York when John first left; Elsie refused to finance it—again, in Barbara's mind, confirming abandonment and rejection by her mother. Elsie commented about Barbara's "bad neurosis"—that term was a keyword of the 1940s to explain many psychiatric abnormalities. Last, I smiled when I read Elsie's comment, "It's a little bit harder to disappear though with two babies." In 1952, Barbara disappeared with five children, and eight years later, in 1960, with nine children.

In the chickenhouse I found several books dealing with mental illness. They all had Elsie's margin notes and underlined text. The pages of *Mental Illness: A Guide for the Family* (1945 revised, sixth printing) were dog-eared and worn. Elsie must have searched for answers. One passage Elsie underlined was probably alluding to the "stupid Doctor" in Las Vegas that she had written about on September 6, 1944.

> Just as your family physician is able to tell whether an infection has really been conquered or whether disappearance of symptoms is only temporary, so your psychiatrist has means of gauging whether a mental disorder still exists despite periods of apparent sanity. Intervals of normality—which in even the most serious cases of mental illness can occur either briefly, several times a day, or for as long as several days or a week at a time —may be only superficial and have no more significance in indicating the patient's real condition than drops in temperature during certain hours of the day.
>
> Most misleading of all, to the inexperienced, is the intellectual brilliance of many mental patients: their remarkable memories, their ability to talk persuasively and to answer questions sensibly, their penetrating criticism, their alertness to their surroundings. Perhaps none of this fits in with your idea of mental illness, but your doctor knows that it is quite characteristic of certain of its types.

Elsie had been unsuccessful in seeing or dealing with Barbara and was returning to New York. I include her diary entries for the next few weeks for two reasons. First, they illuminate a page from our collective past—WWII, train travel, social mores from that era. Also, the angst my grandfather must have felt living with the knowledge that Barbara was troubled and he was thousands of miles away, at sea, with no communication. Because of extreme secrecy about convoy routes and weeks at sea, he went for several months without a word from home.

Elsie's 1944 Diary entries continue:

Sept 13, 1944: *On the Northern Pacific Western late— resting after being so tired from packing and getting off. The ticket man was grand, but the baggage man was awful—*

almost made us miss the train. I'm going to miss dear little Gram so much.

Sept 14, 1944: Slept late to rest after getting off. I really was very tired not having any men to lift anything—The Carpenters are still on to Butte, Montana. We played Bridge until dinner. When they left, I wrote a long letter to Ruth and Gram.

Elsie left the West Coast with no attempt to see Barbara—again confirming Barbara's sense of abandonment. Twenty years later, the summer of 1964 when I was sixteen, I left a foster home and rode the rails out west—no doubt the same rail route Elsie traveled returning to New York.

Sept 15, 1944: North Coast Limited. Very rainy day going through North Dakota and Minnesota. Wrote letters to all the family saying goodbye to them after a grand and glorious summer. Really have visited with so many people the last six months I can't be bothered to make acquaintances on the train. Got off in Minneapolis at 11 p.m.—strange not to see Marie but to have to go out to Lake Minnetonka at this time of night.

"Marie" was Marie Andrews Commons, author of *The Log of Tanager Hill* (1938). Marie was Henry's aunt—his mother's sister. In the chickenhouse, I discovered an autographed copy of her book. *To Elsie and Henry Philips whose visits at Tanager Hill are remembered with affectionate appreciation by the author. Marie Andrews Commons, July nineteenth, 1938.*

Sept 18, 1944: *Chicago-Broadway Limited. I had a bedroom on the Broadway Limited at 3:30 for N.Y. Did a little more shopping and luncheon at Fields and had a grand finale for my six months of seven thousand miles and 26 states visited. Lovely comfortable room on beautiful compartment —after a delicious dinner, listened to Dewey talking in Seattle, going 100 miles an hour through Ohio!!*

Sept 19, 1944: *Arrived in New York again after nearly six months. Jewish Holy Day—New York looks empty. Broadway Limited one hour late. Arrived at Kath Wiman's at 10:30 a.m. she and Suzi had breakfast awaiting me. We visited all day—so nice of her to have me here—good way to break into New York alone. I took Kath to dinner at "Stockholm"—good as wartime will permit. Kath and Suzi told me about the hurricane last night. I heard about it first on the train—damaged almost as bad as '38 no such loss of life. Wind very high knocked down many trees in Central Park. Almost blew Suzi's dog, "Buddy" away!*

Sept 21, 1944: *It's fun being here with Kath and Suzi— good for me—recalls the times when I enjoyed being with Polly so much. No one could ever have been more fun than she up to eighteen—I wonder why they both (Barb and Polly) went off at sixteen and eighteen. Emotionally controlled it must be.*

Interesting entry. Elsie had been dealing with Barbara's issues for almost ten years. In reading Elsie's diaries, warning flags about Polly—her illness as an infant, her extreme forgetfulness later in adolescence, and then her sudden drop in academic performance must have raised concerns.

Back to Elsie's diary:

Sept 22, 1944: *Back at 538 East 89th N.Y.C. Arose leisurely. I'm not in the least looking forward to going back to my apartment alone. I know all sorts of depressing memories will return to me which I have been away from for nearly six months. Life hasn't turned out the way I planned it at all.*

Sept 24, 1944: *Seven years ago today Barb and Polly and I sailed for Europe. I stayed up last night until one o'clock reading Pol's and my diary about it. Now I don't like being here in New York alone, Henry in dangerous war zones, Barb no better, and Pol in a marriage I don't like. What dreadful years we've lived through!*

Henry's V-mail letters to Elsie reveal his angst and sense of helplessness. The fact that he could not receive letters from Elsie compounded his disconnect. I share excerpts from Henry's letters, of his concerns for Barbara.

Dearest, It seems so strange to go along from one day to the next and not to be able to have an inkling of where you are and how the Barb case is progressing. I try not to worry too much about it, as I know you are doing everything humanly possible—if we could only see the outcome, but not being able to, all I suppose you can do is that which you are doing. The war news is certainly gratifying.All My Love To You Dearest As Always, Henry

From Elsie's diary:

Sept 29, 1944: *Had the best cleaning woman today. Ida Smith sent from Cameron Agency, colored. She's worth every cent of the seven dollars. "Mail" from Henry saying he won't be back for over a month. He's still "enroute" and very cold. He must have gone to Russia poor dear. What a monstrous jaunt but he's touching on many different places on the globe.*

V–Mail from Henry to Elsie:

Dearest, Another Sunday and we're still enroute. It is a perfect sunshiny day—the first in days, but quite cool. It makes me think of the lovely Fall days in the country and we'd drive towards Danbury and how the girls loved it so and we would stop for cider and honey. How different it all is now. I haven't the faintest idea where you are now but can only presume it's about time for you to be with Barb. I'm reading some fascinating books and am keeping a list of those I know you'd enjoy. It's amazing to find novels with characters somewhat similar to Barb. And to come upon them unexpectedly, too. Love to you always, Henry

Elsie's diary continues:

October 9, 1944: *A nice letter from Henry—he's still "enroute"! A letter from John announcing the arrival of the second son weighing 11 lb 2 oz. The doctor shouldn't have let it get that big. Henry could have gone all the way around the world. I sent a money order for $40 to Barb. Reported for Air Warden Duty and registered to vote for president. It's awful—Henry won't be able to vote because he can't have his war ballot mailed to him.*

October 16, 1944: *Red letter day. Letters from Henry, and Polly, and John—Henry is still "enroute." He must have gone halfway around the world. John says Barb is getting better—what a relief! I took the apt. at 316 E. 58th I hope Henry won't mind.*

Oct 26, 1944: *Moved into 316 East 58th St. Packed all a.m. Mover men took things from 558th and moved it in the new apartment. It's going to be very nice. Spacious and wood burning fireplaces.*

Elsie lived in that apartment until the summer of 1960. When we were children on the Minnesota farm in the 1950s, most of us memorized that New York address because we often wrote to our grandmother. She always returned our letters—red pencil corrections on grammar, punctuation, spelling—and included a dollar. It was a great source of income for little kids.

On November 28, 1944, after the liberation of Antwerp, the seaport was opened to Allied shipping. Henry's troop ship was one of the first U.S. ships to enter. After the troops debarked, Henry must have spent several days in port and toured Antwerp and Brussels. He sent this postcard to Elsie. It's chewed at the top and weathered from decades in the chickenhouse.

Postage mark is December 5, 1944:

Merry Christmas Dearest, I certainly am wishing I could be with you for it. But we'll see you shortly thereafter. Does this look familiar to you? It is a lovely city and I hope we can do it together after the war. I am quite keen about it – it reminds me a lot of Philadelphia. All my love, H.

With the troops safely debarked, the ship and crew left Antwerp but was torpedoed by a German U-Boat and sank in the North Sea on December 12. The ship's crew and Henry's army MP contingent escaped in lifeboats.

Elsie wrote in her diary:

December 25, 1944: *Christmas Day. So wonderful—Henry home from Europe—Antwerp, North Sea, London, Edenborough.*

1945

In Europe and in the Pacific, the Allies raced toward victory. Did the constant barrage of war news affect Barbara—reminding her of lost friends in Poland? Shortly after the New Year, she returned to New York. For the next four years Barbara distanced herself from her parents, yet often contacted them for money and help. Unlike the wealth of letters during 1944, Elsie's diary entries illuminated the next few years; and it wasn't only Barbara, Elsie agonized over. After several years of erratic behavior, Polly had her first schizophrenic break while on duty as an army nurse cadet. She was hospitalized and diagnosed with paranoid schizophrenia.

Elsie's New Year entry:

January 1, 1945: *If only all New Years could be so pleasant. We were having a marvelous party to celebrate Henry's safe return and usher in '45. His ship went down in the North Sea. He was picked up by a British Corvette and taken to London and flew home for Christmas.*

In 2010, after I boxed up the chickenhouse treasures, there

were still loose letter pages lying on the cracked concrete. I tossed the pages in a tote and tucked them on a garage shelf when I got home. Years later, long after I had catalogued the bulk of the documents, I went through the tote of miscellaneous pages. As an old sailor writing about my grandfather's ship being sunk in WWII, I was curious at just what had happened. In that tote, I discovered this letter dated May 18, 1945, five months after Henry had returned to the United States. He was on a cross-town bus and met a soldier who had served under him two years earlier. After the chance encounter, the soldier sent my grandfather a letter. An excerpt: "Your experience in being torpedoed must have been an unenviable one, and I am very happy that you came through it without serious results to yourself."

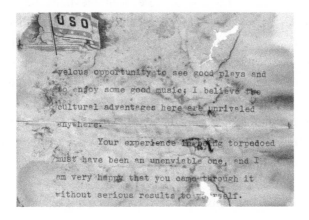

On January 2, 1945, Henry reported to his new army duty station at Camp Shanks, thirty miles north of New York City. Almost two weeks later, Elsie wrote in her diary:

Jan 13, 1945: *Henry here, stayed overnight to help paint baby buggy for Barb.*
　　Jan 14, 1945: *The famous day Barb was to fly with the*

two babies from Las Vegas, Nevada. A big snowstorm here.
I don't think she left. But Suki left because Barb is coming—
I will miss Suki but I think it is for the best because with
Henry coming and going it will seem more like his own
home now—even when Barb and the babies are here.

Jan 19, 1945: Barb and babies arrived about 10 a.m.
and this began a most strenuous and very difficult two
months and a half.

If Elsie wrote the preceding entry the day Barbara arrived,
how could she know that Barbara would stay in her home for
"two months and a half"? Many times, as I worked with Elsie's
diaries and letters, I discovered comments and notes made after
the fact, painting Elsie in a more desirable light. So, like her
daughter, just how reliable a narrator was my grandmother?

Barbara was on public aid for the next five years—until she
disappeared from New York. I imagine Elsie pushed her to apply
as soon as she arrived. I try to imagine Barbara moving into a
three-bedroom third floor apartment in New York City, trying to
shelter her children from their loving grandmother. Barbara was
completely dependent upon Elsie and Henry for food and shelter.
I wonder, with Barbara's history of violence, how soon did it
erupt?

Two and a half months later, Calvin sent this letter to his son:

March 3, 1945 Calvin Philips Seattle, Washington

Dear Henry, I am glad to learn Elsie has found a
physician who is willing to try to cure Barbara. I will
anxiously await the result of the cure. Barb's letters show
intelligence sufficient to know right from wrong and her
treatment of you and Elsie has the earmarks of childish
peevishness that is totally unwarranted. Some electrical or
other type of medical shocks may set in motion the brain
cells of love and affection the parents are entitled to receive.

Some good common horse sense advice from a nonmember of the family such as this woman doctor may have beneficial results.

I hope John will carry out his declared intentions to send all of his paychecks to Barbara. I have formed a good of opinion of John from the letters he has written to me.

Both of you are brave and trying hard to solve our most difficult problem and in time it will be solved. It will require a continued patience for a while. I am a great believer in time solving most problems and in holding tempers and avoid explosions of speech. Leave that for the physician. I am enclosing another $25 to help out. It is not much but may help—my income is continuously lessening. I arose at 5:30 this a.m. to get this letter off to you and Elsie for I am thinking of both of you a great deal these days. My best love to both of you – Father

Calvin's statement, "electrical or other type of medical shocks" gives the reader a glimpse of his first-hand experience with his son Calvin Jr., who struggled with abnormal behavior. Recall what Elsie wrote in a letter dated September 6, 1944: "He [Calvin Jr.] is a real neurotic case—similar in many ways to Barbara."

Vulnerability to mental illness can be passed from one generation to the next. Martha "Pattie" Thomas Garstin (1888-1935), Calvin's cousin, had been committed to Normansfield Hospital, Teddington, England, and spent her life institutionalized. How *did* genetic vulnerability affect the Philips family over multiple generations?

On March 31, 1945, Polly enlisted in the Women's Army Corps (WACs) and began training at Fort Oglethorpe, Georgia. I include this next letter, written by Polly, because she mentions that Barbara is now living in New Jersey.

May 5, 1945 "Polly" Katherine Batten Fort Oglethorpe, Georgia

Dearest mother, I got a card from you the other day. So Barb may go to California. Well that's a shame for you, because it must be nice having her in New York or at least New Jersey. I should think if she has a house, it would be difficult to sell it. I saw "Meet Me in St. Louis" that was a good show I thought. I have moved to a different company it's Company 4, 20th Regiment. That was just a few days ago. Well I must close now. Love Polly

Above picture enclosed with Polly's letter. Caption on the back side:

April 1945, Timothy age 6 months, Christopher age 23 months. 12A Hurd Street Mine Hill, Dover, N. Jersey

(Why the bow in Chris's long curls?)

Barbara, obviously unhappy and financially destitute, ran

again. Polly's letter was the first mention I found that Barbara wanted to return to California and John.

Elsie wrote in her diary:

April 25, 1945: *Henry had a long talk with Dr. Kalui about Barb's situation—she has a piano and is playing now and charming the neighbors.*

For the moment, after being evicted from her apartment in New Jersey, Barbara and her children were back in New York, living with her parents. Over the next few years, she often disappeared for months at a time.

Again, for historical context, I include Elsie's diary entries as WWII in Europe ended. Germany surrendered on May 8, 1945.

May 4, 1945: *A very wet day and we have no heat. Almost all of Europe is free now. Hitler and Mussolini dead but no VE Day yet. Henry called from Camp Shanks in evening.*

May 8, 1945: *These reports have been coming along so gradually that it's impossible to realize that after seven long years the fight in Europe is over. Henry had to be at Shanks in case there were special orders.*

Soldiers, sailors, and airmen began returning home. Thousands of American prisoners of war gained their freedom. Europe struggled to find a new normal after millions of people had been murdered or displaced.

Elsie's diary illuminated those hectic happy days:

June 1, 1945: *Barb called for me to send her a little money. She says she is out. Had to cash a check at the Vassar Club and send it special delivery. Dear Henry in from Camp Shanks for dinner and a lovely evening.*

June 5, 1945: *Dear Henry left here at the usual 6 a.m. I cooked breakfast for him before he left. Henry left at 2 p.m. with train load of young aviators who had been shot down over Germany and had been prisoners, to take them to St. Louis.*

June 8, 1945: *Went to Barb's apartment to see the painter. Then looked for furniture for her and chairs for me.*

In a later entry, Elsie commented about Barbara living in an unheated apartment. Over the next few years, Barbara lived in four of five New York City boroughs; she never made it to Staten Island. I wonder if a part of her moving so often was due to being evicted. When we were children and Barbara ran away from the farm in Minnesota, I remember fleeing in the dark of night, motel bills unpaid.

Elsie's diary continues:

July 4, 1945: *Polly in Fort Oglethorpe, Georgia, learning to be a nurse. Barb with her babes in N.Y.C. Too bad it's so hot there but, with little children, Barb is better off not near water.*

July, 9, 1945: *Henry probably arrives in Seattle today. What excitement after so many years away! I wrote a letter to Barbara trying to help her regain her cheerful outlook.*

July 28, 1945: *10 a.m. An Army bomber crashed into the Empire State Building's 80th floor killing many and setting many floors on fire. I cry watching through the fog, very dense. It shows we shouldn't build buildings that high —no German bombs did it in all these years. We had to wait for one of our own. Late afternoon the fog still so dense we could hardly see the building two blocks away and as I left, I walked to 34th to the building and home on the 5th Ave. bus. The fog so dense at the building you couldn't see above the 30th floor. Talked to Agnes about Suki—Alcoholics Anonymous is really curing her. I wish*

Church of the Truth would cure Barb before she ruins the children.

Elsie's comment about "Church of the Truth" indicates that Barbara was attending church meetings. A forerunner of the "New Thought Movement" which Elsie was probably alluding to, Church of the Truth taught individuals to tap into her own well of physical, mental, and spiritual resources, referred to as Universal Principles. For example, through the Principle of Polarity, hate might be transmuted to love. According to Steiner's research, in her book *Where Do People Take Their Troubles?* "Each individual is expected to be loyal only to the 'Truth he/she sees.'" A dangerous concept for Barbara's reality.

We can never know just what Barbara's truth was. After she died in 2010, I brought her two Bibles home—both "Authorized (King James) Versions." As I thumbed through them, I was surprised; in the years I visited with her and interviewed her, she never revealed a spiritual side. Yet, one Bible had several *Radio Pulpit* pamphlets tucked between the pages; the pamphlets were dogeared and, at times, paragraphs circled. In the second Bible, a *Gideon* (1954) I found several obituaries and news clippings, and envelopes from Moody Bible Institute and Dallas Theological Seminary. I discovered a marked-up flyer from *The Bible Stories in Ten Volumes* by Arthur S. Maxwell and a *Tape Ministry Catalogue* (audio) order form. Just as her mother Elsie had done through the decades, clipping news articles and tucking them away, so her daughter Barbara had done in her later years.

Elsie documented the final days of WWII in her diary:

August 4, 1945: *Congress signs the United Nations Charter —one of the great events in history.*

August 5, 1945: *President Truman announces the Potsdam Ultimatum sent to Japan as a peace proposal.*

August 6, 1945: *Pres. Truman announces the use of the*

first atomic bomb which blew up a whole Japanese city. The next, Nagasaki.

Polly sent this next letter to Elsie:

August 10, 1945 "Polly" Katherine Batten Fort Oglethorpe, Georgia

Dear Mother, Do you see Barbara very much? I should think her living so nearby would make it convenient for you to visit with her and the children since both John and Dad are in the service. Those lonely evenings could well be filled up with a pleasant chat with your oldest daughter. It seems a shame that me being your youngest daughter should be gone for these many years. To think Barb will be 25 the 11th.. I must get her something for her birthday or at least a card.

Lots of love, Polly

Elsie's diary continues—more than one million U.S. military men and women were killed or wounded. The country's euphoria was wild, yet for families of those lost and maimed, victory was bittersweet.

August 10, 1945: *Word came over the air at ten a.m. that Japan had asked for peace. Great excitement—six long years of war.*

August 11, 1945, *Barb's Birthday. The first birthday I've had with Barb since she was fifteen years old. Took all birthday things with me—cake, candles, and presents. She is on 94th St.*

August 14, 1945: *Japan accepts the Potsdam Declaration. World War II ends—claim the atomic bomb did it—also Russia entering the war. I happened to be in the government district at 2 p.m. when it was announced—*

went there to shop at Macy's. Suddenly the whole sky was filled with little pieces of material as all the workers in all of those tremendous buildings threw their scraps out of the window—making the whole sky black with tiny pieces of material and what a tremendous loud cheering!! I'll never forget it.

Polly sent this next letter to her mother. It's rather sad. She no doubt is alluding to Victory over Japan (VJ) Day on August 14 that Elsie wrote about in her diary. That celebration was also famous for "The Kiss" in Times Square.

Dear Mother, I got your nice letter today thank you so much. I imagine you must have celebrated a good deal. Peace is something we haven't heard about it in so long. I think it's too good to be true. It's nice you and Dad got a chance to listen to Truman's speech. How is Barbara? It's too bad she didn't get in the spirit of things. But then for her I guess this war has lasted longer than for most. So you must have been glad to see her. It must have been an awful crowd on Times Square. Lots of love, Polly

Elsie's diary continues:

August 15, 1945: *We are having a wonderful holiday celebrating the ending of the war.*
　　August 16, 1945: *Still a holiday for War's end.*
　　August 21, 1945: *Hot summer day. Saw my Dr. McCombs, N.Y. Hospital—Barb's psychiatrist, Dr. Scott. Talked to Henry on phone to Camp Shanks. He's very tired with many troops—then to Pier 90 to watch Queen Mary come in with 16,000 troops—great thrill—such an interesting screaming singing crowd.*
　　September 9, 1945: *Hot day—Henry slept. I made a*

dress for Barb. Read Sunday Times by East River. Later took the dress to Barb and did a big washing for her. What a day!

September 14, 1945: *What a day! Cleaned the whole house—marketed. Sewed some clothes for Barb, went up there and visited with her until one a.m. taxied home dead!*

September 30, 1945: *Such a lovely day. Henry and I had luncheon at noon then went for a long walk in the sunshine in Central Park, watched the sailboats sail. Went to Barb's to get my things, she wouldn't let us in. She really is inhuman.*

October 1, 1945: *Monday morning work and talking on the phone. Bad note from Barb—It just seems as tho we hit our heads against a stone wall.*

October 2, 1945: *I'm not going to Barb's much anymore. It seems useless.*

October 6, 1945: *To Barb's in the eve—we had a nice visit but she does not improve. Always has to get something out of everyone she comes in contact with.*

October 24, 1945: *Did laundry for Barb and children.*

Did the end of the war trigger depression for Barbara as she watched millions celebrating? Memories of her lost friends in Poland must have been forefront in her thoughts. Again, Elsie mentioned doing laundry. I recall, as a child, doing my own laundry in the old Maytag ringer washer. The alternative was to wear filthy clothes to school. As I reflect on it, there were household jobs that Barbara seemed incapable of performing: laundry, cooking, cleaning.

Elsie's diary continues:

October 31, 1945: *In the evening I took Halloween cookies and cakes to Barb. She didn't open the package—she said she'd give it to the boys the next day.*

November 1, 1945: *A beautiful day—I slept late because*

I was so tired from staying up at Barbara's until midnight. I couldn't sleep a wink.

November 6, 1945: *What a wonderful day. Went to St. Barts, then dashed to go on noon shift at Troop Transit Canteen Penn Station, from there we were all taken on board the Missouri, saw where the Japs signed the Peace ending World War II.*

For the past ten years, Elsie had struggled with Barbara's problems. Sadly, in this next letter, Polly has been admitted to the hospital—so began her battle with schizophrenia and my grandparents' lifelong commitment as Polly's caretakers.

November 8, 1945 "Polly" Katherine Batten Augusta, Georgia

Dear Mother; Well no letters lately, what happened to your correspondence? I suppose it's partly my fault for not writing like I should. How is Barbara? I must get a letter off to her soon. Also how is Dad? I'm in the hospital right now of all things I don't know why. I just didn't feel so good so they put me in here. After all I have been doing a good deal for eight months in the Army. And that's one thing I can say for the Army they seem to give you a lot to do. Well I've no idea how long I'll be in here. Lots of love Polly

Elsie's diary continues:

November 15, 1945: *Polly is in the hospital sick at Augusta, Georgia—Oliver General. I hope it's nothing serious. Barb has found a heated apt—unbelievable and is moving today. It takes a huge load off my mind. I took up a few things but of course she wouldn't let me help on account of not wanting me to see the children—isn't it a sad thing but*

Henry and I are determined not to let it get us down—to look at it objectively.

November 18, 1945: *Walked through Central Park—a telegram from John Curry saying he had arrived in San Francisco from Tokyo and was leaving for New York on Friday.*

November 19, 1945: *Dashed back for an early dinner then up to Barb's new apartment. In a downpour to measure her curtains. But she didn't seem to want them. She has heat but otherwise it isn't much better.*

November 22, 1945: *Still Roosevelt's Thanksgiving. Probably a good idea to not make it so near xmas. Barb turned down our invitation to come to dinner with the babies, so we determined to enjoy ourselves anyway. Had cocktails here first then went to the Ambassador for a delicious dinner. We really had a happy day and found lots to be thankful for even though not everything.*

November 27, 1945: *John Curry called me much to my surprise—he's a nice boy. He said he'd call again.*

Chris, Barbara, Tim
(December 1945)

This Japanese flag must be a "war trophy" John purchased while in Tokyo. John was a ship's cook and must have gotten a few days off while in port—Tokyo Bay. This picture, taken in Barbara's apartment, is very telling: Note the bare bedsprings— twelve days after moving in—and the cracked plaster wall. Barbara loved Chris's "Little Lord Fauntleroy" look.

Elsie's diary continues:

December 2, 1945: *A great event happened today. Barbara, John, and the 2 boys drove up in their car and spent the afternoon with Henry and me. Henry was very favorably impressed with John. He looked very well in his Naval Petty Officer's outfit. The little boys are so cute—they were very good but rushed into everything. Barb did pretty well but she is not all right yet. I think John managed very well with her. She's thrilled over the car—I gave her the lovely auto robe grandfather gave us—Henry was thrilled it all went so nicely.*

December 8, 1945: *What a day! I went to the bank early, did my banking, paid up town bills then went to Barb's to tell her about Polly's illness. John not there. We went riding in the car. What a ride. Barb had Timmy in his go-cart in the back seat. We stopped for gas and lunch which I paid for— Then went to park on Riverside. Christopher ran into the street Barb shrieked then was very cross. Drove through Central Park—relieved to get home. Got out at N.Y. Hospital —dispensary closed. Barb should take nerve medicine. Henry is going to Newton D. Baker Hospital Martinsburg, West Virginia, tomorrow morning to see dear Pol who has been in the hospital more than a month.*

December 9, 1945: *Went to dinner at Alcoholics Anonymous and stayed to the meeting afterwards. Very interesting—all these AAs are neurotics who have a purpose, in other words have found themselves and now help others—I wish Barb and Polly could.*

"I wish Barb and Polly could" is Elsie's first acknowledgement that Polly's illness is not physical but psychiatric. Why did Elsie go to an Alcoholics Anonymous dinner? Was she considering AA as a possible therapeutic program for Barbara and Polly, or did Elsie recognize that *she* had a drinking problem? She loved her "skoosh" or "tea" as she euphemistically called hard liquor. I recall the times I lived with her in the 1960s, we would go out to dinner and, although I was underage, she would order me alcoholic drinks, but never allow Polly to drink.

In 1967, a few months before I went to Vietnam the second time, I took thirty days' leave, and Elsie, Polly, and I drove from Seattle to Minnesota; I did the driving. Our first day on the road, Elsie sat beside me, her "skoosh kit" resting on the floor between her feet, beneath a lap robe. In the kit were ice, bourbon, and quinine water.

Early evening, after almost three hundred miles and several skooshes, just before we reached Spokane, I was pulled over by a Highway Patrolman. "Have you been drinking?" he asked me.

"Are you kidding," I replied, pointing at the passenger side and back seat, "With my grandmother and aunt riding with me?" The Patrolman gave me a warning ticket and told me not to cross the centerline again. So, I ask again, why was Elsie going to an AA dinner twenty-two years earlier?

In this next diary entry, it sounds as though Elsie is in denial about Polly's illness:

December 10, 1945: *Our Wedding Anniversary. Telegram from dear Henry saying when he would be back from Newton D. Baker Hospital seeing dear Polly who is ill. Was up writing xmas letters when Henry arrived. Reported he had arrived at just the right moment for dear Polly—had a wonderful day with her. The dear thing is really wandering in a fog. So many young people of today are—the brave new world of New Deal, Women Suffrage, and two World Wars and Great Depression was not right for them—there is no credibility to it.*

December 11, 1945: *Beautiful sunny winter day. Went to Barb's to see how John was getting on—he seems to be so well balanced he's managing all right. Barb is really awful—nice to John because he's a good money provider. She plays nicely for him. She never plays for us—unwilling to let her father play with the darling children.*

This photo of Barbara, cradled in her paternal grandfather's arms, is labeled, "Barbara Ann, Dec 1920." It was probably taken at Greenbank Farm. On the back, Elsie wrote, "This is how grandparents enjoy their grandchildren. Please return." I found this picture up in the old farmhouse attic after Barbara died. I suspect that Elsie wrote that note and sent the picture to Barbara in the mid-1940s after my two older brothers were born and Barbara denied her parents time with their grandsons.

Calvin Philips holding four-month-old Barbara. Seattle,
Washington. (December 1920)

Elsie's diary continues:

December 12, 1945: *A year ago today dear Henry went down into the sea or rather his ship did, coming out of Antwerp about six o'clock at nine they all got off in lifeboats, were picked up about 11 at night by a British Corvette. This year Commander and Barbara Foster were here and came in from Shanks and we all drank to the occasion.*

December 24, 1945: The busy "Day before Christmas" this year Christmas is on such a day that most all shopping and delivering of presents is accomplished ahead of time. It would have been a perfect day except that Barb ran in some things for me to do at the last second—I had to run all over town. We started trimming the tree, stuffing the turkey, doing the last presents for stockings, all Barb's family came over about five.

December 25, 1945: Christmas Day always seems too busy a day to write up. This year it was a lovely one. We arose about nine and so thoroughly enjoyed opening our presents. Dear Henry's presents to me were so thoughtful and lovely—pearls, pretty lingerie, my new fur coat was my principle present. And Gram's present of the check was certainly the most marvelous. Our decorations and red stockings by the fire and tree were beautiful. The turkey dinner was delicious—Barb and the children didn't come at the last minute—snowstorm.

December 27, 1945: Barb came down early with Timmy and Chris and spent the day—a postponed xmas day. They opened their presents under the tree and had a very good time. They all stayed to a delicious turkey luncheon. Henry came in but was so upset that he nearly spoiled it—I don't blame him but finally we all had Tea together in the living room. The boys made quite a bit of havoc in the house.

1946

The spring of 2010, as I explored the chickenhouse treasures, an ossified mouse skeleton tumbled from wadded curtains. Beneath, lay a Zales Jewelry store bag. The bag caught my attention because in 1967, as a teenaged sailor stationed in Bremerton, Washington, I dated a young lady who worked at Zales across the harbor in Seattle. In the Zales bag I discovered a packet of later-1940s documents that detailed Barbara's life and her failing marriage, including the final divorce decree issued November 25, 1947, in Las Cruces, New Mexico. That document opened an amazing door for me—the door to my paternal roots, but I jump ahead.

Again, Elsie's diary illuminates the United States' early postwar experience from a fifty-year-old New Yorker's point of view. Her diary is also the best window into my mother's activities.

Jan 1, 1946: *This year began very happily. I did my shift of the Troop Transit Canteen in Penn Station. Almost no one else came—I poured nearly eight hundred cups of coffee in about two hours. There were many more soldiers and sailors than usual.*

Jan 3, 1946: *Barb arrived early in her car with Timmy and Chris and we drove down the East River Drive across Manhattan Bridge for her to shop in Brooklyn. It was a beautiful day. I dashed back, mailed some packages rushed some dinner up to Barb's. I folded clothes for her and sewed for her until eleven—I was very tired when I reached home.*

Jan 4, 1946: *What a thrilling day. I went to Camp Shanks for the day—sun and mist and warm. The Queen Mary at Pier 90 having just brought in her last famous load—the 82nd Airborne—all stationed at Camp Shanks. The troops are very colorful with all their fourrageres [braided cord military awards] and medals and ribbons of valor. They spearheaded Italy, Anzio, D-Day—Holland and Germany, the Rhine—Belgian Bulge. I met Henry and Colonel Keater at luncheon—a jolly chap. The snow is quite deep.*

Jan 9, 1946: *What a hectic day. Barb called for me at 10 in the car to take the children to Macys to shop. What a day we had—parking the car—in and out of shops all day long in the rain. I treated most of it.*

Jan 12, 1946: *The Great Victory Parade. The weatherman was kind today tho the radio said rain. Henry went out the night before to work on getting the boys started in—We had good seats and oh! What a sight they were, the whole 82nd Airborne, nearly fifteen thousand of them—Full battle array—2 fourrageres, Holland and Belgium, many gold overseas stripes and battle stars and stripes and ribbons followed by vast numbers of great tanks.*

Jan 28, 1946: *Finished things for Barb—Reached the apartment about 12:30. Went to Charlie's for Carnation milk for Barb. Taxied to Barb's, cleaned her house, came home. Tired but did Barb's laundry so Henry wouldn't have to go in the evening. We had cocktails—about 10 p.m. Henry started*

going on a tear. I don't know what possessed him. He kept it
up until nearly 5 a.m.

Was Henry disgusted with Barbara? As I worked with these old diaries, I reflected again about how, when we children, from the age of six years old, cleaned the house—not just a room, but scraped tracked-in cow manure and clay mud off the floor after it built up, because Barbara never attempted to clean the house.

Jan 30, 1946: *Polly came home. Dearest Polly arrived home today the first time in nearly three years. We had a grand leisurely breakfast then Henry left for Camp Shanks. He may be out in a few days and become a civilian. After lunch dear Pol and I went shopping. She bought a winter coat at Bloomingdales, very pretty brown. Then Pol and I went to the bank and on to Barb's for Tea. Timmy and Chris were so cute playing with the turtles I brought them. A delicious dinner and lovely evening, but dear Pol is so very quiet.*

Is Polly's silence caused by psychotropic drugs? Henry later speculated in a letter that Polly's mental breakdown was the result of caring for severely wounded soldiers who had been shipped home from Europe. Though, as I've mentioned, she was diagnosed with schizophrenia, Henry thought health care workers were affected by the carnage they witnessed—which is a recognized PTSD risk for law enforcement, first responders, and emergency room workers today.

John Curry must have been discharged and returned for a second time to New York. The following diary entry is the only reference to his return:

Feb 2, 1946: *John telephoned that he, Barb, Timmy, and Chris would be down with duck for dinner. Soon after, Barb telephoned, "no."*

Feb 14: 1946: *Valentine Day. Polly and I went shopping then went to an auction at Plaza Galleries. I brought a Valentine cake and flowers. We were going to take them to Barb, but she turned us down.*

March 26, 1946: *Henry and I had a letter from John Curry saying that he could not go on with Barbara any longer. I can't say I blame him—he really has tried. We all went up to Barb's in the evening, but she acted her usual rude self. If she put as much effort into being generous as she does into some things, entertaining, washing, caring for the children, and piano, she'd be a wonderful person.*

Elsie and Henry could not understand that with Barbara's mental illness, she had an abnormal brain, and all their best intentions couldn't change that reality. The letter they received was probably not a surprise. The few weeks John Curry spent with Barbara after his discharge must have sealed his decision to seek a divorce. Again, Elsie mentioned Barbara's inattention to laundry. Ten years in the future, when I was about eight, my younger sister, Laurel, was helping me feed my wet laundry into the wringer. The wringer caught her hand and her arm was pulled through almost to her shoulder before I hit the emergency release. Moments later Barbara knocked me down and kicked me aside.

In this next entry from Elsie, we glimpse Barbara's rage:

April 8, 1946: *Pol and I took a lot of things to Barb and had a perfectly awful time because I insisted on coming in and seeing the children. Someone told me that's the best thing to do with neurotics. Everybody pussy foots and lets them have their own wrong way and that is bad for them. But she set upon me and pounded me to pieces. I really can't take such treatment at my age—it's awful.*

There were no documented repercussions from Barbara's attack on her mother. Elsie was fifty-three when she wrote that. Short temper and intense rage are borderline personality disorder symptoms. I wonder if Elsie and Henry had pressed charges against their daughter for assault, would Barbara have reformed her behavior? Probably not. As a child, I often took the brunt of Barbara's rage; depending on the depth of her anger, she would sit on my head and pummel me with her fists until she was worn out. More than once I lay half suffocated when she finally stopped. Late spring, Elsie's mother Idalia wrote to her. It's a long, rambling family letter, but this excerpt jumped out at me:

> *April 15, 1946* Idalia Fratt Seattle, Washington
>
> Dearest Elsie, …. It is certainly awfully sad about dear Barbara. It is hard for me to write about it as I have constant interruptions. John's letter seems a very straight forward decent letter and we can understand his feelings and how he feels a responsibility for the boys. That should be encouraged. Do you think it better to let him get a divorce right away if he is willing to help the boys or linger along? Does Barb still care for him?
>
> Happy Easter, Bushels of Love, Mother

At first glance, Idalia appears to be a meddling old lady, but old letters confirm that she cared about her grandchildren, and over the years she had spent much time and money helping Barbara, so I imagine she felt invested in the problem.

Elsie's diary continues:

> May 1, 1946: *I think Barb has taken a place on Long Island. She gets Polly to drive her around. Henry went back to Wall Street, Lee Higginson from where he left four years ago— how fast time flies—he is glad to be there.*
>
> May 3, 1946: *Barbara moved out on Long Island,*

*Selden, near Patchogue. Polly helped her. It's a nice little
house. She should be very pleased as they are very hard to
find, in fact there are none.*

*May 25, 1946: Beautiful day—The railroad strike on—We
bought lots of food then drove out to Barbara's, beautiful
ride in Polly's car. Since the muffler is fixed it runs very well.
Barb's little place in Selden is very cute. The boys look fine
but Barb's no better and she surely is teaching them to
dislike us. It seems like a problem with no solution.*

Barbara cut herself off from her parents, so I was at a loss
trying to reconstruct her life. After reviewing the documents I
had linked to Barbara from 1946, I began reaching out: I sent a
Freedom of Information request to Suffolk County Social
Services, Long Island, New York, where Barbara had been on
welfare. Request Denied: Records didn't go back that far.

I reached out to Manhattan and Bronx Social Services, no
response. I had 1947 letters from Holt & Holt Law Office, Las
Cruces, New Mexico, the law firm that Elsie had hired to represent Barbara in her divorce from John. In 2018, I contacted Holt
Mynatt Martinez P.C. Law Office in Las Cruces, thinking that
Holt might be the grandchild of the 1947 Holt family—no
response.

On a long shot, I sent a message, including Barbara and
John's date of final divorce and case number to Dona Ana
County Court Administration, explaining that I was doing
research for a book. I received a prompt response from Jodi, a
Judicial Specialist Supervisor, 3rd Judicial District Court, Las
Cruces, New Mexico. She took the time to dig into seventy-year-
old records for a stranger.

Jodi sent me forty-two pages of priceless information that
illuminated a very troubled time in Barbara's life, including two
depositions and hints that a yet unknown genealogy wizard
would use in an amazing discovery that changed the course of

my life, enriching it in unexpected and surprising ways—but I'm jumping ahead again.

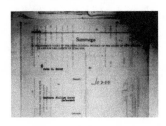

John Curry Files for Divorce.
(April 25, 1946)

On the following pages I summarize information and deposition transcriptions that helped elucidate Barbara's situation and the forces she felt were aligned against her.

John [plaintiff] petitioned court for divorce:

Excerpts from the summons:

"Statement #4: That, by reason of difference in temperament of the said parties an incompatibility exists between them that has steadily grown worse... That plaintiff is a resident of the county of Dona Ana, State of New Mexico and for more than a year last past has been a resident of said county and state; that defendant [Barbara] is a nonresident of the state of New Mexico, and that personal service of summons cannot be had on her, that her residence is 303 E 94th Street, New York City.

"That said plaintiff and defendant intermarried at Yuma in the State of Arizona in April 1942, and that two children were born as the issue of said marriage, Bruce Nicholas [Timothy] seventeen months old, and John Curry Jr. [Chris] thirty-six months old, both in custody of defendant."

On April 26, 1946, Barbara received Summons and Notice that John Curry has filed for divorce:

"Unless you enter your appearance in said cause No. 10200 on or before the 14th day of June, 1946, judgement will be rendered in said cause against you by default."

On May 24, 1946, John Curry placed Legal Notice for divorce in Las Cruces Citizen Newspaper

June 13, 1946, Barbara [defendant] answered through her attorney, Holt and Holt:

> Barbara ... "denies that she is a non-resident of New Mexico and avers the fact to be that she is temporarily absent from the State on account of physical illness. She denies allegations and, "...avers the fact to be that she is now pregnant and with child as the result of cohabitation between herself and plaintiff [John Curry]."

Either this is not true, or she miscarried. The answer continues:

> "That since the birth of the first child of the parties hereto, defendant has been and still is in ill health; and that since the alleged separation of the parties, defendant has been in New York, in contact with her parents; and has been and is under treatment of physicians for her physical illness.
>
> "That she is without means to support herself and the two minor children of the parties and is physically unable to earn a living for herself and said children, or to provide for her care during the existing pregnancy or for the expenses which will necessarily be incident to the birth of the expected child; or to pay a fee to attorneys representing herein.
>
> "WHEREFORE defendant prays judgement:
>
> "That the prayer of plaintiff's Complaint be denied. That an order may be entered herein requiring the plaintiff to provide for the adequate support and maintenance of defendant and the aforesaid children of the parties hereto, and for expenses incident to the affordsaid existing pregnancy of defendant and the birth of the expected issue;

and for payment of a reasonable fee to her attorneys herein, in such an amount as the court may deem proper."

June 26, 1946, John Curry's attorney replied:

"Comes now the above-named plaintiff, replying to the defendant's answer filed herein and states; "That if defendant is now pregnant, she has not made her condition known to the plaintiff; that he has not seen her since the 26th day of Feb. 1946; That because of the nature of the relationship between plaintiff and defendant when they were last together, it is impossible that she is pregnant from any act of his. He therefore denies that the defendant is pregnant by him.

"That defendant is in physically as good health as plaintiff and is physically able to earn her living. That she has refused, the last time, April 1946, plaintiff's request that she come to New Mexico and live with and be supported by him.

"Wherefore he prays that she be denied the relief prayed for."

Through their attorneys, Barbara and John sparred back and forth through 1946. Barbara, living in Selden, New York, was on welfare and had no vehicle. She walked to the local store for her groceries and other needs. It must have been a struggle, pushing two small children along the shoulder of a dirt road in a baby carriage and carrying groceries. Elsie apparently told the extended family that Barbara was doing great.

John Curry wrote to Idalia, Barbara's grandmother, while she was visiting in New York:

December 6, 1946 John Curry Las Cruces, New Mexico
Dear Gram: I am glad to hear that Barbara and the

children are enjoying good health. I wrote Barbara recently asking for two photocopies of the children's birth certificates. The government has held up more than three months subsistence checks from my G.I. training because they need this proof of dependents. I hope Barbara has taken this pain in getting these photostatic copies made, because it is for her own benefit. I hope you enjoy your stay in New York. Please write again when you find time. I enjoy your letters very much.

Love to all, John [Curry]

Christopher Curry, Photo Studio, Selden, Long Island. (1946)

Barbara's "photoshop" instructions attempted to make Chris into "Little Lord Fauntleroy." Her directions on the back of this proof photo: "Please color this hair as golden as possible, fair rosy complexion, white teeth, light brown eyes." Chris had dark black hair and brown tinted skin—his father was Hispanic. Why did Barbara want to alter Chris's appearance?

1947

M aking sense of Barbara's life during 1947 was like assembling a jigsaw puzzle without the completed picture as a reference. I started with what appeared to be disparate pieces, but eventually they came together and formed a Greek tragedy scene gone wrong, with Barbara as protagonist.

A few months after Polly was divorced and discharged from the army, she was admitted to New York Hospital psychiatric ward on September 17, 1946. Did Barbara witness the side effects of Polly's electric and insulin shock therapy treatments? If so, I believe what Barbara saw terrified her and influenced her future decisions when Elsie threatened to have Barbara committed.

The two depositions I received from Dona Ana County Court Administration were done early in 1947: The first with Elsie Philips; the second with Barbara's case supervisor Mae Sloane with Suffolk County Social Services, Long Island. There was a flurry of correspondence over the next several months, beginning with a series of letters between Holt & Holt Law Office and Elsie (Mrs. Henry O. Philips). I include them for the reader to see Barbara's struggle—how borderline personality disorder controlled her life.

It must have been very frustrating for the attorneys because Barbara refused to answer any correspondence and had apparently frozen Elsie out. Also, unknown to Elsie or Barbara's attorney, Barbara was in a new relationship.

LAW OFFICES

H. B. HOLT
E. L. HOLT

HOLT & HOLT
FIRST NATIONAL BANK BUILDING
LAS CRUCES, N. M.

January
20,1947

Mrs. Henry O. Philips
316 East 58th Street
New York 22, N. Y.

Dear Mrs. Philips:

Your letter of the 15th instant reached us this morning. From a perusal of its contents we infer that you did not fully comprehend what is necessary in connection with your daughter's pending divorce suit, as outlined in our letters to your daughter and to you. Under date of October 4th, your daughter wrote stating that she accepted $40.00 per month for her children but her letter indicated that she was under the impression that the decree had already been entered, which of course was a mistake. Under date of October 11th last, you transmitted a written statement from your daughter dated October 5, 1946, reading as follows, to wit:

"I acknowledge the $40.00 the Court has decided John Curry shall pay for the support of his children. I agree to accept this sum with the understanding that when he is earning more he will send more."

The letter continues:

"I [Barbara] have decided I don't want a divorce. Please hold it off. I think I refuse the divorce. I've written to my husband to tell him that since he has to send half his money to us anyway, he might as well come back and live with his family. I think divorce is a very serious matter when there are two children involved and I think the judge realizes this."

Under October 28, 1946, prior to receipt of your daughter's letter of November 3rd, we wrote her relative to the support money for the children, a copy of which was mailed to you.

Under date of November 13, 1946. Your daughter wrote to us, among other things, she said:

"*Please disregard all my previous letters. I absolutely refuse to divorce my husband and I wrote you of this several weeks ago. I will not under any circumstances sign a divorce decree. I wish you would speak to my husband and ask him why he does not come back and live with his family. After all he has done, we are willing to take him back. I see no reason he should not come back and live with his children and his wife. I will never give him a divorce because of the children. They need their father. He realizes now that he can't get out of supporting them so he might as well come back and make a success of the marriage.*"

On November 25, 1946, she wrote us [Holt & Holt] another letter in which she said, "*...I absolutely refuse to divorce my husband. I am his wife, and I will not consent to a divorce.*"

Mrs. Philips, Since your daughter is determined to resist the divorce suit, it will be necessary, under the circumstances, to take her testimony by deposition, which means to take her testimony under oath based upon written questions which we shall prepare and which will be attached to the commission, to be issued by our Court here [in New Mexico] to some Notary Public in New York authorizing him take such testimony or deposition in the form of written answers to the several questions.

In our letter of November 29, 1946, we asked your daughter whether or not you and her father, Mr. Philips, would bear the expense of taking the necessary depositions, but thus far we have no reply to the inquiry either from her or from you. Without full and proper cooperation by you and your daughter we can not hope to successfully resist the divorce suit.

The failure of your daughter to answer our letter on the 9th, and the contents of your letter on the 15th cause us to fear that your daughter's mental and or physical condition may have become aggravated to such an extent as to preclude her answering our inquires.

We feel assured that you must recognize our difficulty in attempting to handle this case at such a long range, and that full cooperation by you and your husband is essential.

Very Truly Yours, Holt and Holt Law Firm

Barbara was spiraling out of control. Elsie's reply to Attorney Holt in Las Cruces:

Feb 1, 1947 Elsie Philips, New York, New York

Dear Mr. Holt, Your long letter of January 20 has just come to me. I so much appreciate your untiring effort in this most intricate case, advising her to stay in New York as a trip would be a very wrong thing to do.

I did not receive the supplement to your letter of Nov 29. I can give you the name of Mr. Giaino who is the attorney for our building here in New York as a notary to whom I could give my deposition—his address is....

Since our daughter, Barbara Curry, lives in Selden, Long Island, seventy miles from here and has no telephone nor is there near transportation, it is difficult for us to get in touch with her because with us, like you, she does not answer the letters. Mrs. Sloane, the Welfare Case Worker lives about ten miles away in Bay Shore and is in fairly frequent touch with Barbara.

I will immediately send this letter of yours on to her [Mrs. Sloane] in the expectation that she will arrange you a notary for Barbara and for herself and let you know the names so that you can prepare the commissions. I think it will be possible for Mrs. Sloane to get Barbara to answer the inquires.

The doctor has not considered her illness severe enough to hospitalize her and considers she is well enough to take care of her children therefore I think it would be feasible to take her deposition. We will be willing to pay the fees for Notary Public. We think it well that you filed a court order for John to pay both alimony and support of the children.

We very much appreciate the difficulties under which you are working and your untiring patience in handling this case. We will do everything in our power to help you speed its conclusion. Sincerely, Elsie Philips

The above letter is significant in that Elsie mentioned the possibility of Barbara being hospitalized for her psychiatric issues. When we were children, one of the triggers that sent Barbara into a violent rage was when Herman, my stepfather, threatened to have her committed.

On January 31, 1947, Elsie received the interrogatories [questions] for her scheduled deposition. In 2010 I found her answers in the chickenhouse—seventy years after the deposition was taken, I received the questions from Dona Ana County Court. Elsie's deposition, taken early February 1947, in New York City, revealed new information and confirmed other:

Interrogatory No. 13: Did you receive a letter from the plaintiff [Curry] after his last voyage with the Merchant Marine containing any statement as to his intensions relative to his wife and family?

Elsie's answer: Yes.

Interrogatory No. 14: If you answered the preceding in the affirmative, state whether or not you now have that letter in your possession: and if so, please produce and identify same in order that it may be marked as an exhibit to and made a part of your testimony.

Elsie's answer: I received this letter from John, and same to him at once telling that he should [inform] Barbara directly of his intensions and I have now in my possession his instructions about delivering this letter.

Interrogatory No. 16: If you have any information upon the subject, state your daughter's condition of health and if you state that she [Barbara] has been and is in ill health, state the nature of her infirmity so far as known to you, and how long she has been afflicted.

Elsie's Answer: My daughter has been emotionally ill since sometime during her first pregnancy, possibly during a period when John was not earning money. The nature of her illness is hard to determine even by experts since the field of neuropsychiatry is only beginning its discoveries. Her trouble is sometimes described as a psychological block.

Interrogatory No. 17: Has your daughter any source of income: and if you say she has not, state approximately how long that situation has existed.

Elsie's answer: She has no income and has had none since her husband left her in February 1946.

Interrogatory No. 18: Is your daughter physically capable of earning a living for herself and her children?

Elsie's answer: It is very doubtful.

Interrogatory No. 19: If you know, state who or what organization, if any, has been contributing to the relief and care of your daughter and her children....

Elsie's answer: Suffolk County Public Welfare has contributed to her relief from May 1946 to the present time.

Interrogatory No. 21: Since the marriage of your daughter to the plaintiff, to what extent, if any, have you and your husband contributed to the support of your daughter and children?

Elsie's answer: About $2500 over a period of time. Some before 1944, completely while he was in training for the Merchant Marine, January to April 1944, and some to present.

Interrogatory No. 23: ...if you know, state why your daughter and her children have been and are dependent on relief [from Suffolk County Public Welfare].

Elsie was not truthful in response to question 16. As we know, Barbara had been psychiatrically unstable for more than a decade before this deposition was taken. According to Elsie, John was in Merchant Marine training from February-April 1944, the exact months Barbara wrote so many letters accusing him of abandoning his family.

By January 1947, Barbara was under tremendous pressure. Alone and abandoned, she reached out for companionship. Impulsiveness and promiscuity go hand in hand with borderline personality disorder. Nine months later, I was born.

Two weeks after Elsie's deposition, Barbara was awarded child support:

February 13, 1947: Alimony/Child Support Decree: It is therefore ordered by the Court here, that decision as to alimony pendete lite shall be, and the same hereby is, reserved pending final hearing upon the merits; and that, dating from and after September 10, 1946, until further order of the Court, plaintiff shall pay toward the support and maintenance of the two minor children of the parties hereto the sum of $40.50 per month, same to be paid into the hands of the Clerk of this Court for delivery to counsel for defendant. Future monthly payments to be made as aforesaid on the 10th day of each succeeding calendar month.

I include this next letter for two reasons: First, it is representative of hundreds of the letters I transcribed—the result of decades of neglect in the leaking-roofed chickenhouse. The second reason is to show that John Curry was 2,000 miles from Barbara during the timeframe during which Barb became pregnant with me. Here is the first contact Holt & Holt Law Offices, Las Cruces, New Mexico, made with Mae Sloane:

February 14, 1947 Holt & Holt Law Office Las Cruces, New Mexico

To: Mrs. Mae L. Sloane Case Supervisor Suffolk County Welfare

94 Fourth Avenue, Bay Shore, N.Y.Re: Barbara Curry---ADC 6496

Dear Madam:

Referring to your letter addressed to us under date of July 5th last [1946]. We have recently written Mrs. Henry O. Philips, mother of Barbara Curry, requesting her to communicate with you and ask you to furnish us with the name of a Notary Public located near your place of business, for purpose of taking your deposition and also that of Barbara Curry. Mrs. Philips wrote us that she had complied with our request; but not having heard from you, we take the liberty of writing this letter.

We are desirous of taking your deposition as promptly

as possible; and we also wish to take the deposition of Barbara, if her mental condition will enable us to do so.

Under date of November 29th last, we wrote Barbara asking for some specific information regarding the separation between her and her husband, but she never answered the letter. On January 9th last, we again wrote her asking for the information and explaining the necessity of taking her deposition as well as yours; but for some unexplained reason we have not heard from her. In two or three previous letters from her she was very earnest in her declaration that she wished to resist the divorce suit and she definitely instructed us so to do.

Please advise us as to Barbara's physical and mental condition; particularly as to whether or not her mental condition is such that she can intelligently testify by way of answer to the interrogatories which would accompany the commission for the taking of her deposition,

Awaiting your reply,

Yours truly, By: H. B. Holt

In the same envelope, the same date, Holt & Holt sent a copy of the above letter and questioned Barbara's mental competence to receive back child support the Las Cruces Court had awarded. I include an excerpt:

February 14, 1947 Holt & Holt Law Office Las Cruces, New Mexico

Dear Mrs. Philips, For your information we enclose a copy of a letter written to the Case Supervisor, Mrs. Sloane.... We shall appreciate it if you will inform us as to whether or not your daughter's mental condition is such as to justify turning the money over to her. If not, favor us with your suggestion as to how it shall be handled.... Not having heard anything from your daughter since last November

[1946], we are concerned about her condition. As you know, in our letters to her, we requested her to answer certain questions in order that we might intelligently prepare interrogatories [for her deposition], but she has never answered.

Also, you may know, she definitely instructed us to resist the divorce , but in order to do so her testimony is essential especially upon the issue of whether or not she abandoned her husband or as to whether or not there was a mutual verbal agreement of separation.

Yours truly, By: H. B. Holt

This next piece of the puzzle came to me from the young lady who worked with Dona Ana District Court; without her, much of my mother's story would have gone untold. On March 3, 1947, Mae Sloane received Notice of Intention to Take Deposition. Sloane's deposition helped clarify events of 1946; the report is rather like the *Jeopardy!* game show—we have the answers in the deposition, but no question. Again, I gained new insights to my mother's struggle and the tremendous pressure she must have been under. How far along was Barbara before she realized she was pregnant with me?

March 6, 1947: Deposition with Mae Sloane, Case Supervisor; some information was redundant. I include only what moves the narrative forward.

Interrogatory No. 6: How long have you known Barbara Philips Curry and under what circumstances did you became acquainted with her?

Answer No. 6, Mae Sloane: We have known Mrs. Curry since May 8, 1946, when she made application for an aid to Dependent Children's grant. She had moved to Suffolk County on May 4, 1946, from New York City where she had been receiving aid. In making her application, she stated that she moved to Suffolk County because she could not find suitable living quarters in New York. She stated that she had not seen her husband for several months and believed that he did not intend to return to the family and that he was in New Mexico with his parents.

Interrogatory No. 7: If you know, state the present address of the defendant, and approximately how long she has resided at her present address.

Answer No. 7, Mae Sloane: Mrs. Curry's present address is Magnolia Drive, Selden, New York, and she has resided at that address since May 3, 1946.

Interrogatory No. 14: If known to you, state her present condition of health, both physical and mental, or otherwise.

Answer No. 14, Mae Sloane: As to Mrs. Curry's mental health, she appears to be a mentally unstable person, because of this, we had her examined by a psychiatrist, Dr. George M. Lott, on August 1, 1946. He stated that she is not mentally ill but that she has a personality disorder which is primarily manifested by a hostile attitude toward her parents. In her relationship with others she has a tendency to be opinionated and obstinate, however, she is well oriented, above average intelligence, and appears to maintain a satisfactory home for herself and her children.

Dr. George M. Lott, head psychiatrist of Suffolk Mental Hygiene Department, Suffolk County, Long Island, New York, was prescient in his conclusion. Though Dr. Lott recognized that Barbara had a personality disorder, Borderline Personality Disorder was only defined as a separate diagnostic condition in 1980, when it became an official personality disorder in the Diagnostic and Statistical Manual of Mental Disorders III, or DSM-III. (See page xiv, Borderline Personality Disorder criteria.)

Deposition continues:

Interrogatory No. 15: Since you have known the defendant, has her state of health been such as to render her employable; and if not, why not?

Answer No. 15, Mae Sloane: Her health is such as to render her un-employable, but there is a question of her employability because of her personality difficulties.

Interrogatory No. 16: If you have stated that the defendant has been physically and/or mentally ill since you have known her, state whether or not there has been any improvement in her condition since you have known her.

Answer No. 16, Mae Sloane: There has been no change in her mental attitude, namely emotional instability.

Interrogatory No. 20: Have you in your possession, any letter addressed by the plaintiff to the defendant relative to his intension to institute suit for divorce? If so, please produce same, explain how it came into your custody, and from whom, and have same marked as an exhibit to be attached to your deposition, and if you have the envelope which enclosed such letter, please also produce that and have it also marked as an exhibit.

Answer No. 20, Mae Sloane: The following letter is an absolute facsimile of one addressed to Mrs. Curry by her husband, John, dated April 20, 1946. Said copy of letter was made due to the fact that Mrs. Curry would not release the original to our possession: We will hereby quote the letter as exactly duplicated.

Barbara, April 20, 1946

I hereby notify you that papers for a divorce are on file here in Court. This is a last and final step and I am sure if we look at it in a sensible way, it is going to be best for both of us. You are to have custody of the children since they are too young yet to understand and I know you will take good care of them. I don't know more to say except that our life in the past has been a complete mess and I have decided not to hurt you or me by this very foolish marriage of ours. Please disregard all previous letters and I would advise you to stay in New York as a trip here would be a very wrong thing to do. The papers will be served you within the week or so and a divorce will come through regardless. You may as well find work to do at present. The lawyer is charging me a considerable fee and I am in debt with Dad. I have done my part in the past.

Very truly John.

Interrogatory No. 21: Since you have known defendant, has she been physically or financially able to journey from New York City to Las Cruces, New Mexico?

Answer No. 21, Mae Sloane: Defendant has been physically able but financially unable to journey from New York City to Las Cruces, New Mexico.

Interrogatory No. 22: If you know of any other matter or thing relative to the issues involved, in the pending divorce suit, please state same.

Answer No. 22, Mae Sloane: We know only that Mrs. Curry at first was agreeable to the divorce provided Mr. Curry contributed toward the support of the children and that now she opposes the divorce because she feels that she would prefer to reconcile herself with her husband feeling that the children need their father in the home.

Suffolk County District Attorney issued an extradition order for John Curry to be brought to New York on charges of abandoning his family. On April 25, 1947, the *Las Cruces Sun-News* published the following article:

SANTA FE, April 25 [AP] Governor Mabry today refused to extradite John C. Curry, Las Cruces, whose wife sought to have him returned to Suffolk County, New York, on charges of abandoning her and two children. Curry is grandson of former Territorial Governor George Curry.

Mabry said in recent Las Cruces hearing by Dist. Atty. W.T. Scoggin, Jr., found Curry repeatedly had asked his wife to join him there. Scoggins informed the governor that the state law provides that "only the husband" has the right to designate where his family's home is to be.

An attorney with Suffolk County Welfare helped Barbara officially contest the divorce. Mae Sloane submitted Barbara's request to Dona Ana County Court:

August 7, 1947
We are enclosing Mrs. Curry's notarized statement that she is contesting the divorce. We regret that we have been unable to persuade her to sign the deposition. Her argument is that if she signs the deposition the divorce action will come into court—by refusing to do so she will in that way prevent the divorce reaching court. We don't know how she arrived at such a conclusion. She only insisted that the enclosed statement should be enough to stop the divorce. As of this date we are writing to Mr. H.B. Holt of Holt and Holt.

Barbara, as she did all her life when overwhelmed, ignored the problem. Holt & Holt Law Office withdrew their representation of Barbara's case; a copy of the letter was sent to Elsie.

August 18, 1947
NOTICE: You are hereby notified that your attorney H.B. Holt has withdrawn from the case and has filed his withdrawal as attorney for you; unless you appoint another attorney to represent you in this cause the plaintiff will apply

to the Court for an order to proceed without attorney, or to appoint an attorney to represent you.

Signed, E.G. Shannon, Attorney for the plaintiff, Las Cruces, N.M.

Barbara, eight months pregnant, moved back into New York City and stayed at her parents' apartment for a short time. I was born October 30, 1947, in New York Hospital, Borough of Manhattan. My birth certificate listed John Clifford Curry as father. On line #11, *Usual residence of mother*: Barbara wrote: 320 W. 34th St., New York. *Length of residence?* 4 days.

According to a Dona Ana County Court document (below), John Curry's attorney, E. G. Shannon, had attempted to reach Barbara at Selden, Long Island, New York, and at Los Angeles, California. When I saw the Los Angeles postal contact, I thought it was a mistake, but soon learned an ominous detail of another abandonment—an abandonment that explained why the natural maternal bond between Barbara and me was absent.

November 19, 1947: State of New Mexico, County of Dona Ana: E.G. Shannon, being first duly sworn, deposes and says that he, on the 18th day of August, 1947, deposited in the U.S. post office in Las Cruces, New Mexico, securely bound, postage prepaid, addressed to Barbara Philips Curry, at her post office address Selden, Long Island, a copy of the above notice, that the envelope bore the affiant's post office address, and has not been returned to the affiant.

November 19, 1947: To the defendant, Barbara Philips Curry; You are hereby notified that the undersigned will, on the 25th day of November at ten o'clock a.m. at Dona Ana County Court house, in Las Cruces, New Mexico, or as soon after said date as the attention of said court can be secured, take up for trial on its merits, the above entitled cause.

I the undersigned attorney for the plaintiff herein do hereby certify that I, this day deposited in the post office at Las Cruces, New Mexico, sealed, postage prepaid, and addressed to defendant's last known post office address, Los Angeles, California, a copy of above notice; that I delivered to the Clerk of this court a true copy of said notice.

Attorney for plaintiff, E.G. Shannon, Las Cruces, New Mexico

Three weeks after I was born, John and Barbara's final divorce decree was issued.

November 25, 1947: ...final disposition on the 25th day of November 1947, before the District Court of Dona Ana as shown by proof of service filed herein County, at Las Cruces, New Mexico, as required by law and the plaintiff being present in court and represented by his said attorney, demanding a hearing on the issues, and the defendant being called and answering not, the plaintiff offering his evidence, and the court having heard same and being fully advised in the premises doth find that the plaintiff and defendant are husband and wife; that there was born as issue of said marriage two children, Bruce Nicholas Curry [Tim] born October 2, 1944, and John Alexander Curry [Chris] born April 24, 1943, who are now in custody of defendant, that a condition of incompatibility exists between the plaintiff and defendant by reason of which they are unable to live together, and that the plaintiff should be granted a divorce from defendant; that heretofore on the 13th day of February 1947, this court entered an order directing that the plaintiff pay into court for the support of his minor children $40.50 monthly, that no part of said amount has been paid as required by said order.

Two children were listed on the divorce decree: "Bruce Nicholas Curry [Tim] and John Alexander Curry [Chris]." The court recognized that I was not John's child. How did Barbara react when she received the final decree? Did she suffer post-partum depression, compounding her other psychiatric problems? The final decree must have elevated her sense of failure.

Mother Kills 4 Children, Self By Gas in Connecticut Home

Elsie was terrified that Barbara would commit suicide and take her children with her. Elsie's "Mental Health Journal" contained several articles about mothers and suicide, including this clipping of a tragedy which took place on November 19, 1947.

In early November 1947 Barbara somehow acquired money for train tickets for herself, two young boys and a two-week-old infant from New York to Los Angeles. (Possibly from delinquent child support that came through as a condition for granting the final divorce decree.) Documents indicate that Barbara spent a few days in Los Angeles, and then traveled to Las Cruces. She was psychologically and financially destitute. In desperation she again reached out to her parents.

Elsie documented her first flight—her diary entries and a few letters reveal just how distraught Barbara was:

December 17, 1947: *Day before flying to El Paso to help poor dear Barbara with her many problems. She called long distance collect twice so Henry made the reservations. I simply threw things in my suitcase as they were.*
December 18, 1947: *Ten Most Crowded Days of My Life.*

Flew to [New] Mexico. A beautiful gleaming white star on a mountain when we arrived at midnight at El Paso. Arrived Barbara's hotel one a.m. We talked until four.

December 20, 1947: Left at 9 a.m. by bus for Las Cruces. Beautiful day, gorgeous scenery. High snow-capped mountains and desert cactus. I had written John we were coming. Barb showed me the way to his father. He saw me right away.

December 20, 1947, Henry wrote this letter to Elsie:

Dearest, Will be glad to hear all your news about Barb and the boys and your "trip back plans." Tell Barb we are all ready for her, glad she is coming home, and will all work together for a new fresh life. "Upward and onward" it is good for her she is coming home. There is much here to revive her interest in living and life and renew her enjoyment of all those things that go toward a versatile, well-rounded out personality. She may even soon find a new husband— stable and solvent. At least she will have the opportunity here of looking over a broader field. Take good care of yourself and write only when you have time. Love to Barb, love to you darling, Henry

Henry's comment, "versatile, well-rounded out personality" jumped out at me. Lee R. Steiner, author of *Where Do People Take Their Troubles?* (1949) wrote in the chapter "Personality on Sale," about the "Cinderella Schools" and "Success Schools" who cured depressed overweight young women of their "Inferiority Complex" and promised them a wealthy loving husband. Perhaps Henry had read the following advertisement or a similar one in *Mademoiselle* magazine: "She came to the Success School a timid, unsure girl, with a strong Inferiority Complex! You should have seen her, this girl of twenty-three.... Her face reflecting so clearly her depressed state of mind, her sense of failure! ... And now today, the miracle of rebuilding that the Success School wrought ... So if you have any feelings of inadequacy, write or call...."

From Henry's point of view, Miss Delafield's Success School may have sounded like the perfect solution for his troubled daughter.

 From the floor of the chickenhouse, I had salvaged a severely damaged letter dated December 1947. I sent it to David, an amazing man who, as the future unfolded, played a pivotal role in this story.

David's expertise made a scrap of unreadable paper—a letter from Elsie to Henry, sent just a few days before Christmas—into a clue.

Sunday, December 21, 1947

Dearest Henry, So much has been happening that it seems as tho I've been away from home three months instead of three days. Barb has been mostly good. But of course, she realizes I've made some sacrifices for her or rather we have.

On Thursday I got into El Paso at eleven and Barb talked until nearly four in the morning—all about how she was to try to get John back. I let her go on and on.

Friday, we shopped all day for all necessary things because she had had no baggage for two weeks.

Saturday, we went to Las Cruces in the A. M., it's a beautiful ride. In spite of the fact that it was Saturday, I saw everyone. First, Mr. Holt; such a sweet man—just as I imagined him—I talked to him for an hour and a half. His wife called him for lunch, but he excused himself, saying, "Mrs. Philips is here from New York." I won't attempt to tell you all the things they told me, but it was pretty hard to hear such awful things about my daughter. She's been chasing John so hard I think the father finally had her run out of town to El Paso—45 miles from Las Cruces.

I'll tell you about that too, but she was so determined to get John back here. I saw the father, Clifford Curry, at the Police station. First, he had determined to be gruff, but soon he was smiling and pleasant. He would not tell where John was. But just as we were walking to the Bus Station along came John. Chris discovered him in a crowd. John took us over to the Amador Hotel. There in the cocktail lounge over beers we had it out and I was really surprised how well Barbara took it. He told her there was no way she could get him back. He said, for goodness sake have her go home without him. She was determined to persuade him to come to New York with us. Well that's settled and she says she doesn't suppose she will ever see him again.

She still intends to go to Los Angeles and get the baby which she says is in a hospital in L. A. We're leaving this afternoon by bus—another 800 miles. It's thirteen dollars. Barbara hopes to be in L. A. for one night, get the baby, & then home—probably Friday. Its 24 hours by bus to L. A. from here so the earliest we would leave for New York is Tuesday, but we're lucky not to have to stay here longer.

I'll write you from L. A.

Arms full of Merry Christmas Love, Elsie

"She still intends to go to Los Angeles and get the baby...." Interesting choice of words Elsie used. Had Barbara considered leaving me in Los Angeles? As I read and reread the letter, I came to a realization as to why she treated me as she did when I was a child— I believe she blamed my existence for her not reconciling with John. I wonder, if John had taken her back, would she have just abandoned me in that Los Angeles Hospital?

And a question looms: How is it possible that I was admitted? What illness or injury did I have? Did the hospital staff admit me because they recognized that I was an "at risk" infant with a mentally unstable mother?

On November 19, Attorney E. G. Shannan stated in Dona Ana County Court, "I, this day deposited in the post office at Las Cruces, New Mexico, sealed, postage prepaid, and addressed to defendant's last known post office address, Los Angeles, California." From that information, I extrapolate that Barbara had left me in Los Angeles Hospital for at least six weeks. After abandoning me, how could she just have me discharged back into her custody?

Memory is an interesting thing: In the chickenhouse I discovered a letter that Barbara had written to her mother sixteen years after her divorce from John Curry.

An excerpt…

April 7, 1963. Dear Mother, …. I truly apologize that you never had a fine son-in-law. How well I remember you tried to stop me from divorcing Curry.

By 1963, Barbara was again destitute, isolated on the little farm in northern Minnesota, with nine children, forced to live with a man she despised. Apparently, Barbara had created a memory, that it was *she* who had sought the divorce from John Curry.

1948

S oon after returning to New York, Barbara met a new
man, Francis Xavier Schoenwandt, through a Lonely
Hearts Club catalogue, and two weeks later, on January
26, 1948, they got married and moved to Schoenwandt's farm
near Cooperstown, New York. My oldest brother Chris remembered Schoenwandt's name, which was very helpful in my
research. In 2015, I contacted the New York State Historical
Association to see if I could learn more about Schoenwandt. I
received a reply with this newspaper article:

Barbara's marriage to Schoenwandt was annulled less than a
year later. Chris, six at the time, remembered Frank as an old
man who was rarely home. On April 2, 1948, according to *The
Otsego Farmer,* Cooperstown, New York, "A charge of second
degree assault has been placed against Francis Schoenwandt,
Town of Middlefield, as a result of a complaint that he beat his
16-year-old daughter and stabbed her in the leg with a pitchfork.
Schoenwandt is in the Otsego county jail…. The arrest was made
on complaint of the daughter and a deposition signed by Mrs.
[Barbara] Schoenwandt." As happens too often in domestic
assault cases, the charges were dropped.

Cooperstown, N. Y.   Friday, April 2, 1948

Arrested For 2nd Degree Assault

A charge of second degree assault has been placed against Francis Schoenwandt, Town of Middlefield, as result of a complaint that he beat his 16-year-old daughter and stabbed her in the leg with a pitchfork.

Schoenwandt is in the Otsego county jail at Cooperstown. He was taken there by State Police after he waived examination before Justice of the Peace H. D. Carpenter of Cooperstown on Wednesday. He was ordered held for action of the grand jury.

The assault, police said, occurred Sunday night at the farm where the Schoenwandt family lives near Roseboom. Mr. Schoenwandt is charged by State Police with beating his daughter, Grace, then throwing a pitchfork at her. One tine of the fork pierced the girl's leg.

State Police of the Cooperstown sub-station were called. Schoenwandt was apprehended Tuesday by the Oneonta State Police. The arrest was made on complaint of the daughter and a deposition signed by Mrs. Schoenwandt.

HIST. ASSN. TO GIVE SPECIAL COURSES HER

Seminars Are Planne For July 11-17; Amer. Culture

Seminars on American Culture a offered to provide adults intereste in five specialized historical fiel with an opportunity for exchangin ideas and for meeting with disti guished leaders in these areas. Th Seminars will be held at Fenimo House, the Central Quarters of th New York State Historical Ass ciation, and at The Farmers' M seum, which the Association operate in Cooperstown, N. Y., on July 11-1 1948.

The Seminars will be divided int five fields of interest and it is ex pected that no participant will enrol for more than two of these. Thre will be held in the morning two i

Tim, Wendell in buggy, Chris. This is the earliest photo
of author—about six months old. Schoenwandt farm
near Cooperstown, NY (Summer1948)

In Barbara's 1960 psychiatric evaluation, when she was committed to Fergus Falls State Hospital, her report stated, "[Schoenwandt] actually carried a gun and was brutal in his treatment of his previous wife [who had died] and the patient [Barbara]. He was 16 years older than the patient...." During interviews I had with Barbara a few years before she died, she confirmed Chris's memories of Schoenwandt being a violent man, as does the news clipping. Again, I think it's impossible to comprehend Barbara's sense of despair and abandonment.

This next excerpt is from a letter draft Elsie wrote in April 1951 to the former First Lady. It offers clues to Barbara's movements late in 1948 and early 1949. As I mentioned earlier, Barbara absolutely was *not* schizophrenic. Was Elsie trying to dramatize Barbara's condition, or did she assume that Polly's diagnosis applied to Barbara, too?

> Dear Mrs. Roosevelt,
>   ...the second husband [Schoenwandt] got an annulment. She [Barbara] tried suicide (second documented attempt). We used up what savings we had trying to rehabilitate her. Scz. [schizophrenia] causes one to withdraw from the World of Responsibilities and people. She started disappearing and going on welfare. In Cooperstown they put her in care of a Psychiatric Nurse when her fourth baby was coming and had her delivered here to our care for convalescence after.

Although Elsie's "diagnosis" was not accurate by today's definition, her statement does contain a symptom of a personality disorder: "Scz. [schizophrenia] causes one to withdraw from the World of Responsibilities and people." At some point in 1948, Barbara changed her name to Linda. Why?

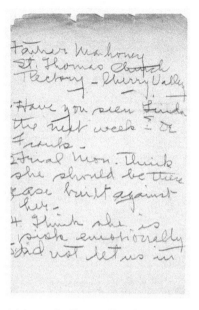

Father Mahoney, St. Thomas Church Rectory—Cherry
Valley [New York]

In Elsie's "Mental Health" folder, I discovered an undated, faded scrap that she had written, referring to Barbara as "Linda" for the first time.

1. *Have you seen Linda the next week or Frank—*
2. *Trial Mon. think she should be there*
3. *Case built against her*
4. *Think she is sick emotionally*
5. *Did not let us in*

Barbara would use the name "Linda" for the next five years. In my earlier book *PAWNS*, in one of my interviews, I asked Barbara why she liked that name so much. She told me that she had attended an operetta in France—couldn't remember the name of it or the composer—but she had considered one of the characters, Rosalinde, to be a sophisticated, clever lady.

I did a bit of research and discovered that the character Barbara venerated was from "Die Fledermaus" (The Bat). It was originally written as a farce by German playwright Julius Rodrich Benedix in 1851. The operetta was composed by Johann Strauss II in 1874. I wonder if what impressed Barbara most was Rosalinde's success with manipulating men.

Just months beyond her second divorce and second suicide attempt, Barbara and her three children were living with her parents again. She was under psychiatric nursing care and, no doubt, ruminating on traumas she had been through over the past decade. This undated "Worry Clinic" (see next page) clipping came from Elsie's "Mental Health" folder. Dr. George W. Crane, author and syndicated columnist, was a psychologist who, over several decades, published self-help pamphlets, three books, and countless advice columns.

Elsie studied psychology from the mid-1930s through the 1960s, including classes at City College of New York, searching for answers for her two daughters' mental illness issues. By 1948, Elsie had been dealing with Barbara's erratic behavior for thirteen years. Elsie's younger daughter Polly had been diagnosed with schizophrenia three years earlier. Elsie must have been at wit's end. She sent a letter to Dr. Crane about Barbara aka "Linda C." [Linda Curry].

WORRY CLINIC

Kindness Often Halts Insanity

BY DR. GEORGE W. CRANE

Linda C., 21, is an attractive brunette about whom her mother is greatly worried.

'She has grown less and less interested in the world around her. I have noticed the change for nearly a year.'

'She stays around the house brooding, or sitting at the piano, which she used to play a great deal, but now hardly ever plays.

'Occasionally she'll smile, as if somebody else is talking to her. If I speak to her then, she may ignore my voice.

Warned of Schizophrenia

'Another psychiatrist told me she is a schizophrenia case and recommended shock treatments.'

This other psychiatrist diagnosed her case very well. I gleaned from further conversation with both mother and daughter that the girl is markedly withdrawing from reality.

She is retreating into a shell, as it were, where she apparently lives in a dream world. I did not recommend radical treatment at this time, for she is not yet insane but certainly is headed in that direction.

Build Pleasant Ties

What Linda needs is to be gently led back into an enjoyment of this world. For people flee only from that which is apparently cold, cruel or forbidding!

On the other hand, we like to remain where we enjoy ourselves! The best antidote for Linda is to build up so many pleasant ties between the patient and the world around her, that she is firmly attached to her environment.

To combat such mental illness, see that you and your children have many happy bonds to fasten your interest upon the external world. Give the younger children toys and puppies, kittens or gardens of their own.

This next letter I had translated from French. It was written by one of Barbara's school friends from Europe. The first paragraph...

Dear Linda

Because Linda is in fact your new first name, isn't it? Anyway, I believed you had really disappeared! I thought you busy with so many things that you no longer knew how to write me... You're married, and on top of that, mother of two children and now here you are a farmer!

Barbara had "disappeared." Linda was now in charge. The phrase "here you are a farmer" places her with Schoenwandt. The phrase "you no longer knew how to write me" is telling. By 1948, Barbara's life was a disaster.

When "Linda" wrote the 1948 letter to her friend, I was eight months old, living with my grandparents. Correspondence from that timeframe reveal that Barbara was under psychiatric nursing care. Why had Barbara changed her name? Why did "Linda" deny my existence? Throughout our childhood all my siblings were very aware—as was I—that I was the black sheep. My stepfather referred to me as "the nigger in the woodpile," ironic because I have a lighter complexion than my older brothers. It's an archaic euphemism similar to the milkman theory for bastard children.

On October 16, 1948, Idalia wrote to Henry:

My Dear Henry, I had a lovely long letter from Barbara (I haven't yet got accustomed to her new name). Is there any special reason why she made the change and chose Linda? How I wish I could see her with those three lovely boys! She certainly has enough now to keep her busy and interested and happy also. Grammy

Elsie's 1948 diary had only sixteen days filled in, and Barbara was not mentioned once. I did find a scrap with notes on it that may have been written in 1948, because Elsie alludes to Barbara's second husband.

1. *Inadequacy very bad—Brings on depression*
2. *Very gifted daughter*
3. *Medicine will cure at some time*
4. *Children suffer*
5. *Communist anti-parents drive all over U.S.A.*
6. *Long since used up all of our funds—not only gave her great musical education, because her instructors always told her.*
7. *The state welfare cannot buy Rehabilitation just with dollars. Never saw Barb—never got into house.*
8. *Nearly destroyed first husband—also second, quarreling.*
9. *Became psychotic early—fluttery type.*
10. *Too dangerous at times for children*
11. *Do a rehabilitative work—have Barb at Euthenics Institute.*

Among the treasures in the chickenhouse, I discovered detailed class notes Elsie had taken while attending psychology classes at City College in New York. One notebook was dedicated to questions for both Barbara's and Polly's psychiatrists. I think Elsie carried forward some Victorian theories about sex. Here is a note she posted in her notebook:

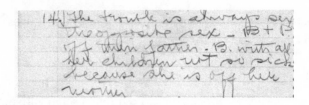

*14. The trouble is always sex. The opposite sex—B.+P.
[Barbara and Polly] off their father. Barb with all her children
not so sick because she is off her mother.*

George W. Crane, author of the "Worry Clinic" advice
column, also published small pamphlets that sold for twenty
cents each. Was the pamphlet titled *Sex Differences Between Men
and Women & Nagging Wives* the basis for Elsie's observations?

For era medical context, I asked a retired psychology
professor for her take on Elsie's note. Dr. Marsha Driscoll's
reply:

*"Of course, I'm not certain what your grandmother means,
but the classic psychoanalytic theory which would have
been popular in the 1940s suggested that in the Oedipal
stage (ages 3-5), a child would be strongly attracted to the
opposite sex parent and hostile/jealous toward the same sex
parent. The resolution of this stage requires the child to
learn to identify with the same sex parent and eventually
establish adult sexual relations with someone appropriate of
the opposite sex. If a child is fixated in this stage, then as an
adult they will have some problem with adult relationships.*

*"It's possible that your grandmother saw Polly as being
closer to her father and perhaps "taking after him," while
Barb "took after" her mother. Perhaps that's what she meant
by "off." She might have attributed Polly's worse condition
to this "Oedipal Complex." (Although, in classic*

psychoanalysis, Barb's personality is more typical of the complex. A kind of search for a father figure, heightened sexuality followed by a retreat from sexual relations, and a rather dramatic presentation are all classic signs of hysterical neurosis from a fixation in the Oedipal stage.)

"Please take all of this with an entire shaker of salt! The theory is now so far out of the mainstream that it's embarrassing to describe it. But it would have been almost gospel in 1947-1950. And of course, your grandmother was trying desperately to find an explanation of why all this happened."

Marsha is probably correct about the meaning of my grandmother's note. Elsie, for the past twelve years, had been the victim of Barbara's sporadic, violent outbursts toward her.

Elsie struggled to find a cure for Barbara. Another note Elsie wrote while attending psychology classes documented Barbara's struggle over the preceding two decades:

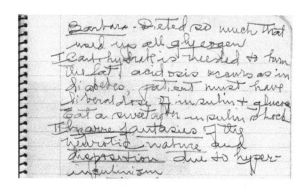

Barbara—dieted so much that used up all glycogen.

1. *Carbohydrate is needed to burn the fat, acidosis occurs as in diabetes, patient must have liberal dose of insulin and glucose. Eat a sweet after insulin shock.*

2. *Bizarre fantasies of the neurotic nature and disposition due to hyperinsulinism.*

3. *Must restore proper nutrition to the brain in order to proceed with psychiatric treatment.*

4. *A hopeless neurotic—Freud blamed the subconscious.*

5. *Zest, interest, stimulates the secretion of cortical hormones.*

Over the years, as I studied the chickenhouse discoveries, I learned of my grandmother's efforts to understand Barbara's and Polly's mental disorders. From the 1930s, when Barbara began acting out as a teenager, my grandmother was obsessed with studying the mental health field, searching for a cure for her daughters. Sadly, my grandmother never found the resolution she hoped for. Eventually, she transferred blame to *her* mother.

Here is a letter Elsie, living in New York, wrote to her mother Idalia, summing up the past two decades. By then Idalia was a resident at Sylvia Ann Nursing Home in Seattle, Washington.

Wednesday, August 5, 1953 Letter number six

Mother dear, The sixteen years of strain we have had from the frightful expense of having our children so dangerously ill have certainly taken their toll. We have had to go it all alone. We have not had your help in all of this dangerous illness as the other ones of your children have had in their troubles. I figure that in the past twelve years you have spent over sixty thousand dollars, most of all which you have spent on them. To Norbert and Ruth, I would say the value is over forty thousand or even more than you could put any value on. It enabled Norbert's career-woman-wife to pursue her career, and she never would have been happy without it, while leaving their little babies at home, not with a careless maid, but with the most wonderful Grandmother in the world. Any psychiatrist will tell you that the value to the home in security and stability and emotional uplift of a grandmother, especially where the mother is a career woman, is priceless.

Without me, Nick would not have had his children for seven more of the formative years of their lives. Because if I had not taken them when I did, they would have settled down with Marie and Ed and then you could not have had them later with Nick as you did. Without you Dee could never have gotten rid of her alcoholic husband as she did. [Recall that Nick and his three sons lived with the Philips family during the Great Depression.]

No, as I see the picture, I have had more severe and dangerous illness to deal with for sixteen years which is worse, you must admit, than any of them have gone through, I have had to go it alone. If I could have had you with me as they had, you probably could have pulled us through these dangerous illnesses and my children might now be well as theirs. Imagine how terrible it is for Barbara's five children, that their mother is so ill. They will surely catch it from her. No, you have not sent Barbara anything in five years or any of your five great-grandchildren of hers. I know it is partly because of her schizophrenia and her desire to hide that you have not sent it. [Elsie still thought Barbara was schizophrenic in 1953.] But you should know something more of these illnesses than their characteristics. Just as this morning you enclosed a letter to Polly in my letter. She stomped and stormed and wouldn't read it because you hadn't put it in a separate letter to her. Some of the marked characteristics are extreme secrecy and almost catatonic silence. I used to think quite a bit of it was inherited from the Philips side of the family, but the more I see of behavior of my own family the more I think quite a bit of it comes from them. I learned quite a bit when I studied Psychology

at City College this year. In the beginning of Barbara's
illness when something in the way of therapy might really
have been done, they [the Fratt family members] refused a
penny of help.

    Arms full of love to you, Elsie

In the letter, the reader can glimpse Elsie's struggle as a
mother and her frustration. By 1953, when Elsie wrote that letter,
Barbara had moved to Minnesota and isolated herself from her
family. And yes—there were five of us by then.

1949

By 1949, Elsie's diary had no entries. Notes in her appointment calendar were very sporadic—she mentioned Barbara four times, twice in January. Barbara was again divorced and eight months pregnant, living two hundred miles from New York City.

Entries on Elsie's appointment calendar:

> January 4, 1949: *N.Y.C. Housing Authority—City Hall for Barb.*
>
> January 8, 1949: *Drove around looking up housing for Barbara.*

My sister Laurel was born February 1949. Her birth certificate placed Barbara living in Cooperstown, New York. No father was listed. Barbara used the name "Linda" as mother's name.

This letter from Henry's British cousin Eloise helps illuminate Barbara's situation.

> *March 30, 1949,* Eloise Garstin, Brighton, Sussex England
> My Dear Henry, Your letter of March 23 reached me on

March 28. No matter how bravely and cheerfully you may write, I cannot get out of my head the idea that you and Elsie are beset with very great problems indeed. For once in my life, if never before, I read between the lines. Do you mean that Barbara and her four children have come home to stay for good? Please don't think I am asking for more information than you wish to give me, or that I am just displaying a vulgar curiosity. I do indeed hope you will not think that of me, but it really grieves me more than I can possibly say for both you and Elsie if my surmise is correct. I cannot think of any more unselfish, patient, and loving parents then you have both been, and it hurts me terribly if you have more trouble on your hands.

In writing thus plainly, you will of course let no one but Elsie read this, and will tear it up when read, and you may be sure I shall make not the slightest allusion to anyone in the family.

Last time I heard of Barbara she had two children—now you speak of four, but I never knew she had had two more. I don't know anyone at all so brave over problems as you and Elsie are.

With much love to you both, Ever your devoted cousin, Eloise

Just weeks later, Elsie's mother wrote to her daughter:

April 22, 1949 Idalia Fratt Seattle, Washington

Dearest Elsie, Your long letter came shortly after I mailed my note to you for Polly's birthday and I think you are wonderful the way you face such difficulties and if anyone needs help it is you. I had no idea you were carrying all these difficulties. I was rejoicing that she [Barbara] was on a farm as that is what she has been asking for a long time.

What became of that butler who was supposed to be so

fine? I didn't know Frank [Schoenwandt] was at home much of the time so Barb could do about as she pleased. It was a wonderful dream; too bad it was so short a one. Wasn't Barbara married by a priest? Then how can they get a divorce? Couldn't Barb sue him for support? When was the last baby born? I mean what date and was she at the farm?

I will send you the money as soon as I get to the bank. I wish you would give me the birthdays of all the babies. I have Chris's but not the others. Now I must go to sleep. God Bless you dear child and I know he will take care of you. Bushels of Love to you all, Mother

Who was the "butler who was supposed to be so fine" that Idalia asked about? Three days later, Elsie's mother wrote another letter. There are a few curious statements in it that I found no supporting documents to confirm.

April 25, 1949 Idalia Fratt Seattle, Washington

Dearest Elsie, You are in my mind all day long, I can't see how you can manage, especially with financial worries. I got off a bank draft to you yesterday but didn't register it. I will be anxious about it until I hear you have it.

Between Barbara's troubles, and now Polly, one can't tell what I might do I am so absent minded. I keep thinking Barbara should try to hang onto that property. If Frank [Schoenwandt] goes to South America, he can't bother her for the present and what good will a divorce do her? He has to provide for her as long as he is her husband.

New York, so they say, is a hard state to get a divorce and the Catholic Church is against it. Were they not married by a priest? And wasn't Barb's first marriage by a Justice of the Peace? Well it will all work out some way only we must find the best way. I'm trying to get the bundle off to Barbara. Bushels of Love to you all, Mother

As I've mentioned, when we were children on the farm in Minnesota, we used to receive "bundles" of clothing from our rich, overweight cousins in Seattle. We went to our little eight-grade school in Nebish, twenty miles from the nearest town, wearing too-big Princeton and Notre Dame sweaters and baggy city slicker trousers and cringed as local farm kids snickered at us.

I wonder if Barbara, with four children, was back living with her parents, the five of us in one room.

On May 24, 1949, Elsie sent this next letter to—

The Honorable Archibald Douglas, As a four-times eager volunteer worker for Governor Dewey and yourself, may I ask a favor. A young mother with four small children is forced to live in one small badly ventilated room. She should be on the emergency city housing list. Could you give me a letter or put me in touch with someone in proper authority? I should think both the Housing and Health Departments. Cordially—Elsie Philips

Elsie's diary entry:

August 11, 1949: *Barb's Birthday. Henry, Polly, and I took birthday cake, candles, and presents to Barb's pretty apartment on 1871 Walton Ave. Bronx—Dear Timmy put the candles on the cake and then blew them out himself.*

Left to right, standing, Tim, Barbara, Chris. Stroller,
Laurel in front, Wendell in back. (August 11, 1949)

It was the last time Elsie and Henry would see Barbara and
us children for four years.

In the 1940s, singles periodicals were referred to as "catalogues"—universally as "lonely hearts clubs." Barbara had met
Frank Schoenwandt through a lonely hearts club catalogue. By
mid-1949, she had advertised herself again. After Barbara died
in 2010, I discovered several catalogues from different organizations in the attic of the old farmhouse in northern Minnesota. The
earliest was from 1945 and had been ordered by my stepfather
Herman upon his return home from WWII. It took him four
years to find a woman.

In her lonely hearts listing my mother wrote:

Charming, attractive, pretty, refined brunette. 28, 5 ft. 4 ½
in., 129 lbs. College educated. Plays piano and sings. I am
wonderful cook and housekeeper. Know how to farm or
ranch. Would love to correspond with farmer or rancher, or

any respectable gentleman who loves children. I have 4
children, 7, 5, 3, 1. Would like to meet someone who would
sincerely love my children and make them his own and be a
good father to them, since they lost their own. My children
would be a great help to a farmer or rancher in later years,
however any gentleman who thinks he could love my
children will be considered. Am willing to go any place in
the world for the right man.

Barbara is #472, listed as "Linda Curry, 1871 Walton Ave,
Bronx 53, NY." (The same address Elsie had written in her diary
for the birthday picture.) Below is the key identifying "Linda."

473—Mrs. Bertha Stafflin, c-o C. R. Van Dolsen, Harwood, Md.	454—E. Weisend, 607 N. Main, River Falls, Wis.
472—Linda Curry, 1871 Walton Ave., Bronx 53, N. Y.	455—Ethel W. Brown, 356 Lincoln, Lexington. K»
469—Leila Cummings, Box 372, Flint, Mich.	456—Dolly Ann, Box 14, Detroit 31, Mich.
468—Jane Montell, Box 26, Wilmette, Ill	457—Vallia Bennett, R. 3, Box 3107X, Edmonds, Wash.
	458—Frances H. Carroll, 2294 - 5

Shortly after the birthday picture was taken, Barbara disappeared from Walton Avenue. She told her parents she was
moving to Far Rockaway on Long Island, New York.

*Armistice Day—Henry and I
went out to Far Rockaway. B [Bar-
bara] is not there. (November 11,
1949)*

Barbara was "not there"
because, through *Cupid's Columns,*

she had met two prospects. Chris remembers that we first moved to a dairy farm in Missouri. He said it was a dirty place. Chris recalled being bitten by a spider and it got infected, but he said, "We kept playing with the spiders and lizards." During one of my interviews with Barbara, I asked her about it. She told me that the man—didn't remember his name—had put us in one of his worker's cabins and expected Barbara to leave us children alone each evening when she went up to the main house to prepare his supper. (Chris told me his name was Harvey but didn't remember his last name.)

We must have been there after school started because Barbara also recalled that she had to traverse long steep hills walking Chris to school. Was this picture taken during one of those walks across Missouri hills? Perhaps we've stopped at a well for a drink and a break.

Left to right: Chris, Wendell, Tim. Laurel out of view,
probably sitting in the stroller. (Early September 1949)

A few weeks later, Barbara and her four children boarded a Greyhound bus for Bemidji, Minnesota, and met her second prospect, Herman Affield. Thus began Elsie and Henry's frantic three-year search for their daughter and grandchildren. During one of my many interviews with Barbara, I asked her why she had come to Minnesota. She told me that she needed a safe warm home for her children. She had lived in unheated apartments while in New York.

How had this woman with four young children, living on the edge of homelessness, purchased tickets to escape her parents and the New York streets? Again I found an answer in the letter draft Elsie wrote to Eleanor Roosevelt, dated March 15, 1951.

> Dear Mrs. Roosevelt, As one mother to another mother, I address you—my daughter has S. [schizophrenia]. She is the mother of four children—three sons and a daughter. She has been missing for over a year ... She disappeared from the Bronx over a year ago. The Welfare there was in that communist section. They completely washed their hands of any responsibility. They had just handed her a check for $250. *(An equivalent of $2,606.15 in 2021 dollars.)*

In visiting with my oldest brother Chris and resurrecting my own early memories, I think at first Barbara and Herman were happy, but as with past relationships, Barbara soon found faults with Herman, who, by nature, was a mild-mannered man. Herman came into the marriage as a forty-three year-old bachelor who, his sister said, "was bashful around women." Herman had very limited financial resources and had no idea the cost to feed and clothe four children and a high-maintenance wife. Less than three years after moving to Minnesota, Barbara loaded her *five* children onto a Greyhound bus and escaped from the farm, first to Elko, Nevada, then to a little cabin on Lake Chelan in Washington. Eight months later, we returned to the farm, destitute and homeless.

The hard years began. Remember Barbara's promise, "My children would be a great help to a farmer...."? Herman expected Chris and Tim to do the work of men, and within a few years, I grew into working full days with them. Herman and Barbara's verbal and physical abuse soon became our normal, with Barbara almost always sporting bruises. In Herman's defense, Barbara would torment him until he lost his temper. Sixty years later, Herman's youngest son remembers watching Barbara taunt Herman, until eventually Herman would say, "Enough is enough," unbuckle his leather belt, and lash out at Barbara.

PAWNS, The Farm, Nebish, Minnesota, 1950s picks up where this story ends.

PAWNS documents our life on the farm and the eventual breakup of our family. An excerpt:

1954 "Stew"

By 1954 Herman knew that Barb wasn't the "wonderful cook and housekeeper who knows how to farm or ranch" as described in Cupid's Columns five years earlier. He reverted to many of his bachelor habits. For example, Barb wouldn't sew his clothing, so he used "bachelor buttons"—metal two-piece buttons that locked together. He shared them with Chris, Tim, and me, even though we knew how to sew on our own buttons. I don't recall if my brothers used them, but I did.

Naturally, having to provide three meals a day put stress on the family. It became a collective effort as we children grew into jobs. Stew was a staple—Herman called it Mulligan stew. During the Depression he and our Uncle Charlie had traveled out west, probably spent time in hobo jungles, and that's where he picked up the name. Our stew generally consisted of about six pounds of meat— usually beef, but pork, raccoon, or squirrel could be substituted. (Allow two hours extra cook time for adult raccoon.) We started it early in the day and after adding water, salt, and pepper, the concoction simmered until suppertime.

A typical stew day went something like this. A halved beef carcass hung in the granary, a cull cow that wouldn't have survived the winter. After morning chores Herman brushed mouse and sparrow droppings from the dehydrated blackened surface, took the ax or Swede saw and hacked out two brick-sized pieces from the frozen carcass. He didn't pay any attention to basic beef cuts. The bricks might be suet or prime rib—actually the cows we butchered rarely had any fat cover so bricks of suet is an exaggeration— more likely grisly flank and shoulder cuts. He carried them into the house and dropped them onto the table.

"Today we make Mulligan stew," he shouted over the tune coming from the piano where Barb sat, Chris on one side, Tim on the other. Laurel, Randy, and I, sat on the floor nearby, playing marbles. The tune drifted off as Barb paused and twisted irritably, awkward in her fifth month of pregnancy.

"You boys," Herman nodded toward Chris, Tim, and me, "go to the basement and get vegetables."

"Make them do it, Daddy," I complained. "They'll shut the light off and lock the door. The boogeyman will get me."

"If I hear him screaming again, you two will spend the whole day down there with the light off," Herman said, as he pulled the stew pot out from under the sink. "Jesus Christ why wasn't this washed after the last time it was used?" he yelled at Barb.

"I'm giving my sons piano lessons." Belly protruding, Barb rose from the bench and shuffled toward the kitchen. "Get your own vegetables and make your own swill."

"They eat, they can help cook. Chris, scrub this pot." Herman set the dented aluminum container in the sink and

turned the faucet on. "Tim, take Windy and get the vegetables."

"I won't have my sons doing your nigger work." Barb grabbed the crusted pot and slammed it against the sink. Water splashed on the floor. "You think you're still in the army giving orders? That's probably what you were—a cook." She swished a washcloth around, dumped the water, and threw the pot on the table. "Here's your damn stewpot. Now leave my boys alone. Make that ignorant Irish stew yourself."

Herman spit his snuice wad in the garbage. "You better settle down. I'm not going to take much more."

Barb grabbed Chris by the hand and stomped across the room toward the piano. Chords from Mozart's "The Marriage of Figaro" echoed through the house as she slammed keys and stamped pedals. "Don't spit your filthy tobacco in my house. Culture—we need culture in this hell hole," she screamed.

Herman shook his head as he scrubbed the stew pot. "You boys go get the vegetables."

Tim and I collected a few pounds of potatoes, two handfuls of carrots, several onions and rutabagas from dirt floor bins and stacked them in a pail. Heading for the stairs, Tim took the lead. Two carrots fell from the bucket and I bent over to pick them up—Tim shot up the stairs, shut the light off, and slammed the door.

I screamed in the blackness. No words—curdling, primordial screams. Finally, "Daaaaaddy," came out of my six-year-old mouth.

"Damn, I told you not to scare him. Damn!" shouted Herman from above. "You're getting the belt."

In the darkness I went silent and listened.

"You're not belting my sons, you bastard," Barb shouted.

"Get the hell out of my way," Herman yelled. "I warned him."

I listened to the belt slap flesh.

Tim howled, "I'm sorry, Daddy. I won't ever do it again. Don't let him hit me Mommy Darling—help me."

The floor echoed as feet raced.

"Don't you hit him again, you bald bastard."

The belt slapped flesh. "You'd hit a pregnant lady—that takes a real man."

"That damn kid better start listening. Tim, go down and get your brother."

I listened to feet cross the floor.

The light went on and Tim came down the steps. "You're going to get it when he goes out to milk the cows. Mommy is mad and you made me get strapped."

Between sobs, I sniffled out Tim's threat. Herman grabbed Tim by the arm, "You touch him and you'll get the buckle end next time. Now peel them damn spuds."

Barb sat in the front room looking across the field toward Maple Lake, humming a tune, hands on her belly.

Late December 1959, ten years after arriving at the farm, Barbara, nine months pregnant with her ninth child and hemorrhaging, loaded all of us into an old car, and drove into the black December night. Less than two months later, homeless and hungry, we returned to the farm from Texas with a new baby brother.

This court document excerpt reveals just how out of control our family was by summer 1960. At the bottom of our names, the document continues "(Re: Brothers: File No. 2103 and 2114). Chris and Tim had been removed earlier; both were on probation for petty crimes. Chris was sentenced to Red Wing Reform School, and Tim was sent to a foster home.

JUVENILE COURT REGISTER "E" 565

```
                                    FILE NO.    2170

State of Minnesota,        In the matter of the Welfare of Wendell George Curry,
                           Laurel Rosalinda Curry, Randoloh Leonard Affield
   COUNTY OF BELTRAMI  ss. Bonita Rose Affield, Linda Darlene Affield, and
   IN JUVENILE COURT        Lawrence Roswald Affield, Minor Children.
                                         Daniel   AJohn Affield
                           (Re: Brothers: File No. 2103 and 2114)
```

June 30, 1960. Petitions of Vera Graves alleging neglect of the above named
children, received and filed.
July 1, 1960. Affidavit of Vera Graves showing need for immediate custody of
the above named children.

The summons continued...

July 1, 1960. Summons to Barbara Ann Affield and Herman Arthur Affield, parents of above named children, and order for immediate custody also directed to the parents, issued, and delivered to the Sheriff for service. A Representative of the Beltrami Welfare Department accompanied Sheriff to the Affield home and took children into immediate custody.

July 7, 1960. Hearing held, present in the court were all of the seven Affield children concerned who were excused from remaining at the hearing because of their age; Mr. and Mrs. Affield, Douglas Cann, counsel for Mrs. Affield; Paul Kief, Assistant County Attorney: Vera Graves, Beltrami County Welfare Department; Reverend Daniels, of Puposky, Minnesota; Pastor Thompson of the Community Church of Nebish; and later Russell Schrupp appeared. (Schrupp was Chris and Tim's probation officer.)

Reverend Daniels and Mr. Russell Schrupp presented testimony substantiating the filthy condition in which the home was maintained. Reverend Daniels also recited his part in getting her returned from her escapade in Texas and also how he urged her to desist from embarking on her new proposed escapade.

Upon questioning Mrs. Affield herself, the story of this escapade was for the most part substantiated and she also substantiated that she was making arrangements to go on a vacation, anticipated going to Red Wing where her oldest son is incarcerated, and that she was going out west to visit relatives and she intended to take all her children on this trip, as well. Mrs. Affield indicated in her testimony that her husband was not providing her and the children with adequate support.

The court determined that the children are neglected because they are without proper parental care because of the faults and habits of their parents and custodians and that they are without proper parental care because of the emotional and mental instability and state of immaturity of their parents and custodians, and that the legal custody of the children be and hereby transferred to the Beltrami County Welfare Board to and until October 7, 1960 at 1:30 P.M., and that the hearing be and the same continued to and until that time when further disposition of the children will again be considered.

On July 1, 1960, a Beltrami County deputy arrived at the farm along with another car driven by Vera Graves. The seven of us were placed in foster homes. Randy and I in one; Laurel, Bonny, and Linda in a second; Larry and Danny in a third. A week later Barbara and Herman appeared in court and she was committed to Fergus Falls State Hospital.

1964

In the chickenhouse, among the thousands of letters, I discovered one I had written to my grandmother when I was fifteen—an excerpt:

March 10, 1964

    Dear Grandma and Polly, ... In school I have to write a report of my family ancestry. I would really appreciate it if you would send me all the information you can. Mother was telling me Calvin Philips knows quite a bit on this subject. Also, I would appreciate it if you could tell me about some of Grandpa's achievements from when he was in the Army. I don't know what I should do on my father's side. I don't know who he is, I think you do but don't want to tell me (no offense). I almost know for sure John Curry isn't my father, even you said that last summer. You don't know how much it would mean to me if you told me. If you don't tell me I may never find out. Love, Wendell

Little did we know Calvin Philips had died five years earlier, and Barbara had used her share of his estate to escape the farm in 1959. Five foster homes and six years after the sheriff removed us from the farm, the court emancipated me.

May 10, 1966. Order Terminating Jurisdiction on Wendell George Curry for the reason that the youth has been out of the home in the service for over a year and can be considered to be emancipated and no longer in need of supervision.

My class graduated from high school that month and I was midway through my first tour of duty in Vietnam.

1966

I think back to a Sunday morning in 1966. Just home from Vietnam, I stand in my rumpled uniform, tired, hungry, and nervous, at the front of a small ranch style house in Las Cruces, New Mexico. The Greyhound bus ride from Long Beach, California, was, no doubt, the same route my mother and two older brothers had traveled eighteen years earlier, after she abandoned me in a Los Angeles hospital when I was two weeks old.

I knock and the door opens. John Curry, the man listed as "Father" on my birth certificate, stares at me: Hispanic features, graying hair, medium build, low voice.

He knows… "Chris?" he says.

I shake my head, no.

"Timothy?"

Again, I shake my head.

"Wendell?"

I nod and he waves me in. He motions me to a seat in the living room and sits across the room. His wife Ella brings us coffee, then disappears. Two inquisitive little girls peek into the room but retreat. John chain-smokes three cigarettes while we force small talk.

"Your grandmother Elsie asked me about you many years ago," he says.

"I know. I wrote to her while I was in Vietnam and told her I'd like to meet you when I got home. She told me you lived in Las Cruces and thought perhaps you still did because your parents lived here. I got your address from the telephone book," I reply.

"My parents are both dead," John says.

A lifetime of taunts and innuendo prompt me to ask, "Are you my father?"

"Why do you ask?"

"Because you are listed as "Father" on my birth certificate, but Chris and Tim look different than me and have always teased me," I explain.

"I will not impugn your mother's honor." John snubs his fresh-lit fourth cigarette out, stands, and calls Ella. "I'm leaving for work," he says, and walks out without acknowledging me. I pick up my duffle bag and ask Ella to call me a cab.

"Please stay," she says. "You caught him by surprise—he needs space to think. He'll be back." She takes my bag and guides me to the bedroom of one of her girls.

Ella calls John's nephew, a young man home on leave from the Marine Corps. He, too, has just returned from Vietnam. We drive around Las Cruces, drinking and visiting his friends. After a few days, burned out and broke, I bid farewell to Ella and the girls and return to California without seeing John. I feel hollow and angry at John's rejection of me and his disappearance.

John died eleven years after my visit. His death certificate, dated April 18, 1977, shows that he was fifty-eight years old, divorced again, and living with his sister. Usual Occupation: *Unemployed.* Kind of Business: *None.* In the box asking for "Cause of Death" I found this statement:

MEDICAL CERTIFICATION

I. DISEASE OR CONDITION
DIRECTLY LEADING TO DEATH* (a)
ANTECEDENT CAUSES
DUE TO (b)

Self-inflicted gunshot wound to the head.

In retrospect, I wonder, what kind of man would leave his wife and two young daughters with a stranger? Through the 1940s, Barbara had written so many untruths to her family, yet was there some veracity to her accusations about John's gambling, drinking, and not holding a job? Did he walk out on her as she claimed, just as he had done to me? Did my visit reawaken old demons and contribute to his death? I hope not; in 1940s correspondence, my grandmother wrote kindly of him. She acknowledged that it was my mother's mental illness that had destroyed the marriage.

PART III

DNA DISCOVERIES—MY NEW FAMILY

2014

Fast forward forty-eight years: By the spring of 2014 I had been exploring the chickenhouse treasures for four years and knew that at some point I would begin telling my mother's story. As I dissected and compared the old letters, diaries, and documents, I knew I had to answer a fundamental question: Who was my father? Chris, Tim, and I had John Curry on our birth certificates; Laurel had no father listed on hers.

I suspected that Laurel and I might be full siblings; we share a similar personality, and both have brown hair as we move into our eighth decade. She and I submitted DNA samples to GTLDNA Laboratory, ironically, in Las Cruces, New Mexico. The results revealed that we, in fact, are half siblings. It was a busy summer and autumn.

Statement of Results. Based upon the statistical analysis of the above data, it is 32.53 times more likely (or a 97.0173288588% chance) that Tested Sibling 1 (Wendell) and Tested Sibling 2 (Laurel) are half biological siblings versus being full biological siblings. These results do not supercede testing involving additional participants related to Tested Sibling 1 (Wendell) and/or Tested Sibling 2 (Laurel).

Client has indicated that a common biological mother is shared between the test participants listed as siblings on this report. Results are implicitly based upon this assumption. If the assumption of a biological parent is incorrect, it is possible the reported results are inaccurate.

Statement of Results: Based on the statistical analysis of the above data, it is 32.53 times more likely (or a 97.01732895858% chance) that Tested Sibling 1 (Wendell) and Tested Sibling 2 (Laurel) are half biological siblings versus being full biological siblings. These results do not supercede testing involving additional participants related to Tested Sibling 1 (Wendell) and/or Tested Sibling 2 (Laurel).

Client has indicated that a common biological mother is shared between the test participants listed as siblings on this report. Results are implicitly based upon this assumption. If the assumption of a biological parent is incorrect, it is possible the reported results are inaccurate.

Laurel and Wendell explore a 1908 photo album from their great grandfather Calvin Philips' farm, Greenbank Farm, Whidbey Island, Washington. (Summer 2014)

My Vietnam memoir, *Muddy Jungle Rivers,* was published in 2012, and I was busy with speaking engagements.

2015

Early spring 2015, Laurel and I drove down to Illinois to get DNA samples from Chris and Tim: The results confirmed what I had always suspected.

Statement of Results: Based upon the statistical analysis of the above data, it is 165,446.98 times more likely (or a 99.99939558040% chance) that Tested Sibling 1 (Christopher) and Tested Sibling 3 (Timothy) are full biological siblings versus being not related at all. These results do not supercede testing involving additional participants related to Tested Sibling 1 (Christopher) and/or Tested Sibling 3 (Timothy). Inclusion of the Known Parent(s) may lead to additional results relevant to this relationship and is highly recommended if at all possible.

The existence of a common parent was neither reported by the client, nor assumed by the laboratory, during the generation of these statistical results.

Statement of Results: Based upon the statistical analysis of the above data, it is 165,446.98 times more likely (or a 99.99939558040% chance) that Tested Sibling 1 (Christopher) and Tested Sibling 3 (Timothy) are full biological siblings versus being not related at all. These results do not supercede testing involving additional participants related to Tested Sibling 1 (Christopher) and/or Tested Sibling 3 (Timothy). Inclusion of the known parent(s) may lead to additional results relevant to this relationship and is highly recommended if at all possible.

The existence of a common parent was neither reported by
the client, nor assumed by the laboratory, during the
generation of these statistical results.

Statement of Results: Based upon the statistical analysis of the above data, it is 1.34 times less likely (or a 42.75320047976% chance)
that Tested Sibling 1 (Christopher) and Tested Sibling 2 (Wendell) are half biological siblings versus being not related at all. These
results do not supercede testing involving additional participants related to Tested Sibling 1 (Christopher) and/or Tested Sibling 2
(Wendell). Inclusion of the Known Parent(s) may lead to additional results relevant to this relationship and is highly recommended if at
all possible.

The existence of a common parent was neither reported by the client, nor assumed by the laboratory, during the generation of these
statistical results.

Statement of Results: Based upon the statistical analysis of
the above data, it is 1.34 times less likely (or a
42.75320047976% chance) that Tested Sibling 1
(Christopher) and Tested Sibling 2 (Wendell) are half
biological siblings versus being not related at all. These
results do not supercede testing involving additional
participants related to Tested Sibling 1 (Christopher) and/or
Tested Sibling 2 (Wendell). Inclusion of the Known Parent(s)
may lead to additional results relevant to this relationship
and is highly recommended if at all possible.

The existence of a common parent was neither reported by
the client, nor assumed by the laboratory, during the
generation of these statistical results.

Chris and Tim were full siblings. Laurel and I were their half
siblings. So, Barbara had gone to her grave with the secret of
who our fathers were.

Laurel and I filed the DNA information on *Ancestry.com*. I
continued to organize and study the chickenhouse treasures.

Five generations: Author holding his great grandson
Aden, Granddaughter Sabrina, Barbara (died less than
six months after this picture was taken), and my son
Jeffrey, who died in 2015. (July 2009)

On a July morning, my wife Patti and I bumped into our son Jeff
at a local store. After visiting for a bit, as we had done since he
was a little child, we gave him a hug goodbye with a, "Love you
—see you later." Two hours later he collapsed and died from a
sudden heart attack. It was a sad summer, as his children, his two
sisters, and Patti and I struggled with the shock of losing him.
Only a parent who has lost a child can truly understand losing a
part of yourself. Six years later as I write this, I am thankful for
the time we had together.

Veterans Day 2015, I was invited to participate in an event,
the 50th Anniversary of the Vietnam War in Rockford, Illinois.
Over the course of three days, I spoke to several groups of
students and veterans. I connected with an army man who had
ridden my riverboat forty-seven years earlier. I also had a special
guest: Brian, (Snipe in my Vietnam memoir *Muddy Jungle
Rivers*) who had been the engineman on our riverboat in Vietnam. It was the first time I had seen him since I was medevaced
out of an ambush in 1968. It was a very special three days as we
reconnected.

The DNA tests done early in the year were not on my radar.

2016

Winter 2016, I audited a class at our local university as I worked on what eventually became the first two books in my *Chickenhouse Chronicles* series. Besides honing my writing craft, I met a student whom I eventually hired as first developmental editor—she did such a phenomenal job that my regular developmental editor charged me only half her regular fee, because "The manuscript is so clean." Through the summer I did several readings, workshops, and other book events.

Over the past few years, I have written hundreds of pages documenting my family's past. The bulk of the information focused on my mother's side of the family, information salvaged from the chickenhouse. In the old farmhouse attic, I discovered a trunk with some of my stepfather Herman's early documents. After studying them, I interviewed a few people who remembered Herman. I also ordered his WWII military records which turned out to be a goldmine of information.

Autumn 2016, Veterans Day week, I did a book presentation on *Muddy Jungle Rivers* and an all-day workshop titled, "Writing

Your War" for veterans struggling with PTSD who were interested in expressive writing therapy, to explore old trauma memories.

The DNA tests Laurel and I had done two years earlier slipped further back in my mind.

2017

As I moved back and forth between the present and the past exploring the chickenhouse treasures, I struggled to find a door into our family's story. I came to realize that my stepfather Herman, through *Cupid's Columns*, had made first contact with Barbara, so the story must start with him. I spent the winter working on *HERMAN*, Book One in the *Chickenhouse Chronicles* series.

Indiana University South Bend was using *Muddy Jungle Rivers* in a history class, and I was invited to come down, speak to students, and do an evening reading. Through Facebook I reconnected with several men I had served with in the navy—including two I had done my first Vietnam tour with. Ron, Chris, and I reconnected in South Bend—it was an awesome reunion, sitting around the fire late evening, visiting, reminiscing, for a few hours not three old men, but young sailors steaming the Gulf of Tonkin, hanging out on the fantail of our destroyer, USS *Rogers* DD 876, in the dark of night. Tragically, Ron died in an auto accident two years later—Chris and I still visit on the phone occasionally.

Laurel called me early May. "I received an email that there's a match for my DNA test," she told me. "From a man named David, who lives in Cincinnati, Ohio."

An excerpt from the first message Laurel received, May 4, 2017:

Hello [Laurel], I am Dave, administrator for the DNA tests for my sister-in-law and her mother, Grace.

You show an 'extremely high' confidence match for Grace for a close relationship such as first cousin or niece. I would like to help determine your precise relationship to them. Could you add or attach a tree to your DNA result? I hope you can add a tree, share the names of your known ancestors, or recognize a name above to help find the connection.

Thanks for any help you can provide. [Dave]

Laurel, in researching her past, investigated Frank Schoenwandt. She had uncovered information about his past, including the 1948 New York newspaper article about Frank being arrested for stabbing his daughter with a pitchfork. Through Grace's information, Laurel recognized the last name and replied:

[Hi David], *Glad to finally make a connection. Isn't DNA amazing! Hello and nice to hear from you. My mother Barbara A. Philips was married to Francis Xavier Schoenwandt on January 26, 1948. I was born February 13, 1949. I am Grace Schoenwandt's half-sister. I would very much like to meet her. My mother moved to Minnesota in 1949. Grace should remember my mother, Barbara Ann. They were friends. Grace was 16 years old when my mother was married to Frank. Do you know if Grace would like to connect with me? Thanks for reaching out to me.* [Laurel]

We had grown up aware of the Schoenwandt name because

our oldest brother Chris remembered Frank as a grouchy old man. Suddenly, after more than sixty years, Laurel had a new half-sister. Grace lived in Cincinnati and Laurel's new half-brother Frank, Jr., lived in Florida. On June 8, 2017, Laurel and Grace visited on the phone for the first time.

In that first conversation, Laurel asked Grace if she was the girl who Frank had stabbed with the pitchfork. "Yes," Grace said. "Your mother called the police on him." She went on to tell Laurel about how Frank had come home one day with a new wife—that she, Grace, remembered three little boys Frank's new wife brought to the farm. Laurel and I discussed that she should travel to Cincinnati to meet her new family—she was hesitant yet excited. Who were they? Would they accept this stranger into their circle?

First meeting, Grace (left) and Laurel. Cincinnati, Ohio
(June 26, 2017)

Serendipity or some other power at work? Six months before Laurel's connection with her new family, I had been invited to be keynote speaker at a military reunion in Chattanooga, Tennessee. As I studied my route south, I realized that Cincinnati was not far out of my way. I called Laurel and told her, "Pack your bag.

We're going on an adventure." From northern Minnesota, I drove to Edina, Minnesota, and spent the night at Laurel's house. On June 24, 2017, we left Minneapolis early in the morning and drove to Cincinnati. Grace was at a granddaughter's wedding, so Laurel and I spent the night in a hotel. The next morning, I spent about an hour with Laurel and Grace and then left for Chattanooga.

In Chattanooga I reconnected with men I hadn't seen in more than fifty years. One of them, Larry, was an army man who had been riding my riverboat the day in 1968 when we got ambushed. Larry and I didn't know each other in Vietnam, but we had shared a life-altering experience that day when we both were wounded. Five decades later, we felt that bond as we sat by the pool and exchanged memories.

Following is a summary that Laurel wrote about her visit and what she learned about her new-found family:

My stay with Grace was awesome. I rented a sedan for the duration of my stay to accommodate her leg disability when we went about. Sunday night we went to her church for about 1/2 hour to pay her respects to a friend who passed away. Drove around the countryside and out to Sherry's so she could show me the house. Did not stop in. About 6 pm we went to Ruby Tuesdays to meet and greet her daughter Sherry and her extended family.

Monday, we stayed at Grace's home and visited all day. Visit in the evening from Sherry and family including daughter who was married on Saturday and who also is the tv news reporter and anchor.

Tuesday, we went to Panera for lunch and met David. Dave is fascinating. He is a guru in genetics. Sherry also had lunch with us. We reviewed the DNA connections. Grace was fascinated and had lots of info on the people showing DNA matches. Later in the day Grace and I went grocery shopping at Meijer's. She was ecstatic to get out of the house and drove the motorized shopping cart with great skill around the grocery store.

Wendell arrived Wednesday morning. We went to Panera again and met with Dave. We were there for about 4 hours. Dave signed on to connect Wendell's DNA alleles. I took Grace home after a couple hours since she was tired, but returned to Panera to learn more about family history from Dave. Dave came back to Grace's house with us when we left Panera and he continued sharing his wealth of genetic knowledge. Sherry also came over after she was done with work. We had pizza for supper and Dave left late in the evening.

The specifics of the Frank Schoenwandt/Barbara Philips story. Frank's first wife Sara Rowley died in 1946. He remarried (name unknown) in 1947 for a short time. He married Barbara January 1948. I was conceived May 1948. I was born February 1949. Barb and Frank's marriage was annulled, and Frank remarried March 1949 to Helen Regan. They moved to Florida and stayed together until death. Frank was born in 1904 and died in 1998 at age 93. Helen was born in 1911 and died in 2004. Older brother Francis, Jr., never went to the farm [in Cooperstown, New York].

Beyond the excitement of meeting Laurel's new family, I was overwhelmed by David's knowledge of genetics. After retirement, he had continued to explore the fast-paced technological advances of that world. When David learned that I didn't know who my father was, he offered to search and I readily agreed, skeptical that he would find anything. Over the next several months he sent me updates on his search.

July 23, 2017, David emailed me. In this message excerpt he mentions a Mr. William Spollen (2nd Cousin):

[Wendell]...your father's lineage in the Americas is old and prolific; there are many, many clues out there. It appears that about half of your totals may be on your mother's side (as shared with Laurel), but there is still a lot there to work with. Matches closer than third cousins have a 95% or greater chance of being shared with other close relatives....

So, I have started with close matches where the chances of quick and significant progress are highest. If those efforts fail or need confirmation, I will have to move to more distant matches. You have 6 third cousins or closer; 4 of those are shared with Laurel as we saw when looking at your results at Panera that day. This leaves Mr. Wm Spollen (2nd Cousin) and Mr. Robt Quintin (3rd Cousin) as likely paternal matches. Both have French Canadian lineages - perhaps explaining your extensive match list. David

As summer moved along, I didn't spend time thinking about David's search, because I was busy with book events and writing. While writing my Vietnam memoir several years earlier, I had come to understand the power of writing about trauma. When speaking at book signing events, I often discussed how my writing had helped me understand and integrate my time in Vietnam into my life experience. A doctor at our Bemidji VA Clinic invited me to facilitate a writers' group for veterans. Several years later the group thrives. Veterans, strangers new to the group, have made friends and have found new meaning and purpose.

On September 11, 2017, at University of St. Thomas in St. Paul, Minnesota, I was honored to receive the "Veterans Voices Award" from the Minnesota Humanities Center. "For Outstanding Contributions to Communities & Society" is inscribed on the crystal award. Later that autumn I was invited to participate in a Twin Cities PBS documentary about the Vietnam War.

On September 13, 2017, David emailed me and explained his "Mirror Tree" search results; again he mentioned William Spollen, and this time, with his expanding search, a new name had entered the scene—LaChance.

Hi Wendell...I have worked some more on the search for your father using 'Mirror Tree' techniques. This involves attaching your DNA results temporarily to some trees I have built and extended which 'mirror' your DNA matches' family trees to see what turns up in terms of your DNA matching the DNA of people they are related to. As I mentioned to you before it seemed I was getting some French Canadian names doing that previously. I recently extended my tree mirroring the much smaller tree of your closest non-maternal match, William Spollen, and it returned some interesting results. Now six of your DNA matches connecting to his tree this time. From that result I am gaining confidence that your father's last name was LaChance, related to Mr. Spollen's mother. Still need to narrow possibilities and check the DNA 'math' to give you a likely candidate or candidates. Dave

My life continued its established flow. Autumn 2017, while working a shift at Bemidji Community Food Shelf, I was helping a customer with her shopping list and commented on her last name. I asked if she knew four brothers: Peter, Lance, Lars, and Ervin. Her eyes widened and she replied, "Yes, they were my brothers. Only Ervin is left." I told her the story about the summer of 1960 when I was twelve, my mother was committed to a mental hospital, and we children were placed in foster homes. My younger brother Randy and I went to an old farm couple's home that had four little Ojibwe boys. I shared with her the story about how the little boys were forbidden to speak the Ojibwe language. Ervin, three years old, was often sent to bed without supper as punishment. After the old couple went to sleep in the evening, I would sneak downstairs and make a sandwich and glass of milk and bring it up to the bewildered, hungry toddler.

As the months rolled by and David, Laurel, and I exchanged email messages, I came to realize that history was replaying itself through correspondence, just as Barbara, her parents, and my great grandparents had done, beginning almost one hundred years earlier. But I fear that with this new mode of correspondence, unlike the faded letters from the chickenhouse, much of today's family history will be lost to the "Delete" key.

And those DNA tests we'd done a few years earlier drifted farther back in my mind, even though David was working with them.

2018

The year started with my new release, *PAWNS, Chickenhouse Chronicles Book II*. Mid-February Patti and I attended a private viewing of the Vietnam War documentary I had participated in at Twin Cities PBS. I connected with some amazing Minnesota Vietnam veterans who had also been a part of the project. Mid-April, Patti and I had a full house at our book release event for *PAWNS*.

Through the year, I spoke at several events. Jean, a lady who has taken an interest in my story and is an amazing researcher, dug into the links I had of Barbara's time in Poland the summer of 1939. Jean discovered that Barbara's school friend Eva Barbacka had survived WWII, married quite a famous Polish artist, and had a son, Thomaz, living in northern Poland. Eva died in the mid-1990s. I find it sad that she and Barbara never reconnected. When Jean reached out to Thomaz, he said that he remembered his mother talking about an American girl. I sent him a letter and emailed but he never responded.

In October I received a message from David—an excerpt:

Wendell, Happy Birthday! I am 99.999% certain that I have identified your paternal grandparents, based on all of the circumstantial data (dates, places, etc.) and the DNA match data and its analysis. One of their two sons was definitely your father; however, only testing of one or more of their grandchildren can prove which son is your father and which is your uncle. (I have a strong suspicion of the 'culprit' but no real evidence).

After a lifetime of not knowing, I found David's message hard to believe. On November 10, 2018, he sent a very long message explaining his discovery of my paternal family along with several graphics. For the reader interested in DNA research, I include David's complete message in the Appendix, but it began:

Hi Wendell,

Before I send the DNA results and graphics which prove your connection to the Grignon and LaChance families, I would like to present a brief description of the methods involved.

Over the next month I received two more lengthy email messages and graphics and several documents supporting Dave's discoveries. Another email—an excerpt:

.... The final and necessary evidence that the Grignon and LaChance families are your paternal lines is evidence that they were in the right place at the right time and moving in the same social circles. As I already described that circumstantial evidence in my first email, I won't repeat it here. The fact that the Lucien Grignon family lived in Selden, NY, at the right time for interaction of one of their sons with

Barbara fits in well with the DNA proof provided above.
Dave S.

PAWNS kept me busy with presentations and book signings through 2018. Laurel and her husband Jerry traveled to Cincinnati to visit her new family. Meanwhile, David was closing in on my paternal family links.

2019

The year started with several speaking engagements, two writing workshops that I taught, and an amazing email that I received from David on New Year's Day 2019.

Wendell, I hope you are well and enjoying the holidays. Happy New Year! I got your last email, and yes, as I stated earlier, I am providing you advice on how to contact the Grignon siblings and (eventually) ask at least one or two of them to do DNA testing at Ancestry for you. There are six who are therefore either half-siblings or first cousins to you depending on whether you are Guy's son or the son of his brother Yves Joseph Grignon.

A short summary: The DNA evidence strongly supports that you are the grandson of Lucien A Grignon (4 Jan 1893 Quebec - 25 Jun 1955 NY) and Yvonne Eva LaChance (29 Nov 1892 Quebec - 28 Jun 1971). Lucien was the youngest of 12 or 13 children of Louis and Lucie Grignon. Yvonne was second youngest of 6 or 7 children of Francis X and Sara

LaChance, your great grandparents and the great grandparents of your closest DNA match William Spollen.

Lucien and Yvonne Eva Grignon were married in 1919 in Montreal Quebec and emigrated to the U.S. in the early 1920s to Pittsburgh. There they had two sons: Guy Louis Roland Grignon and Yves Joseph Lucien Grignon. The family had moved to Brooklyn by 1930 and Selden by 1940. Lucien was a photoengraver at a NY newspaper by trade (like Frank Schoenwandt). Lucien was naturalized in 1941, Yvonne in 1943. Lucien and Yvonne lived at 70 Adirondack Dr in Selden and are buried in Holy Sepulchre Cemetery in adjacent Coram NY (plot 1-E-84/88).

The DNA evidence and circumstantial (documentation) evidence strongly supports that one OR the other of Lucien and Yvonne's sons is your father.

Dave S.

David sent me a family tree which now included my paternal family and provided me with a short summary (that he had gleaned from public information on the internet) for each of my possible "six …half-siblings," children of Guy Grignon.

Laurence "Larry" was the first-born son. He was married with two daughters. It turned out that Larry's daughter Laurie had a tree on *Ancestry.com* under the name 'Harinsky,' which helped to connect the LaChance and Grignon families. It would be Larry and daughter Janine whose DNA tests with *Ancestry.com* first confirmed the Grignon connection.

Guy, Jr., was second-born, married with one child.

Louis, third-born, also had two daughters. David provided LinkedIn information and a web address for Louis's business.

Michael "Mike" fourth-born son, divorced, with two sons.

Gene, the youngest son, divorced, with one son.

Yvonne, the baby of the family, widowed with one son and two daughters.

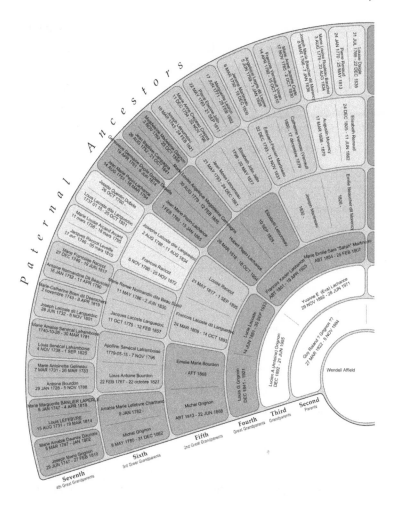

After studying each profile, I reached out to Louis because I realized we had a link in common—our early years on small boats—me, on the riverboat in Vietnam and Louis, on a fishing trawler in the Atlantic Ocean.

January 12, 2019

Dear Mr. Grignon,

I recently took a genealogical DNA test through Ancestry.com and learned that my ancestors date back to

Louis Grignon (1841-1921) & Lucie Lacoste (1851-1931). Are your grandparents Lucien Grignon (1893-1955) and Yvonne Eva LaChance (1892-1971)? I have close DNA cousins through both the Grignon and LaChance families, so I am therefore somehow related to your extended family.

My mother, Barbara Philips Curry (1920-2010), was divorced with two young children living in Selden, Long Island, when I was conceived. I was born Wendell George Curry on October 30, 1947, in NYC but grew up in Minnesota. Through a lonely hearts club advertisement Barbara met Herman Affield and she moved her family to Minnesota in 1949. I do not think my biological father knew that I existed. Today's technology makes it possible for me to explore links to my paternal family, so I began a search of discovery.

I am married with two grown children, several grandchildren and three greats. Sadly, our son Jeffrey died from a sudden heart attack in 2015. I am retired, the author of three books, a Vietnam Veteran, do a bit of public speaking, and work with the underserved in our community.

I am searching for my biological father to learn my heritage and especially my medical family history. My DNA shows evidence of significant French ethnicity, but my mother's family is primarily English. I am hoping to find descendants of your great-grandparents to do a DNA test with *Ancestry.com* so that the results can help me narrow my search. I am willing to pay the costs or donate an Ancestry DNA test to any potential relative willing to do a test for me. I have found a tree with your grandparents in it on Ancestry called the "Harinsky family tree." Is someone in your family the Ancestry member who built that tree? Goggle Search shows you as the former owner, but still manager of the Sag Harbor Yacht Yard.

I found a tree on Ancestry by Ancestry member

"Sagyacht" with Yvonne LaChance in it. Is that you? I have researched extensive family trees for the LaChance and Grignon families and will share them with you if you are interested.

You must have a love for the sea and boats. I spent four years in the Navy (1965-1969), most of it sea duty and overseas service. I have taken the liberty of gifting you a copy of my Vietnam memoir, *Muddy Jungle Rivers.*

I hope that you have information or can do a DNA test that will help me to identify my birth father and that you are open to contact with me. I don't wish to upset anyone's life. My purpose in searching for my birth father is to learn my medical history and perhaps see photos or maybe meet biological relatives. You can learn more about me at http://www.wendellaffield.com/

If you go to my website, near the top of the page click on "Press" to learn more about me.

If you have information about the LaChance/Grignon family history that you could share with me, I would deeply appreciate it. I look forward to hearing from you.

Thank you and Happy New Year 2019,

Wendell Affield

Author: *Muddy Jungle Rivers* and Chickenhouse *Chronicles series*

The same afternoon Louis received my letter and *Muddy Jungle Rivers,* he called, and we had a lengthy conversation. After we hung up, I sent him this email:

Louis, Thank you so much for calling and sharing your family history with me this afternoon. I gave David your phone number. As I told you, David found my sister Laurel's father, Francis Xavier Schoenwandt. David discovered that Schoenwandt in the early to mid-1940s owned a farm on

Long Island and worked for a newspaper as an artist or typesetter. You mentioned that your father and grandfather worked as printers—is it possible the three of them might have had a workplace connection? Frank, Jr., my sister's new-found brother who recently passed away at 90, remembered that one of his father's friends affectionately referred to a coworker as "The Crazy Frenchman." Possibly your grandfather?? Have you ever heard that phrase?

You said your uncle was Wendell—my mother loved to play name-games. As I learned about her past, I discovered how she wove old beaus' names into her children's names. I will drop my two latest books in the mail for you Monday—is that the best address to send them to—where I sent the first one? I am excited to see the results of your DNA test— according to my DNA, we are somehow closely related— maybe Wendell Still is the link.

Again, thank you for reaching out to me, Wendell Affield

That same afternoon, on January 11, I sent a second email message:

David and Laurel,

Good afternoon, I just got off the phone after an hour with Louis Grignon.

To sum it up: He said I have the eyes of his father. He had an Uncle, Wendell Still, who lived on Long Island in the late 1940s—married and would have been in his mid-forties when Barb was in Selden. His grandmother Hough (maiden name Dare) had a large old farmhouse in Selden where she took in renters—Barb??? Louis is very excited about the whole thing—he is going to order an Ancestry DNA kit and submit it—his wife Patty just had one done as a Christmas gift, so he is familiar with it.

David, I explained how you had discovered Laurel's

sister, that you were a professional genealogist and that I thought it would be much better if he spoke directly to you because I didn't want to mess up linage explanations. He looks forward to your call. Louis is very knowledgeable—has a degree, I believe he said, in Marine Biology—very interested in history. Fun to visit with.

David, Thank you for all you do for Laurel and me, Wendell

Louis and I began a thread of emails, messages, and phone calls. (Afe was my nickname on the riverboat in Vietnam.) An excerpt from Louis:

Hello Afe, if I may call you that. I will finish "Muddy Jungle Rivers" today. I am traveling now. When I get back, I will be arranging for the DNA test. I have spoken to two of my brothers and they will also take the test. I also have put together some notes and pictures for you. I have enjoyed the book and look forward to reading the others. I would also like to extend an invitation for you and your wife to visit. We have room for you here and Montauk is an interesting and pleasant place to stay. My best to you Louis

Louis Grignon swabbing the deck on a fishing boat.
Nantucket Sound. (Summer 1976)

On March 6, 2019, Louis emailed me:

Hello Afe, I ordered the DNA kit. I will need a little help in figuring out the family tree building. I finished "Muddy Jungle Rivers." You wrote a good book. I have often wondered how I would react under fire. I will save my questions for when we meet. Having spent much time on fishing boats, I can understand the dynamics of a small crew. I will be seeing my various siblings in the next couple of weeks. I have spoken about this to two of my brothers, Larry & Mike. They are OK with all of it. This is me, on the left and brother Mike on the right. He is 14 months younger than me. This weekend I will pull some pictures of my father and his brother and email them to you.

My best, Lou

On March 7, 2019, I sent Louis a reply with several pictures from my Vietnam time:

Lou, I love your pictures—a lot different than the boat I was on. One option I considered when I got out of the navy in 1969 was to work on fishing boats in Washington or Alaska. But other things got in the way. Here are a few pics that I have. Buddha [my riverboat captain] and I reconnected in the early '90s and he shared his pictures, otherwise I wouldn't have any from Vietnam. After I was medevacked, my seabag never caught up with me—all my pics, clothes, camera, etc.—gone. Some Rambo in the rear is probably still using my stuff to tell war stories.

Great on the DNA kit—I'm excited to see the results. I would suggest keeping David in the loop—he is so knowledgeable and I'm quite sure he will help develop your family tree. David did all the

Wendell Affield visiting with Vietnamese children. U Minh Forest Operation, Vietnam (July 1968)

work on me and my sister Laurel's family tree. Thanks for the kind words about Muddy Jungle Rivers. I think that no one knows how they will react when suddenly under fire until it happens. The "Fight or Flight" part of our brain really is a mystery. By the day I got hit, I had seen enough that I'd developed a fatalistic attitude. That's why I sent you the book—because I assumed you could relate to life on the boat with a small crew—their strengths and weaknesses. I'm also excited that your siblings are on board with our project. Do you have a gap between your top front teeth? I have passed that trait down to my daughter and now my grandchildren.

Take Care, Wendell

Louis replied:

[Wendell] I read your books (HERMAN and PAWNS). I don't know if I told you how involved I got reading your books. I felt, and as it turned out, that I was experiencing an anxiousness as part of the crew [Muddy Jungle Rivers] because of our relationship; as an invisible sibling watching the past replay itself in mundane, dangerous and honorable ways.

The next two books I felt the same or even absent from. I think I was feeling guilty for not being there and having such a different experience growing up. I do not know how to address the life you had while young...Our father would have been proud of you. First growing up as you did, not letting that drive your life into anger and violence but instead working through that and looking for the good & peaceful in the years ahead. Following in his footsteps into the Navy, our father would have had someone to educate about life on a steel deck and sleep on a cot. He came out often on my fishing boats after retirement, taking home a cooler full of lobster tails and claws. Always bragging to his friends about me being a captain while butter ran down his and his friends' chins.

March 14 Louis emailed me:

Hello Wendell, I spoke to the same woman at [Suffolk] county Social Services as you did. Records just don't go back that far by only a couple of years. I spoke to my cousin who may be able to help. His brother serves on the Selden public library board. They have a lot of info and pictures there. Like your grandmother, they are all good Republicans and despise the Democrats. Which is why I think my father moved us out of that town. My father was brought up as a devout Roosevelt Democrat. We 6 kids are kind of split. Larry & Gene are Republican. The rest swing to left and vote Democrat. I hope that is not an issue with us. He is also going to contact some friends who work for the town of Brookhaven, which Selden is located in and see who we can use to gain access to the county records. I don't think there is a mile between the house my father grew up in and the house Barb was in on Magnolia. My maternal grandmother's house was between the two, just west of Dare RD. There was a local bar that <u>everyone went to.</u> I will get the name.

*   I will be bringing down the box my mom always referred to as "your father's shit." Many pictures from the navy and*

plenty before and after the war. My father was a camera kind of guy. It was great talking with you last night. DNA test kit got mailed in today.

My best, Louis

My reply to Louis on March 14:

Hi Louis, That's great that you have contacts in Suffolk County. After I sent this first email, I realized it was to your local museum/history center—but that might be a good connection, too. I'm not real political—I try to find humor from both sides of the aisle in this current political theater we are witness to. Here are a few pics of Barb and my two older brothers from the mid-1940s. [I attached several of the pictures earlier in this story, of Barb, Chris, and Tim.]

I began to learn about my father—our father now—through stories Louis shared with me. On March 25 he sent this email:

I found the pictures I was looking for. There is a bunch of [my father] Guy, Joe, their parents, aunts, uncles and cousins. Also, many as young men, in and out of uniform.

In this picture, Joe is on your left, Guy on the right. I do not know the man in the middle or ANY of the women. The woman in

the lower left corner kinda looks like Barb in the picture of her heading to Europe. But I do not see the "Widow's Peak" on her hair line.

Any look like Barb to you? I finished all the books. I read every line, right to the end. I read that there were times when you wondered about who your father was and his attributes. Guy was a good guy. We did not see him much when we were young. He worked the 4 to midnight shift at NEO Gravure in Weehawken, NJ. He would be sleeping when we left for school and be gone by the time we got home. We would see him on the weekends.

Dad did not like guns. Not .22s, shotguns, firecrackers or even water pistols. However, he always said the best time of his life was in the Navy. He wore his Navy ring his entire life and was buried with it. I don't remember him wearing his wedding band.

He told us where he was stationed and what his job was. Other than that, not much. He sailed for N. Africa about 2-3 months after the invasion. He was a radio repairman and machine gunner on a PBY doing search and rescue for downed pilots and boat sinking survivors. And, of course submarine spotting.

There was plenty of PTSD to go around in the family. My mother's brother, Buddy, was in the Merchant Marine. He had the boat beneath him taken out 6 times. My aunt's husband, Uncle Ray, was a Marine corpsman. He had been in the Island battles for Iwo Jima, Okinawa, Saipan, etc. After reading "Muddy Jungle Rivers," I wonder if my Dad didn't have a problem. Perhaps he was busy picking up bodies as you had experienced.

Where you saw Barbara and Herman argue more than what can be considered normal, I never heard my mother and father raise their voices. Which, as a married man for over forty years, I find kinda weird. He taught us to always walk in someone else's shoes before making any judgments and give a lot of slack to those who march to a different drummer.

Not all of us get to choose the path we want, or think we want. However, when it came to the kids, Guy was working. Being the middle child (#3, like you), I had two older brothers who set precedent for the rest of us. I participated in every sport available. Anything to get out of the house, I guess. Football, baseball, track and wrestling. Wrestling is the sport I liked best. No bullshit. You win, you go on to the next round, you lose, you go home. There was no coach's favorite, money or good looks didn't make a difference.

But I always participated alone. Dad did not go to ball games, track meets or matches. Mom dropped us off and picked us up after. Again, never a raised voice in the house, but never a soft voice either. We never knew what mom or dad were feeling or thinking. I, however, cannot complain. I thought that was normal. But after reading your story, my life was fine.

There are a lot more pictures. The boxes are spread out over the siblings, who, by the way, say HELLO to you and are excited about this.

My best, Louis

On March 25, I replied to the message Louis had sent me:

Hi Louis, Thanks for the picture—I printed it out then rescanned at a high resolution and blew it up—I don't think Barb is in the picture.

I facilitate a Veterans Writer Group for veterans who struggle with PTSD—It's kind of interesting, many of us— including you and your siblings-- grew up with a father who survived WWII. Your father sounds a bit like Herman in that the military was the high point of his life. Imagine those guys came of age during the Great Depression, most never leaving the area where they grew up. Going into the military and traveling the world was a huge experience for them. Society recognized PTSD early on, but the VA did not recognize PTSD until 1980.

I think some of us who have lived through war,

*witnessed the horror and the terrible toll on civilians, have a
greater empathy for other people than many civilians do—it
sounds like your father did. About 30 years ago I became
friends with a fellow Vietnam veteran—he died in 1999 and
his family became homeless. Over the past 20 years my wife
Patti and I kind of adopted them. There were two daughters
who grew up and had children—actually, go to my web site
and read "Angie's Story."*

On Monday, April 8, 2019, David's email message to me was
titled:

BOOM! Guy Grignon WAS YOUR FATHER!!
*Wendell and Laurel, I have been in touch with Louis and
gave him some help with his tree but haven't gotten back
with him with full access yet. I will do so asap. (see attached
screenshot of conversation from Ancestry.)*
*BUT, I checked Ancestry today and...... apparently Louis'
older brother Larry and his daughter Janine had submitted
DNA tests already. !!!!!!!!!!*
***AND...... AS YOU CAN SEE ON ANCESTRY AND IN
THE ATTACHED SCREENSHOTS, THEY ARE BOTH
STRONG MATCHES TO YOU !!!***
***Larry Grignon, almost certainly Guy Grignon's oldest
son and Louis' brother, is a DEFINITE HALF-BROTHER
TO YOU !!!***
***And Janine Grignon, likely Larry's daughter, is a
definite half-niece to you!!***
Louis' results will be the icing on the cake.
*BUT THIS CLINCHES THAT YOU ARE GUY LOUIS
GRIGNON'S SON if Larry is Louis's brother.*
*(The DNA test doesn't have a tree attached, but Louis's
brother Larry has a daughter Janine, which fits perfectly with
the Grignon family I've researched)*

You may want to call Louis to confirm that Larry is his brother.....and/or contact Larry to let them know these results !!!

So happy for you and glad I could help !!!! Congrats!!!!

Dave

Two days later Dave emailed again:

Louis Grignon's (Sagyacht) results posted today. Half-brother. 1431 cM shared. No doubts now.

On Saturday, April 13, 2019, I emailed:

Hi David, Sorry I haven't replied sooner—guess I'm just trying to absorb the news. Louis called yesterday and we had quite a long conversation. Thank you for the amazing work you do, Wendell

April 14, 2019, David emailed—an excerpt:

Wendell, No worries. I understand completely. There is intellectual understanding of the news and then there's emotional understanding. Ripples from the impact. Absorb away! You've essentially suddenly doubled the number of siblings you have and resolved a longstanding mystery with potentially deep and unanticipated effects on your psyche. And opened a new chapter in your family life to be written. Past and future have shifted—no doubt your present needs to adjust to that. (Right, Laurel?)

I'm curious. Did Louis confirm the number of siblings he has? I had 'found' Larry, Guy, Jr., Louis, Michael, Gene, and Yvonne, as Guy, Sr.'s possible children. Is that right/all?

All things considered, Guy is no doubt your biological father, and the Grignons appear to be as empathetic and

*welcoming as one would want. (Although there may be
"interesting" large family dynamics there, as yet unrevealed,
as both of you and I know from our own family histories.)*

   My best, Dave

   *PS: I almost forgot. As you saw on a previous message, I
sent Louis an invitation to my/your "Wendell" tree on
Ancestry. I will now send him copies of your Grignon
grandparents' naturalization papers, family tree fan chart,
and DNA match graphics I sent you earlier. (He shares most
if not all those matches with you and Larry, and may wonder
how they're related) David*

Louis and his wife Patty live on Long Island, New York, a
world different from mine here in northern Minnesota. They
invited Patti and me to come out and visit them. I'd sent him my
three earlier books, *Muddy Jungle Rivers, Herman,* and *Pawns,*
so he knew my life story. I'd seen pictures of him—he reminds
me of the protagonist in a Hemingway sea story. We'd visited on
the phone, exchanged messages and emails, but the thought of
finally meeting him and his family was a bit intimidating yet
amazing.

A few weeks later, on April 26, 2019, I heard from my new-
found sister:

*Hi Wendell! It's your sister Yvonne! I just wanted to say a
quick hello and tell you that I am so excited to meet you
this summer. I just finished the Chickenhouse Chronicles
Parts I and II. My heart hurts. I am looking forward to
speaking with you and sharing stories about our Dad. He
was a wonderful man and it DOES sound and look to me
like you did inherit his empathy and good looks! I am so
happy for you that you can get these answers. I know that
my brothers and I were shocked to hear of you as we never
suspected we had another sibling. After seeing your*

picture, I have no doubt we share the same Dad. I just wish things could have been different for you as you were growing up. I'm still in shock and think about this every day. I can't imagine how you're feeling. I'll see you soon! love your sister, Yvonne

My reply:

Good Morning Yvonne, What a gracious note—thank you. After I received your message, I went down by our little lake, watched the sun set as the loons called out, and just reflected on how life is full of surprises. As you know, I grew up aware that I must have family somewhere beyond the Nebish farm. On the other hand, you and your siblings had no idea. I think with my mother and Guy getting together, it was kind of the proverbial "Perfect Storm." Guy had just returned from the war and there was a sense of euphoria and celebration throughout much of society. My mother was in the middle of a divorce, vulnerable, seeking companionship. As I mention in PAWNS, I am quite certain that she struggled with borderline personality disorder (BPD) and a primary symptom is fear of abandonment and making unwise choices. But that is ancient history and it still happens today. Thanks to modern technology—DNA—and David, the genetics wizard who put the puzzle together, you and Louis and the rest of the Grignon family and I have connected.

I was thinking about going to Europe this summer to explore where Barbara had gone to the music institute and then on to Poland and dig into the time she spent there, but now, connecting with Louis and you and the rest of the Grignon family, I think I'll put the Europe trip on hold and just come out by you folks sometime this summer. My wife Patti and I are both retired so pretty flexible. Again, thank you for such a kind note, I look forward to meeting my new family.

   Wendell

Over the late spring we exchanged emails, messages, and phone calls, getting to know each other. On May 1, I sent this email:

Good morning Louis and Yvonne,

   Two questions: First, Patti and I plan to drive out this summer—when would be a good time? Second, in a letter dated April 22, 1949, Idalia Fratt, my great grandmother, wrote to Elsie inquiring of Barbara: "I was rejoicing that she [Barb] was on a farm as that is what she has been asking for a long time. [Frank Schoenwandt near Cooperstown, where my sister Laurel was born.] What became of that butler who was supposed to be so fine?"

   [Yvonne and Louis] Are either one of you aware of any "butler" in the Grignon family?

   Take Care, Wendell

Louis replied the same day:

Good morning Wendell, Any time after Memorial Day. I am kind of busy until then. After that, it is fun & games this summer. Technically, I am supposed to be going into semi-retirement after October 17, 2019. We will see how that pans out. I do not know of a "butler."

   BUT, If I remember correctly, grandpa and grandma Grignon's house in Selden was GREEN. So the green/Grignon house theory might have some relevance.

   I am still looking into Schoenwandt and Barbara's time on Long Island. My customer who is an attorney for New York State (NYS) in the welfare/social services section is coming out this weekend. I intend to give him the info on Barbara and Frank S. and see what happens.

My cousin Parker Hough and I are scheduling a meeting after Memorial Day to visit the Selden Library and go through their microfiche collection.

Did you have a chance to locate a full mailing address for Barbara in Selden? A house number is what I am looking for. She may have received mail by general delivery in those days. If I get the number, I'll visit the location and take a picture and have more info when I go to the Library. My best, Lou

My reply:

Hi Louis, As I work on this latest book, about Barb's life from the 1930s through 1949, I am revisiting all the information I have and might discover some new links including her Selden address.

I think I sent this to you already but attached is a page from the deposition that Mae Sloane of Suffolk County Welfare did. It mentions the Magnolia address but very interestingly, on reply #14—she talks about a psychiatrist's report on Barb and states that Barb "has a personality disorder." Exactly what I theorized more than seventy years later.

Take Care, Wendell

After firming up dates with Louis, I sent David the following message:

Tuesday, May 21, 2019: Hi David, This morning I spoke to Louis. Laurel and I plan to drive out to Long Island the week of June 16-22. We plan to spend the 15th with Grace and leave for LI early on the 16th. I invite you to come along with us. I believe it will be an illuminating and cathartic experience and you can witness first-hand the fruits of your labors. Louis and his wife Patty have 3 bedrooms available and have invited the three of us to stay in their home.

David replied:

Wendell, How exciting!   Thanks for the invitation! Sounds great to me.

I spent the next few weeks preparing for our great adventure. Patti and I assembled a basket of locally crafted and Minnesota-grown products for our hosts—maple syrup, Bob's Honey, Red Lake Nation lake-grown wild rice, Paul Bunyan and Babe coffee mugs, Woolen Mills scarves, and a few other things. I spent two days cleaning up my Google Map app and entered route and address information. I contacted two men I had served with in Vietnam; traveling east, we could do a pit stop, lunch, and quick visit. As our travel plans solidified, Louis and I exchanged many messages—an example:

Hi Louis, Sorry I haven't responded sooner—waiting for David to get back to me. He did this evening and yes, he is excited to come along. I think he may be a real asset in figuring out the past. I look forward to meeting you and Patty and the rest of the family.
    Take Care, Wendell

Louis's reply:

Hello Wendell, Great! We have three bedrooms available. Arrival in Montauk June 18th. I presume that may change as you drive east. I can't wait to meet you face to face.
    my best, Lou

My reply on June 1:

Good morning Lou, Our plan is to leave Cincinnati very early on Monday morning, stop near Pittsburg and have breakfast with a guy I was in Vietnam with (Snipe in Muddy Jungle Rivers) and head on to your house. I look forward to meeting you and Patty and the rest of the family.

Laurel, David, and I are really excited. Take Care, Wendell

After several exchanges, thanks to Dave and Louis, our travel plans firmed up. We would spend a night in Stamford, Connecticut, tour Darien the following morning, and then drive to Bridgeport and catch the ferry across Long Island Sound to Port Jefferson. I made reservations at Stamford Residence Inn for the night of June 17.

The day before I left northern Minnesota, Louis sent the following message:

Hello Wendell, we will more than likely have nice days and rainy days when you are here. I would like to take you sailing on my boat on Friday (supposed to be a nice day). I figure you, youse and ya'll and my wife Patty, sister Yvonne, brother Mike, and maybe even brother Guy. It is a sailboat, 38'. If anybody is a landlubber, speak up now! Other than that, there will be dinners at the house and out and about.

What's your take on seafood? We have plenty of that here. Your choice of lobster, sea scallops, clams, oysters, mussels, fluke, flounder, tuna, mahi mahi, and more. Plenty of farm food, though, a bunch is sent in from NJ this time of year. Our plants are just beginning to sprout. If there are any dietary issues let me know.

Bring bathing suits. We have a pool and of course the bays and ocean.

I figure you would like a tour of Selden. If we can pick a day, I will contact my cousin and get some access to the Selden library records and micro fiche. And of course, we've got some charts to look at and discuss. And some pictures. And you have some siblings that want to meet you. If you have any questions, begin asking.

You will of course need to climb the stairs to the top of the Montauk Lighthouse if you're up to it. I know my knees might bark back at me if I try it.

My best to all, Louis

DESTINATION: MONTAUK, NEW YORK

J une 14, 2019: And so, I embarked on a second great adventure in two years, driving fifteen hundred miles and seventy years into the past. I bid Patti, Fritzie, and Sadie farewell for about ten days. (Patti was recovering from shoulder surgery and didn't feel up to the trip, though she insisted that I go.) She stood on the lawn, Fritzie our Yorkie in her arms, Sadie, the collie, sitting at her feet. I arrived at Laurel's house in Edina—spent the evening visiting with her and her husband Jerry, and to bed early.

June 15: Left Laurel's house at 3:45 a.m. About forty miles east of Hudson, Wisconsin, we passed a semi-truck that had overturned—just happened, State Patrol not on scene yet. A few drivers had stopped, we kept going—nothing we could do. Arrived in Madison, Wisconsin, had breakfast with Chris, a friend from my 1966 Vietnam deployment—nice to visit

with him again. On south through Illinois, stopped at LeRoy, Illinois, for a picture with Elvis—sent to my little friend, Sarah, who is a great Elvis fan.

Early evening, arrived Monroe, Ohio, and visited Laurel's sister Grace at her assisted-living home, Ohio Living, Mount Pleasant Campus. We were just in time for an ice cream social. Grace was so excited to see us—she began introducing us; asked Laurel if she could call me brother. Such a sweet lady.

June 16: Sunday, Father's Day. A storm passed through during the night—branches scratched against my bedroom wall —woke up to church bells and rain and the realization that I was on my way to meet my new family. We had lunch with Grace, who shared stories from her past, about Levittown, New York, near where she grew up in Massapequa on Long Island. I gifted her two sets of my books, *Muddy Jungle Rivers, Herman,* and *Pawns,* for Mount Pleasant Campus library. Sunday afternoon we attended church service with her.

Laurel, Grace, Wendell, Sunday afternoon church
service at Grace's care facility, Monroe, Ohio (June 16,
2019)

Spent Sunday afternoon visiting. Grace retold the story of her and Laurel's father Frank. Seventy years later, she teared up as she shared again how he had stabbed her in the leg with a pitchfork when she was sixteen. "Your mother called the police on him," Grace said. She pulled her pants leg up. "Right there," and she placed her finger near dark puncture scars. "It still hurts seventy years later."

That evening Grace again shared the story about how, during WWII, her father Fredrick Schoenwandt had a fishing boat, *Sand Bar I*, out of Montauk, New York. She told us that he had been stopped and boarded by a German U-boat crew while fishing in 1941. "It was written up in a New York newspaper." (To date, I have not been able to find the story.)

David, the man who had connected Laurel and Grace, came to visit. Late evening, dinner at the Fig Leaf Brewery restaurant. David visited with some "Poet Club" patrons who were into their suds.

June 17: Left Cincinnati at 3:45AM in a rainstorm. Listened to David explain about DNA and the many twists and turns in his search to find my New York family. A few days earlier I had called my old Vietnam riverboat crewman Brian and asked him to join us for breakfast. Discovered Brian and Nancy at "Park and Eat," a small restaurant south of Pittsburg. So sad, Brian struggles for each breath with congestive heart failure—a gift from Agent Orange exposure more than fifty years ago. So many of us are gone. And for the millionth time I wonder, why not me?

David, Laurel, Wendell, Brian (Snipe), and Nancy

It was great to visit with Brian—we first reconnected in 2015 when I spoke at Rockford, Illinois, and he came to visit. Before that, our last contact was August 18, 1968, when we were ambushed, and I was medevaced. We bid farewell and back on the road.

Laurel driving, I sat in the back seat admiring fog-shrouded hills of Pennsylvania, listening to David explain about jellyfish molecules in tissue samples and the double helix that is the structure of DNA and the science that goes with it, and wondering about these new siblings I was about to meet. Arrived in Stamford, Connecticut, early evening, toured downtown, visited the library, and ate at a sidewalk café, "Tiger Irish Pub." Spent the night at Mariotte Residence. Up early to tour Darien, the small town where Barbara grew up, near Stamford.

Wendell and Laurel, standing outside Darien High School that Barbara had attended in the 1930s (June 2019)

June 18: In the 1930s, Stamford, New Canaan, and Darien were individual small towns where Barbara had spent time; ninety years later they blend together. I recognized many of the street names from Elsie's diaries: Five Mile RD, Middlesex, Post RD, Half Mile RD. We drove Cedar Gate, the winding, tree-shaded lanes, searching for the address Elsie had used on her letterhead, but no house numbers.

In 1936, Barbara graduated from Darien High School, now City Hall. I explained to the receptionist that my mother had been a student, and we were given free rein to explore the building. We discovered original murals depicting colonial settlers and Native Americans in the staircases and the preserved auditorium where I stood and imagined Barbara as a sixteen-year-old student, sitting at a piano on the stage, playing her favorite pieces for classmates.

Darien High School auditorium

A few hours later, in a drizzly wind, we boarded the Bridgeport/Port Jefferson Ferry. After off-loading in Port Jefferson, we drove through rain to South Ferry, crossed, and drove east on Long Island through truck farms, vineyards, vegetable stands, and wineries. We arrived at Sag Harbor Yacht Yard about 3:00 p.m., walked into Louis's office and found him sitting at his desk.

Louis (left) and Wendell, first meeting (June 18, 2019)

"Hi there," Louis said. "You made it." He rose and came around his desk toward me. We stood for a moment looking at each other, and I recalled one of his first comments when we'd visited on the phone. "Your eyes are just like our father's," Louis had told me. Now I understood why, as I looked into his. We tentatively reached out for a handshake then suddenly found ourselves in a long hug. I experienced a strange sensation—an instant bond. I think Louis sensed it, too. Louis was the tangible link that I had wondered about most of my life. And as the week

progressed and I met other siblings, that tangible sense of acceptance was there each time.

The four of us—Louis, Laurel, David, and I—sat and visited
for a bit. Louis suggested a tour of the marina. We passed dozens
of sailboats and yachts bobbing on gentle swells as we walked
the floating docks. I was impressed—it reminded me of a mini-
naval shipyard with repair facilities, fueling dock, and even a
ships' store. We reached Louis's sailboat and he invited us
aboard. After a tour of the 38-foot completely self-contained
boat, we went below deck to the cabin and visited over iced
shots of *English Harbor Rum.* David explained to Louis how he
had first made the connection with Laurel and Grace—how I had
met him, and he had learned that I didn't know who my father
was. He went on to explain his search and the Spollen/LaChance
connection that led him to the Grignon link.

David provided the tree that revealed how Spollen was
connected to my new family, going back three generations.

Late afternoon I rode with Louis while Laurel and David
followed us from Sag Harbor to Louis and Patty's home in
Montauk. Patty met us at the door with a warm welcome. It's a
beautiful old home—built in the 1920s, perfectly preserved. That
evening we went out to dinner—seafood. Home again and Louis
spread old family pictures across a table in his living room. We
explored family late into the night. Louis is a historian, very
knowledgeable about his—now *our*—family history. He
explained that we have a saint in our family, Saint Louis Marie
Grignon of Du Mont Forte.

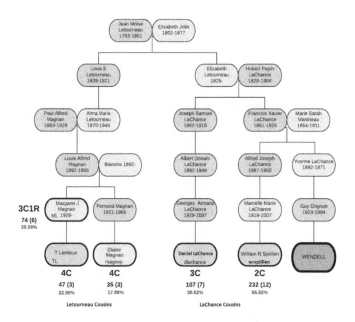

June 19: Woke to an overcast foggy day in a second-floor bedroom overlooking a beautifully landscaped backyard with a swimming pool. Patty is an early riser—she and I visited over fresh-ground dark coffee. I learned that she had grown up in the Bronx—the last place Barbara had lived before she fled New York City the summer of 1949, and later, as I wrote this, I realized that we had returned to New York on the 70th anniversary of the date when Laurel and I had left with Barbara, Chris, and Tim.

Louis gave us a tour of Montauk, including the famous Montauk Lighthouse. Just as logging and Native American culture is central to our northern Minnesota history, so the sea, whaling, fishing, and Native American culture is central to Long Island history. But there is an added layer, our collective colonial history. In 1796, George Washington had commissioned construction of Montauk Lighthouse because so many ships ran aground at the point.

We spent the morning climbing to the top of the lighthouse and visiting the museum. Louis is a great storyteller, and he shared his life as a young man on the fishing boats at sea. Home, and again studied old Grignon family pictures -- several of our father, Guy, Sr., in the late 1940s, but no pictures of Barbara. That evening we discussed politics over Patty's delicious mani-cotti dinner. As I listened, here in this earliest European settled part of our country, it saddened me at how polarized our country has become.

David, Wendell, and Laurel, Montauk Lighthouse in the
background (June 2019)

June 20: Up and showered about 5:15. Coffee, Racine Danish Kringle, and visiting until about 9. Another foggy cool morning. Louis said it's about 10 degrees cooler on the point of Long Island where we are. Today we go to Selden to meet brother Larry. Drove through the Hamptons—Town Pond—Louis explained that the pond was used to ferret out witches in the 1640s. When a woman was dunked into the pond, if she floated, she was declared a witch.

Arrived at Selden Library and met Larry. Again, a long hug

that just felt so natural. He commented how much I looked like his father, then corrected himself, "I mean *our* father." We spent some time at the library exploring old records and 1940s newspapers, then drove to the LaChance grandparents' home where the current owners invited us in. Larry and Louis reminisced about childhood memories from the old house.

A few blocks from the Grignon/LaChance home, we drove Magnolia Drive, the street where Barbara had lived in 1946-47. Larry and Louis explained that, at that time, Selden was all dirt roads with one little store. On Magnolia, small older homes are nearer the main street—as one drives out, the homes become more modern. I took pictures of a few older homes—was it possible Barbara had lived in one of them? If she were with us, would she have recognized it after seventy years? (A few years earlier, when Patti and I drove out to Lake Chelan in Washington state, from our ferry, I had instantly recognized the cabin, perched on the mountainside, where I had lived in 1952 when Barbara ran away from Herman.)

We left Selden and drove toward Middletown. I came to understand how Long Island had earned its name—it's more than 100 miles long. We followed Larry to his daughter's home. It was an amazing welcome. I met Larry's wife Ginger and his two daughters. Janine, whose home this was, and Laurie Jean, who had come from Pennsylvania with her three children. Janine's husband, a New York police officer, welcomed us into their home. Janine and Laurie Jean remembered their grandfather Guy; when I walked through the door, Janine said she thought her grandfather, who died in 1994, had returned because I looked so much like him.

Group picture of Larry Grignon and his family. They were all so
loving and accepting. (Picture credit, Larry's friend Lenny, June 20,
2019)

A group of us walked across the street to greet Janine and
Dave's children when they got off the school bus. Several neighbors gathered—they had heard about the "new uncle" coming to
visit, and they all welcomed me, including the school bus driver
when she delivered the children. And all the kids were so
excited. Dave, an excellent chef, and Janine had a feast for us
including a "Welcome to the Family" cake. The afternoon flew
by as we all visited and took pictures. One day I hope to get back
and spend more time with Larry and his family.

That evening we met Louis and Patty's two daughters,
Camille and Elizabeth Rose, for dinner—two delightful young
ladies. Later, back at Louis and Patty's house, we speculated
about how Barbara and Guy Sr. might have met in 1946. Guy,
just home from WWII, had a car, and lived just a few blocks
from where Barbara lived. Louis gave me pictures of Guy as a
young, handsome man. Louis said he was an outgoing person,
friendly, always ready to help others. As I said, fresh home from

the war, victorious, happy to be alive. There's a picture of him at the beach with several young men and women, catching up on life after the terror of four years of war.

Patty, Elizabeth Rose, her friend, Laurel, Camille, Wendell, Louis
(Picture credit, David)

<u>June 21:</u> Up about 5:30 to bird song through the open window; shower, shave—early morning visit with Patty. Drive to Sag Harbor Boat Yard. Louis's daughter Camille is the yard manger. Louis brought David, Laurel, and me into his Ships' Store and gave use each a gift. I treasure my insulated "Sag Harbor Yacht Yard" sweatshirt—great for northern Minnesota winters.

I met two more brothers and sister Yvonne at Sag Harbor Boat Yard—all but Gene—he couldn't make it. I gifted a set of my books to each. Yvonne set out a delicious lunch for us. First impressions—Guy is stocky and gregarious; Mike is slim and muscular. We visited over lunch then Louis gave us a tour of his

Masonic Lodge and adjacent museum. While at the lodge, I
visited a bit with Yvonne; she recently lost her husband to cancer
and missed him terribly—they must have been very close. The
museum had a maritime theme with displays centered on
whaling and *Moby Dick*.

Louis, Guy Jr., Wendell, Yvonne, Mike -- Sag Harbor
Boat Yard, NY (June 2019)

We transferred leftover lunch to the sailboat refrigerator. In
the evening we sailed Long Island Sound. I helped Mike on the
bow as we cast off; then the two of us lingered up front on the
deck as we moved away from the marina. "You look so much
like Dad," he said and reached out and touched my arm. It had
been an overcast week, but that Friday evening we sailed gently
rolling swells and watched the sun set as we snacked on ham
sandwiches and cold beer. Like the ocean swells, conversation
rolled nonstop. Yvonne, Louis, Guy, and Mike reminisced about
childhood memories as I listened and gained insights into who
my father was. Late that evening, after long goodbyes and
promises of getting back together, we returned to Louis's house.
I do believe that Guy Sr. never knew I existed because Barbara,
as she so often did when in trouble, ran from Selden when she

discovered she was pregnant, changed her name and disappeared into New York City.

Laurel, Mike, Yvonne, Louis at the helm, Guy Jr.,
Wendell, sailing Long Island Sound (June 2019)

Early morning, after a hearty breakfast of eggs, bacon, and *real* New York bagels, we bid Patty and Louis farewell and set out for Minnesota. Laurel drove and visited with David while I sat in back and wrote the last pages of my travel notes. How do I feel about Guy Sr.? Louis said it best—Guy and Barb's natural attraction was their French connection. They lived very close together, they both walked frequently, so it was easy to meet.

We arrived late in Cincinnati, bid farewell to David, and got a few hours' sleep. Early Sunday morning Laurel and I were up, had breakfast and visited with Grace, then homeward bound. Late afternoon we arrived at our oldest brother Chris's apartment in northern Illinois, took him out to dinner, then on to Minnesota and Laurel's home well after midnight. Knowing I wouldn't sleep, I hugged Laurel farewell and drove through the late night, reflecting on our incredible visit with my new family. Home at 9:00 the next morning.

. . .

On July 1, I emailed...

> *Hi Yvonne, I am still trying to process meeting my new family. After more than 70 years, to suddenly learn my paternal roots, is almost overwhelming. And to meet so many wonderful and accepting siblings is truly amazing. I wrote on my blog, but really there are no words. I wish we had had more time to visit—I sensed your still-deep grief about losing your husband. As I told you, Patti and I unexpectedly lost our son four years ago this July 9 and each day we think about him. Death anniversary dates are always very tough.*
>
> *As your husband lives on in your heart, so, too, does Jeff for us.*
>
> *Take Care, Wendell*

Yvonne replied, along with her address and a list of all my new brothers' addresses:

> *Hi Wendell, Thank you for the kind words. I am so sorry for your loss as well. As you know, the loss of someone close just leaves a gaping hole. Time will make it smaller, but it will always be there. I find comfort in believing that I will see him again someday. I just went back to work today after having two weeks off. Just relaxed mostly but I did go visit Mike upstate for a few days. He put me to work trying to claim more of his yard and cutting weeds down! Good exercise. I hope you and Patti are well and enjoying your summer. Yvonne*

Louis and I exchanged several messages—Perhaps I was trying to reconcile how Barbara and my father had gotten together. We recognized that the French language and culture would have drawn them together. When Barbara met Guy, she was in the middle of a disputed divorce from John Curry. In her confused state of mind, did she replace John with Guy? Both were handsome young men.

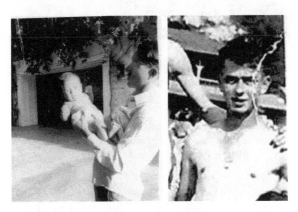

Left: John Curry holding his son Christopher in 1943
Right: Guy Grignon Sr., 1946 (From a picture Louis
shared with the author)

August 14, 2019, Louis emailed:

Ahoy Wendell! good morning to you and Patti. What is the date(s) you would be comfortable with a couple of New Yorkers coming out? Lou

I replied:

Ahoy Mate :) The week of October 5-12 would be great. I am scheduled to speak at our local History Center and think it would be wonderful if both of us were up there.

Give Patty a hug for us—we are looking forward to seeing you both.

Take Care, Wendell

Left to right: Paul Bunyan, Louis, Patty, Patti, Wendell,
Babe -- Bemidji, Minnesota (October 2019)

Louis and Patty flew into Minneapolis/St. Paul Airport Sunday, went out to dinner with Laurel and Jerry, spent the night at Laurel's home, and arrived in Bemidji on Monday, October 7. The first evening we just hung out and visited as they caught their breath from a long day. A few days earlier our local news-paper, *The Bemidji Pioneer*, had published a feature story titled, "Finding his roots: Bemidji man connects with half-siblings through DNA testing."

It was a whirlwind few days: The first morning, we went to Itasca State Park, visited the Mississippi Headwaters where Louis and I walked across on slick boulders. Later into Bemidji for lunch at a local restaurant—Raphael's. Everyone there must have read the *Pioneer* story—we were greeted warmly by so many people. That evening Louis and I spoke at our local Beltrami County History Center to a packed house—Louis, a master storyteller, shared a few tales about his experiences on fishing trawlers in the Atlantic.

The next day Patti and I gave everyone a tour of Bemidji, naturally ending at our iconic statue of Paul Bunyan and his blue ox Babe. In the afternoon a young lady from Lakeland PBS tele-vision came out to our house and interviewed Louis and me—

that evening it aired. The next morning when we went into another restaurant—Minnesota Nice. Again, everyone was so welcoming and warm. Early afternoon we drove out to the old farm.

Selfie outside the Chickenhouse where the search had begun: Louis, Patty, Patti, Wendell --Nebish, Minnesota. (October 2019)

Louis in the basement of the old farmhouse (October 2019)

Louis and Patty had read my earlier book, *PAWNS*, about growing up on the farm in Nebish, so they were familiar with the old homestead. Patty and Patti stood in the yard visiting while Louis and I toured the old blacksmith shop.

It was a lazy afternoon as we wandered the farm—me, telling childhood stories and Louis, asking questions and sharing stories about his youth. Finally, the four of us went into the old house, now abandoned, smelling of bat guano and mouse droppings. I brought Louis down into the old dirt floor basement where I had spent so many hours almost seventy years earlier. And as we visited, I remembered how my older brothers had locked me down in the primordial darkness and yelled from above that Ed Gein, the monster Wisconsin murderer who skinned people, was in the dark basement. Today the crumbling concrete walls are split and leaking, daylight filters through gaps between the floor joists and the foundation, and squirrels had built their winter cache where I once piled potatoes.

On the last day of Louis and Patty's visit, we drove up to Red Lake Nation and visited my friend Ringo at Red Lake Trading Post. Later, back in Bemidji, our family gathered at Giovanni's Pizza for a farewell. It was a wonderful evening of visiting—

Louis and Patty full of questions for our daughter Trish, her husband Troy, and three of Jeff's four children and the grandchildren. Early the next morning we sadly bid our family farewell—until we meet again.

Clockwise, from lower left corner: Louis, Patty, Lexi,
Livia, Troy, Trish, Kadance, Caley, Ella, Zach, Trevor,
Wendell, and Patti at Giovanni's Pizza in Bemidji
(October 10, 2019)

Soon after Patty and Louis's visit, I wrote this letter to my new family—an excerpt:

11 October 2019

Hello to my new family:

Baby sister Yvonne, and brothers Larry, Guy, Louis, Gene, and Mike. This past June it was such an amazing visit when I came out to Long Island and met you all (Gene, next time). I will always cherish your warm acceptance of me into the Grignon family.

I began this letter the afternoon Louis and Patty left our home in northern Minnesota, heading south toward St. Paul, hoping to miss the first snow-blast of the season. Patti and I shared an awesome few days with them. On the first day, about twenty miles from our home, we visited the headwaters of the Mississippi River. Louis and I walked across while the girls videoed us. Another day we drove up to Red Lake Nation, the Indian reservation just north of our old farm. We drove past the powwow grounds where I was honored to participate in the Grand Entry several years ago, and the now abandoned movie theater in Redby where my brothers and I went as children in the 1950s to watch the cowboys and Indians duke it out, bow and arrow against Winchesters.

Another day we toured the farm I grew up on. The first building we visited was the chickenhouse where I discovered the old documents that led me to all of you. It's cleaned out now, the little chicken door still swings in the breeze—I mentioned to Louis how my brother Randy and I played tag when we were little—how we squeezed through the chicken manure-crusted little opening.

Our old house is now abandoned with no back door, so we walked in and stirred ghosts. Louis and I went down into the dirt-floor basement; I showed him where the potato bins once stood, and the table Barb ordered me to crawl under to dig for Hoganson—a fantasy she carried with her from New York. The four of us, Louis, Patty, my Patti and I stood at the upstairs window and looked out over the now overgrown garden—out the window I had jumped from when I was nine years old to escape Barbara's wrath.

Louis and I walked over to where the pig house once stood—now an overgrown slab covered with thorn bushes and nettles; not a lot different except for the little hog house where I had hidden from Herman more than sixty years earlier.

We walked into the old blacksmith shop and I showed Louis where the forge and the anvil once stood, and I remembered the little boy who spent hours slowly turning the crank on the forge billows. We visited as we looked across the field toward Maple Lake—Louis asked questions and I shared my childhood memories.

At our house, late into the night, Louis and I stayed up sipping English Harbor Antigua Rum over ice. He shared many stories of his childhood and memories of growing up with our father. As I listened, I learned that Guy Sr. was a good man—a good father, and I grieve that I never had a chance to meet him.

We can never know how my mother Barbara and our father met. We do know they both lived in Selden at the same time, the time that I was conceived. As I have written in my memoir PAWNS, Barbara struggled with borderline personality disorder. She could present herself as the most normal caring person in the world, but beneath that mask was a smoldering cauldron of dysfunction. I do not say that in anger; having spent most of my childhood with her and now, after ten years of studying old documents, I try to think and write about Barbara's life from an objective point of view, though at times I flash back, and childhood memories trouble me. But I've come to understand the terrible struggle she lived with. As children, we could not know that; her erratic behavior was our normal. Today, as I reflect on her eighty-nine-year journey, I'm amazed she survived so long.

So how did Guy and Barbara meet? During our late-night visits Louis and I speculated again on that. I remember as a child on the farm, our phone was often not working because the bill was delinquent—Barbara, with us in tow, would walk the road up to a neighbor's house to use their phone. Other times, I remember riding into Bemidji with neighbor men whom she talked into chauffeuring us when Herman wouldn't drive her in. And I suspect that is how Barbara met our father; she may have walked from Magnolia Drive to your mother's home or to the Grignon home that I visited while in Selden this past June—both were within walking distance from Magnolia Drive. Barbara was on public aid—she had no vehicle and no money for taxi. Maybe Guy stopped to help a young mother carrying a baby, a bag of groceries, and a toddler in tow. Or she may have asked Guy to give her a ride into New York City for some forgotten reason. The two young people learned that they had something in common—French language and an interest in French culture. Again, Barbara was a master manipulator and could put on the most convincing mask— she may have presented herself as a war widow to gain our father's sympathy. Guy, fresh home from the war, would have been empathetic. Remember—Barbara was divorced and feeling very abandoned. When she discovered she was pregnant with me, again from old documents I retrieved from the chickenhouse, I believe she disappeared from Selden and Guy never knew. On my birth certificate (Borough of Manhattan) she used a new alias—Barbara Olmsted. It's one of the features of borderline personality disorder—to run from your problems. Eight months after I was born, by June 1948, she was Linda Philips; within the year she was Linda Curry, the name she used for several years before returning to Barbara.

Why do I tell you these things? So, you will understand that our father was taken in by a very gifted young woman. Just a couple of movies you may have seen over the years where the protagonist struggles with borderline personality disorder—Girl Interrupted and Play Misty For Me. Naturally, there's Hollywood spin on them, but you get the idea.

I may have mentioned to some of you that the manuscript for my next book in Chickenhouse Chronicles series is based on Barbara's life from the 1920s-1949 when she moved to Minnesota. I thought I was getting close to sending it to my editor last January (2019) when David, the genealogist, first told me about a possible discovery which led me to the Grignon family. That discovery opened a whole new wonderful world to me. This past week, as I listened to Louis talk about our father, a thought occurred to me. Suppose you each wrote me a letter, sharing a few special childhood memories you carry of our father.

Today, my vision for this book I am working on is to have a Part III which will open with the 2014 DNA tests I had done and the five-year journey that brought us together. With your permission, I would include your letters with childhood memories—and maybe a few pictures—about growing up with our father. I would send each of you a copy of that section before getting published for your final approval. If any one of you is not comfortable with the idea, I understand and will not pursue it.

I look forward to hearing from you,

Love you all, Wendell

Louis had shared many memory stories of our father; shortly after I sent the letter, Larry sent me a childhood memory:

October 28, 2019 Larry Grignon

Dear Wendell, A short account of how our Dad (Guy SR.) really helped me out one cold November night in 1972. In 1972 I was in my 4th year of my Electrical Apprenticeship. I went after work two nights a week to "Charles Evan Hughes High School." It was between 8th and 9th Avenue on 18th Street (The west side of Manhattan.) I would drive there and park on the street.

I would get out of class about 8 p.m. then go east across Manhattan to the Midtown Tunnel, which goes under the East River and comes out in Queens onto the "Long Island Expressway" (Rt 495). I would take that home.

Larry Grignon and Wendell, outside Selden Library,
Selden, New York, a few blocks from where Barbara lived
in 1946-47 (June 2019)

So, I was working my way across Manhattan when all of a sudden, the clutch cable in my Toyota Corolla snapped! I coasted to the side of the street with a severed clutch cable. I wasn't going anywhere.

Thank Heaven, I knew Dad was working the night shift at "Columbia Corrugated" in Long Island City, Queens, doing the printing on cardboard boxes.

Long Island City isn't too far from the Midtown Tunnel, on the Queens side. Luckily, I found a working pay phone near where I was stuck. I called our Dad, and a short time later, he was there to help me. He brought a heavy-duty rope, we tied it to my front bumper and his rear bumper. He towed me to the tunnel, then through the tunnel.

Then he pulled up to the pay booth on the East side exit and paid his toll and gave the collector the money for my toll. We continued east, and went to friends of his and Mom's, who lived in "Flushing Queens," which wasn't too far. We parked in front of their apartment building, then I called Ginger and she came and picked me up. Dad went back to work. I took off work the next day and me and a friend towed the Toyota back to my house.

Yes, our father was a good Dad.

P.S. In reading about Herman, I believe had you been in a similar situation, Herman would have also helped you. Larry (Bro #2)

Yes, Larry, I believe Herman would have helped me.

At the beginning of the memory story Guy Jr., sent, he alludes to the 2020 pandemic Covid-19 (Coronavirus). Like millions of other Americans, Patti and I were self-isolating at home in northern Minnesota.

Guy, Wendell, Louis—Selden Library (June 2019)

March 25, 2019 Guy Grignon JR.

Yo Wendell, it's Guy. Yeah, I think everyone's doing what you and Patti are doing, hunkering down. Here's a story I would like to tell you—it's short. In 1956 or '57, I was 6 years old. We were living in Syosset, Long Island. It was the weekend and Dad and Mom and us kids drove to Port Jefferson to visit Mom's sister Dorothy and Uncle Wally.

Their son, Wayne, took me down to the basement and showed me some of the cool stuff his father and mom had accumulated. One of the things they had was from Uncle Wally's brother, who was an avid collector of arrowheads and Indian stuff. I was totally immersed and so excited about these arrowheads because all I watched on TV was cowboys and Indians, so when we got home, I asked Dad, "Where do you find those things?"

Dad said, "Well, you find them in streams and fields, but mostly where water is running on rocks and washes the soil away."

I didn't think about it much, but several days later I was in the backyard getting a drink out of the water faucet and noticed these rocks the water was falling down on, so I bent down and looked closer, and there in the pebbles where the rocks had been washed clean by the water was a beautiful rose quartz arrowhead.

I took it and showed it to Dad, and he said, "I told you so."

Dad had gotten the arrowhead from Uncle Wally, knowing that I would look under the faucet eventually.

Yvonne sent this next message and memory story. As with me, her olfactory sense is a powerful trigger.

March 27, 2020 Yvonne (Grignon) Adolph

Hi Wendell, I hope this email finds you and Patti well. It was so nice speaking with you the other day. Such crazy times we are living in now with this corona virus. I had a chance to read your draft that you sent to all of us. It was very informative. We owe so much thanks to Dave for making all the connections. Without his expertise, we would never have crossed paths.

Yvonne (Grignon) Adolph and Wendell Affield—Selden,
Long Island (June 2019)

So, I was thinking of a memory from my childhood about our father and I kept coming back to the same story in my head. I feel it's a small memory but very strong for me.

I recall being young, maybe anywhere from four to eight years old. My parents and I would go down to the TV room in the evening and watch television. I remember, many times, snuggling up to Dad on the couch and laying my head on his chest. I can still hear his heartbeat, feel his warmth and safety. He always wore a white Fruit of the Loom crew-neck t-shirt. I can still smell the scent of his cotton t-shirt. To think of it, brings back a feeling of warmth and love.

A couple little extra thoughts on Dad...he loved wood working. I remember him making a set of shelves for my room. We went to the store, picked out the wood and the paint. I stood by him the entire time while he made it. Dad was a very handy man and taught us a lot. He also enjoyed taking care of his lawn. His very green lawn was his pride and joy.

Our Dad was a very kind man and I just remember missing him a lot. He worked nights during the week, so for years, I would mainly see him on weekends.

I feel in my heart, if Dad were to see you today, he would be so proud of you, Wendell.

All my love...your little sister, Yvonne

Mike sent this following cover letter along with several vignettes —memory stories—from his early years.

October 20, 2020 Michael Grignon

Mike Grignon, sailing Long Island Sound on Louis's boat (June 2019)

Hi Wendell and Patti, I hope all is good with you and the family. It looks like winter has started for you guys. We've had a couple of frosts and the trees are pretty much bare here in upstate New York—no snow yet, though. Soon.

Yvonne and I are really sorry we didn't get to Bemidji to visit with you and Patti this past summer. Next summer, pandemic or not!!!

Give sister Laurel a hug from me. Can't wait 'til we get together again. Your Ever Lovin Brother, Mike :)

I think of you often Wendell—here are a few of my early memories

Beach Bungalow

It had to have been after Grandma Hough died in 1965. She had owned a bungalow on West Meadow Beach in Stonybrook, New York. So now it was left to her kids; turns out, Mom and her brother

Uncle Buddy would each take a month during summer vacation. They agreed to alternate July and August in the years to come.

Summer School

I think it was 1966, the summer after 4th grade. Mom, Louis, Gene, and Yvonne would be spending a month at Grandma Hough's bungalow on West Meadow Beach. It was the most favorite place to be for us kids. I wouldn't be going. Instead, I had to go to summer school for reading.

I spent the month with Dad. Every evening after he came home from work, we would go someplace for dinner, and a few times we went to Adventure Land—rides, games, and just junk food—another favorite place for us kids. On weekends Dad took me to West Meadow Beach. It was good time spent with Pop.

Dear Old Dad

It was some time in my early teen years. I don't recall exactly how it came up. Dad and I were shootin' the breeze and I asked him, "What would you like us to call you besides "Dad?""

He said, "Papa."

I said, "Nah..., we can't call you 'Papa.'"

Mom was nearby listening, and she didn't like the sound of it, either. We ended up with "Pop." And that was Pop's new name.

Working With Pop

It was the early 1980s—Pop got me a job in the printing business where he worked at Walker Prismatic, located on East 23rd St. between Lexington and 3rd Avenue in Manhattan. Walker Prismatic produced advertisement pages for newspapers and magazines. Dad was a layout artist and Foreman of his department. He worked with photography film the size of magazine and newspaper pages.

Our father, Guy Grignon Sr. at work, in the printing
industry (Circa early 1980s)

*It may have been my first day there. Visiting with Dad, I asked
him, "What is that you're listening to?"*

"Country music," he told me. "After a while you get to like it."

*I worked with Pop for about two years. He was right about
Country music.*

As I read Mike's letter and memories, I watched the video clip of
our June 2019 sailing adventure on Long Island Sound, and I
realized once again how blessed I am to have connected with the
Grignon family.

I received a package from Gene Grignon, who lives in
upstate New York. I smiled as I read the note he enclosed—it
reminded me of the documents and pictures I had found in the
chickenhouse out at the farm in northern Minnesota ten years
earlier.

Gene Grignon 06 October 2020

*Dear Wendell, Here are some pictures I had been looking for.
Please excuse the mouse damage. The large one is of Dad, maybe
in Florida or North Africa. In another, taken the summer of 1946,*

*Uncle Joe Grignon is in front of Soldier Roll of Honor monument,
both their names on lower left. Clarence L. Hough, Mom's brother,
is in the middle column. He either took or is in the picture. And one
picture of Dad relaxing.*

   Your friend and Brother, Gene

Guy Grignon Sr. in Florida (Mouse damage cropped out.)
(Circa early 1943)

   Gene's box included more than pictures. There was a four-
inch iron statue of a sailor holding crossed semaphore flags
above his head, several of our father's books, two maps, and a
compass trainer. From the frayed edges and shop-worn condition, it was obvious that Guy had used the compass trainer
during the war to learn target angles and compass corrections
while a crewman on a PBY and later, on a Ventura—both long
range aircraft that required accurate navigation. I was excited
with Gene's contribution to sharing memories about our father.
Gene's box of treasures gave me a deeper understanding of who
our father was.

   As with so many WWII veterans, the war must have played a
significant role in Guy's life. The books Gene shared with me
provided insights to how our father dealt with his wartime
memories. The most visual of the books was *US Navy War
Photographs,* a 106-page collection of graphic black and white

war photos. As I studied each photo, I thought back to similar situations I had witnessed or had taken part in while in Vietnam. I imagine Guy flashed back to memories of his North Africa war experiences as he thumbed through the book decades earlier.

Guy was an eclectic student of WWII history. Rather than focus only on the North African Theater of Operations where he had served, his choice of books revealed that he explored the global war. For example, the photograph book I mentioned documented the Pacific Theater of Operations. Another book, *Forgotten Soldier* (1967) by Guy Sajer, is a memoir written by a French/German soldier who served with the German Wehrmacht (army) and survived the Russian Front. The angst and waste in Sajer's story are reminiscent of Erich Maria Remarque's *All Quiet on the Western Front* (1929), a novel based on WWI combat, also written by an enlisted German soldier.

One little book piqued my curiosity: Why did Guy have *A Pocket Guide to Vietnam* (1962) published by the Department of Naval Personnel? In a conversation with Louis, he reminded me that our father was fluent in the French language. Guy had shared with his children that during his time in North Africa, he had spent his free time with soldiers of the French Foreign Legion. Did Guy make some friendships that survived beyond the war? At the end of WWII many French soldiers were deployed to Vietnam. Remember that before WWII, Vietnam was a French colony known as French Indochina. Was it possible that French soldiers Guy had met during WWII were transferred to Vietnam, thus Guy's interest in the country?

Or was Guy, as a student of history, educating himself on a

potential conflict at the cusp of a quagmire the United States was
teetering toward, concerned that his sons were coming of age?
During my visit at Louis and Patty's home, Louis told me that
during the Vietnam War, Guy had told his children, "You don't
need to go to war. I've seen enough for all of us."

I treasure the information that each of my new-found siblings
shared with me, and Gene's contribution provided insights into
my father's life that I would never have known.

EPILOGUE

In writing this story, what have I learned? John Curry, the man listed on my birth certificate as "Father," the man who walked out on me fifty-four years ago when I began my search in 1966, left me at a loss, his silence an admission that he was not my father. Since the discovery of Guy Grignon Sr. I've added a new dimension to my life that filled a void I had come to accept. I continue to be amazed by the unconditional love all my new siblings have given to me.

Reflecting on this past year, it saddens me that I didn't connect with my family sooner. As we move into the autumn of our lives, I realize that I have missed so much. But I feel blessed to share this time we have left. Unfortunately, this pandemic Covid virus we are currently dealing with in 2020 is a monster speed bump for getting together.

I now have a touchstone to my past. From my new siblings I learned that our father had a deep empathy for others—I like to think I inherited that gene. The first time I remember consciously reaching out to another, I was twelve years old, in a foster home, and smuggled supper up to a Native American toddler who lay crying in his crib after being sent to bed without food as punishment for speaking Ojibwe rather than English. A few years later, at seventeen, in Naval boot camp, I got into a fight, defending an African American recruit from a southern racist. Fast forward fifty-two years: I received an award from the Minnesota Humanities Center for my work with the underserved in our community. I like to think that sense of compassion is one of my father's legacies to me.

What have I learned about my father? As a young man, he served his country in WWII. I received his complete military record and, after studying it, this is the takeaway that I shared with my new-found siblings:

(To all my Grignon brothers and sister) *I never met our father, but from the military record he left us, I see that he was a high-performing man who did an amazing job under what must have been, at times, very harsh conditions. The military uses an "E" system for enlisted rank; for example, Guy was an E-1 when he entered boot camp. When he was discharged, as Aviation Radioman First Class, he was an E-6. That is very impressive. (After four years during Vietnam, I was E-5 when discharged.) During peacetime it can take more than 12 years to reach E-6. Wendell*

After receiving an honorable discharge, Guy Grignon returned to Selden, New York, and, as with millions of returning veterans, searched for his "new normal" after witnessing the horrors of war. Two years of combat duty in North Africa compromised our father's health and instilled an aversion to guns.

I learned that my father was a hard-working conscientious family man whom his children loved and respected—a father they could always count on. He was a humble God-fearing man.

He enjoyed a good time and had a zest for life. A gift that he and his wife left each of their children is a capacity to care about others.

And Barbara—I've come to realize she was an amazing woman who had a gift for languages and music. Because of her fear of being alone, she made several impulsive decisions on the men in her life, all of which turned out to be unwise. Yet through her darkest hours, she found the resilience to continue.

By 1985, Barbara had only one of her nine children, Lawrence, living with her on the farm near Nebish, Minnesota. Her youngest son Danny had recently gotten married and lived about a mile south of the farm. As I visited with Danny, he recalled a morning that summer when he drove over to the farm for some forgotten reason and discovered the house locked tight, Barbara and Lawrence gone.

A few weeks later they returned. Barbara refused to say where they had been. Lawrence told Danny that he and Barbara had driven out to the East Coast and visited Barbara's childhood haunts in Connecticut and New York. After Barbara died in 2010, I found a family tree in the farmhouse attic. It had been created in 1985 by "THP." Only recently did I realize that THP was, no doubt, a branch of the tree, Barbara's cousin, Thomas Hall Philips. The 1985 address placed him living in Connecticut.

As I studied the family tree, I discovered that Barbara, in sharing our branch of the family, had indicated that her marriage to Herman Affield had taken place in 1942, the year she married John Curry. On the tree, Herman is listed as the father of her nine children.

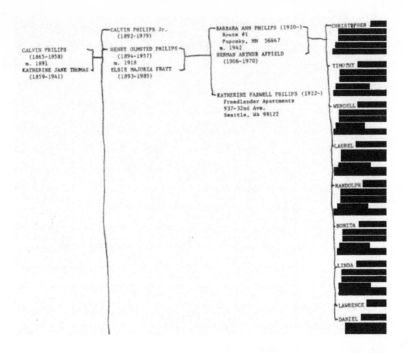

Throughout her life I believe Barbara dissociated at times as a coping mechanism to endure very stressful events. I speculate that she may have had a much more severe form of dissociation known as Dissociative Identity Disorder. For clarification of understanding Barbara's psychiatric illness, I have decided not to focus on this additional notion, but find the possibility fascinating, nevertheless.

I recall a line from Deborah Bray Haddock's book, *The Dissociative Identity Disorder Sourcebook* (2001). Haddock wrote, "An individual never completely forgets what has happened to her in the past. Sometimes, though, those memories have been dissociated and stored very far away, like stacks of boxes packed away in the corner of a basement." Barbara had stored her memories away in the locked chickenhouse.

I spent the last few hours with Barbara as she died in 2010. She went to her grave with the secret of my father's identity intact. Thankfully, a few days before she died, she changed her will and left her probate estate to me. Did she realize that clues in the chickenhouse treasures would lead me to my paternal family?

APPENDIX
DAVID'S DNA RESEARCH / MIRROR METHOD AND RESULTS

Without David's expertise I would never have connected with the Grignon family. Below is a lengthy message he sent me, detailing the technical aspects of his search. The discussion is simplified and incomplete but details some of the work and methodology used to narrow the search for my father, using DNA matching to guide the necessary genealogical detective work for documentation of likely candidates.

1) Ancestry.com - Tools and Data Source

Ancestry was founded as a searchable online documents library for genealogical research; DNA testing and comparisons were added later.

On the genealogy side of things, Ancestry allows users to enter names, dates, places, and other identifying information to search its documents database for information specific to a given family member. It also performs an automatic search function which runs without user intervention to find potential information matches in its databases and other users' family trees. If it finds a potential document or tree match to the entered biographical and family information for an individual, it places a "green leaf" on the user's tree and family member profile pages as a HINT. It is up to the user to determine its accuracy and decide whether to incorporate the suggested information and records into their tree. Unfortunately, some (many?) users just add it, assuming it to be pertinent and true—so these tree record hints are a shortcut which are sometimes abused and can propagate errors in users' trees.

On the more recent and separate DNA side of things, Ancestry collects saliva samples [which Laurel and Wendell had done in 2014] from participating users and tests the DNA obtained against 700,000+ DNA regions specifically known to vary between people. These selected segments vary at single points in the DNA—the variants are known as Single Nucleotide Polymorphisms (SNPs)—and assigned identifying numbers. The more related you are to someone else, the more of these SNPs you will share, and they will be found in "runs" or matching segments of increasing size the closer you are related. This shared segment data can be tabulated and even be visualized by "chromosome painting" on websites such as Gedmatch (Ancestry does not provide this capability. See 3 attached example files for Philips cousins—Peter Philips, Chris Philips and daughters)

Comparisons can be made to population averages of SNPs and their patterns on the chromosomes (averages are created as references defined by Ancestry to 'represent' ethnic groups or nationalities) allowing Ancestry to provide the popular but variably accurate 'Ethnicity' reports. (Recently improved.)

In contrast SNP comparisons with distinct individuals allow detection of family relationships; this application has greater accuracy than comparisons used for ethnicity reports. Ancestry automatically determines and provides a constantly updated list of discovered DNA matches ordered from closest match to most distant. Ancestry also groups these matches as "Parent/Child," "Close Family," "First Cousins," "Second Cousins," "Third

Cousins," "Fourth Cousins," and "Distant Cousins." All group names are imprecise and include relationships not described by the group titles. For example, an identical twin may also appear under "Parent/Child"; siblings, half-siblings, grandparent/grandchild, aunt/uncle/niece/nephew are found under "Close Family"; and more and more diverse family relationships are found under the various "Cousins" categories.

The actual numerical data (total length and number of shared DNA segments (in 'centiMorgans,' cM)) for a given DNA match can also be used with outside resources to more narrowly determine the possible relationships that that degree of shared DNA may represent. Previously hidden from novices, Ancestry now lists this data under each match.

In a manner similar to record hints, Ancestry also features automatic determination of relationship hints for DNA matches. This can only be done IF the individuals being compared have BOTH created family trees AND have both linked their DNA test results to an individual in that tree. Links to these determinations appear as 'green leaves' like records hints, but on the right side of the DNA Match List page. Clicking them leads to an individual Match Page where Ancestry suggests paths from each matched individual through their respective DNA-linked trees back to shared Most Recent Common Ancestor(s) (MRCAs: individuals or couples), (see attached examples Madeleine-PhilipsMRCAhint, calliopeMRCAhint). These 'leaves' are distinct from Records Hints appearing in family trees and are also just suggestions to be evaluated for accuracy by the user. They depend entirely on the accuracy of the two compared family trees—which can vary wildly. Of course, an Ancestry user can always determine or confirm these relationships on their own, using self-verified trees. Additionally, once a genealogical relationship has been determined or suggested, it can be assessed independently for accuracy (to a degree) using outside sources by comparison to the types of relationships known to be possible for that level of DNA sharing. (Tables and websites exist for this purpose, more below).

2) DNA data limitations

Each individual has two parents, so with each generation back the number of ancestors doubles. Focusing just on the math, in the fourth generation back from you, (2xGreatGrandparents) you have 16 ancestors (8 couples). In the ninth generation (7xGreatGrandparents) you have 512. Eventually you are predicted to have more ancestors than the actual number of people known to be alive at a given time. Indeed, going back 40 or so generations (about 1,000 years) predicts you have more than a trillion proposed ancestors—more than the number of people who have ever lived!

The solution to this apparent math-created impossibility is 'pedigree collapse'—historical and archaeological actual population sizes mean that your family lines and other present-day people are actually distant cousins all descended from the same ancestral individuals. Moving back in history population size was obviously smaller, which means that at some earlier time people were even partnering with more closely related individuals. Second and third cousin marriages were very common; the estimated average over most of prehistory is that 80% of marriages were between second and third cousins. Go far enough back and everyone alive shares the same ancestors.

Speaking in terms of DNA, also consider the following. We each get half of our DNA from each parent. We therefore inherit less and less DNA from each individual ancestor as we move back in generations (see dna-inherited, attached). Assuming for a minute there is no variation in the amount of inherited DNA from each ancestor (an assumption proven false by science and 'crossing over'/recombination)—by the time we reach our 512 7xGreatGrandparents, each would only provide us with 0.19% of their DNA. (about 6.8 cM). Specific DNA connections to our ancestors fade and disappear as we move back in time. Those many we do share DNA with only provide a tiny amount of DNA to us, and going back far enough, all living people are descended from the same group of ancestors sharing different but overlapping subsets of DNA 'snippets.'

In reality the amount of inherited DNA from each ancestor is actually just an average due to DNA crossing over and mixing upon formation of each sperm or egg at each generation. For example, people get an AVERAGE of 25% of their DNA from each grandparent. In reality a given person may get only say 18% from Grandpa Schoenwandt and 32% from Grandma OConnor, whereas their sibling may get 27% Schoenwandt and 23% OConnor DNA. To some degree, siblings 'take after' different family lines. This variation continues all the way back and thus means that DNA connections to SOME ancestral family lines drop out SOONER than the math above predicts; the loss begins at the third cousin (2nd great-grandparent) level. So entire DNA connections to ancestors will vary from sibling to sibling. This affects ethnicity estimates as well; Joe may retain a distant DNA link to Native Americans, but sister Suzy may show no such connection.

This means that genealogical family trees can be documented but are not the same as DNA family trees. (see attached example, dna-genetic-tree (lt. blue areas indicate shared DNA, white— none), and linked article, https://thegeneticgenealogist.com/2009/11/10/qa-everyone-has-two-family-trees-a-genealogical-tree-and-a-genetic-tree/).

Eventually many of our known ('provable,' 'documented') ancestors actually share NO DNA with us, but may have passed along some DNA to our siblings and other relatives. When comparing the DNA of living modern people while moving back in time, we eventually lose the ability to trace specific connections to specific past individuals, then to specific families, then to ethnicities. (However, comparing DNA with ANCIENT individuals from archaeological finds can extend our ability to trace connections to ancient peoples; this research has exploded in the past three to five years).

This variable loss of DNA connection to our ancestors affects matching adversely—since each of two compared individuals may lose DNA connections to different specific actual ancestors, the odds of finding shared DNA between them, even if actually related, drops off dramatically. So, in using Ancestry-derived DNA determinations for comparisons, two to five percent of known third cousins will NOT share ANY DNA. Fully one third of known fourth cousins won't share DNA, and two thirds of fifth cousins will share no DNA. (see attached, dna-sharing)

Another effect of the variation in amount of DNA inherited is that as the average amount of shared DNA between cousins decreases, the variation (standard deviation) increases, thus 'smearing' the expected results over a wider and wider range. The DNA relationship groupings will overlap more and more. Overall this means that using DNA to narrow down probable relationships between more distant relations (people sharing small amounts of DNA) becomes more and more difficult. In an attached example, a match at 1300cM has about a 50% chance to be a half-sibling and 50% chance to be a 1C (Y axis is probability in %). Moving to the right on the X axis (amount of DNA shared in cM), note that the groups (colored curves) spread out and overlap more, making prediction more difficult.

3) Using DNA to find relationships in family trees

The good news is that the vast majority of 3Cs, and ALL 2Cs and closer, will always share DNA (albeit a variable amount). And those closer DNA matches have a more narrow range of possible relationships underlying the match than more distant ones, making finding the connection more straightforward. The more DNA you share with someone the easier it is to use the amount of DNA shared to predict or corroborate a specific relationship determined by genealogical research.

Professional and amateur genetic genealogists have collected data to describe the connections between the amount of shared DNA and known family relationships (e.g., https://thegeneticgenealogist.com/2017/08/26/august-2017-update-to-the-shared-cm-project/). Tables and websites are available online giving probabilities and guidance as to what to look for in the family trees to determine relationships (e.g., attached DNA Detective table, and website https://dnapainter.com/tools/sharedcmv4).

Working from 1979 cM shared DNA (such as Laurel's match with Grace) to predict a relationship is relatively straightforward —there is 100% probability it is either a half-sibling, grandparent/grandchild, or uncle(aunt)/niece(nephew) relationship. Ages, family tree information, etc., can then narrow those choices— voila, half-siblings! Working from 232 cM (Wendell's closest non-maternal match—with wrsp0llen) is more difficult—this level of sharing can be explained by many relationships in several groupings (the effect of those variability-caused range overlaps). (See https://dnapainter.com/tools/sharedcmv4/232).

If both matching individuals' family trees are known, shared DNA can be used to find a likely connection, and those possible connection hints found by Ancestry can be verified. However, if both trees are not available or not extensive enough, or the DNA tests haven't been linked to a tree, Ancestry cannot provide a hint. For adoptees and in unknown parentage situations, trees will be completely lacking or only partially known, so in those cases researchers cannot find and Ancestry obviously cannot detect likely ancestors.

Sooo, what to do?

4) **Mirror trees**

A clever and powerful method has been developed as a 'work around' to use Ancestry's MRCA search algorithm (which compares the trees of DNA matches) to find connections, even if one match has no tree or only half a tree provided to us on Ancestry, wherein the researcher builds or extends missing or tiny family trees of DNA matches first. (Note: I use the term 'adoptee' to include any person, such as you or Laurel, who have a partial tree with an unknown paternal line).

In this method the researcher first chooses or, as necessary, creates the tree of one of an adoptee's closer matches and uses it in lieu of the adoptee's tree in the search—copying or 'mirroring' it for use as a temporary surrogate for the missing tree. To be maximally useful, all 'bloodlines' of the tree (in-laws at each generation) must be extended back as far as possible. If one side of the adoptee's tree is known (nearly always maternal, as in your case), then by using Shared Matches lists, paternal-side matches can be found and surrogate trees developed from the 'missing' (paternal) side of the family.

Next an adoptee's DNA raw dataset is then linked either to a 'hypothetical' strategically placed person or to the matching individual in the mirror tree (done under "DNA, Settings" on your DNA results page).

Finally, Ancestry's MRCA algorithm is allowed to run and do its 'magic,' taking a few hours or days to search all of the adoptee's remaining DNA matches' trees for any common ancestors using this 'borrowed' tree (hoping some are extensive enough to return hints). The returned results will show which of the family lines of that mirror tree are in common with or connect up with the adoptee's other DNA matches, thus narrowing the search to lines connected by the shared DNA.

This process can be repeated within a tree and on different mirror trees to gather the most information. The DNA dataset can be detached from one individual in a given tree and attached to another and the algorithm allowed to run again. By moving up the tree and attaching the DNA data to each of your surrogate's parents, grandparents, etc., a path can be traced to detect which of your other DNA matches (if any) share or connect to each line. Generally, the next step is to move to another mirror tree by choosing the next closest DNA match, making a tree, and linking the adoptee's DNA to various people in that tree, and so on.

The end result is a list of family names the adoptee's DNA 'flows through' to connect each of their DNA matches to a common ancestor. The compiled connections can be used to identify the closest relatives which will explain all of the discovered family connections and MRCAs.

The method is dependent on DNA matches having correct and reasonably extensive trees for Ancestry's search algorithm to work on. Trees must go back far enough and extend 'sideways' enough (listing siblings, uncles/aunts, great uncles/aunts, etc.) for connections to be detected. DNA matches without trees, having only 'stumps,' or posting otherwise incomplete trees, won't work. Trees without a match's own DNA linked to them will also not work. So often simply 'borrowing' a tree is not possible—the researcher must build a match's tree for them; creating and extending the match's tree from a 'stump' to make it usable.

An attempt at an analogy—mirror trees as 'nets':

The total number of 'fish' in the DNA 'pool' of your matches that is available to be 'caught' by the mirror tree 'net' affects success rates. Luckily, you have a massive list of DNA matches —52,581 total (as of yesterday), compared to 28,277 for Laurel and 22,416 for Grace. Here is a current tally:

Number of DNA matches

	Total	3C&closer (#paternal)	4C
Wendell	52581	14 (6)	1880
Laurel	28277	17 (10)	417
Grace	22416	29	349

Even more critical is the number of useful 'nets' available (the closer matches and their trees used for mirroring). Third cousins and closer reliably make good nets with no 'gaps' in coverage and make extraction of the 'fish' easier (easier evaluation of the results). Alas, you have only fourteen 3C and closer matches, and worse yet, only six of those are paternal. In comparison, Laurel has a similar number of close matches, but 10 are paternal—including Grace, the 'fish' that 'netted' itself and 'jumped into the boat.'

Another consideration is that the resulting size and relative ease of 'weaving the nets' (making the mirror trees) is limited by the records available for constructing the trees and how far back family lines can be traced before records disappear. As far as 'net' size goes, we were comparatively lucky here—your father's family happened to be French-Canadian, having been in North America since the early 17th century, whereas Laurel's paternal German and Irish ancestors were 19th century immigrants. In addition, the Catholic church records for that group are detailed and extensive, and all available on Ancestry (at least for International subscriptions, such as mine), allowing for construction of large 'nets' (extensive mirror trees).

On the other hand, as far as 'ease of weaving' goes, this luck was offset by research complications and confusions such as the French-Canadian use of two first names (Jean Pierre, Jean Luc, etc,), their common use of two last names ("dit" or 'also called' names, see https://en.wikipedia.org/wiki/Dit_name, https://www.genealogytoday.com/articles/reader.mv?ID=2913), and by a requirement for an ability to read priests' handwriting in French from photocopies of decaying records (see your grandparents' marriage record attached, thank you college French!).

*5) The search arsenal—your matches and their 'mirror trees'

Attached (CloseAncestryMatches) is a list of all of your closest matches up to the 4C level, with a few of the closer 4C matches thrown in as well. I have included Laurel's to show which must be your paternal matches, and many of Grace's closer matches as well for comparison in later discussion and graphics.

For ease of reference, your six close paternal matches are:

2C—Wm. Spollen (wrsp0llen)

3Cs—seisonsmom2589, Joan Dudine Hoffman, jlonghill, lachanced, and Robert Quintin

Unfortunately, most of these six closest paternal DNA matches had no trees or only small trees ('stumps') available on Ancestry; and none were extensive enough to be suitable for use as 'mirror trees.' This required that I build trees for them for use as mirror trees. Luckily, they had just enough information available so that I was able to get a 'foothold' and build trees for them, or I was able to find them in the mirror trees I had already made! (Note: Since mirror trees are 'experimental' research trees, I made them all both private and unsearchable to Ancestry users—currently only my account has access to them. I will share them eventually, perhaps some of these folks may find them useful). Each tree was verified with available records (both Ancestry and online obituaries) to the best of my ability before used in the mirror tree method/ MRCA searches. They are:

Family or tree name (cousins inside)	# of Individuals	# of Records
Spollen (WR Spollen, lachanced)	3527	2705
Seisonsmom	441	175
Dudine (JD Hoffman, jlonghill)	295	603
Quintin	223	298

Additionally I made trees for several fourth cousins at the upper end of your list, including:

Family or tree name (cousins inside)	# of Individuals	# of Records
Schaaf (John Schaaf (JS))	318	548
Fritchen/LaBatt (Arden Fritchen)	196	253

*6) The saga begins....

So, I started with closest match, William Spollen's tree, as my first mirror tree for you, first extending it back 5 generations where possible and ending up creating a tree with 3527 individuals confirmed with 2705 records.

For a 232 cM shared DNA, the Shared cM Project dnapainter website tool gave these likely relationships:

55.52%—Half GG-Aunt/Uncle, 2C, Half 1C1R, 1C2R, Half GG-Niece/Nephew;   33.13% - Half 2C, 2C1R, Half 1C2R, 1C3R;

9.27% Great-Great-Aunt/Uncle, Half Great-Aunt/Uncle, Half 1C,   1C1R,   Half   Great-Niece/Nephew,   Great-Great-Niece/Nephew; etc

Since you and Mr. Spollen are of similar ages (from his Ancestry profile), many of those relationships could be ruled out as unlikely. I thought that 2C, Half 1C, Half 2C, and possibly some "1R" (once removed, one generation from WR Spollen) relationships were most likely.

So I applied the mirror tree method. Linking your DNA to the root person (Mr. Spollen) gave me several hundred MRCA hints, all through the LaChance side of his family through his mother Marcelle, none through the paternal Spollen line. You were likely a LaChance. Linking your DNA to Marcelle in the tree, still gave hints through her father Alfred LaChance, but none through her mother Marie StPierre. Not a St. Pierre.

Marcelle's half-brother Rene LaChance (b. 1913), lived in NYC and worked at a newspaper. (!) Had you been Rene's son it would have made you and WR Spollen half-1Cs, a possibility—both sharing a grandfather, Alfred LaChance, and also explaining the lack of a St Pierre connection.

Linking to him still gave hints through the LaChance grandparents, but none through his mother Irene DeLorme. But a lack of DeLorme hints and a low probability ruled that out as well. This is as far as I had gotten in December 2017.

So I moved back a generation to Alfred LaChance (Marcelle and Rene's father, Spollen's grandfather) and started looking at his brothers and sisters to try and find where a second cousin connection could be found—after all it was more likely. But I had not yet found records for most of his siblings and needed to find their spouses' names and extend their families back to continue. Sisters Aurelie, Ozelia, Alphilia, and Yvonne; and brothers 'Ravil' and 'Kanico'—all were possible. Being the grandson of any of these would make you WR Spollen's 2C, but which? WR Spollen only had their names listed in his tree and no spouses. Records searches for the women failed, as usual, due to name changes upon marriage. And no Ravil, no Kanico. Stuck.

So I then switched to spending time making mirror trees for your remaining close matches at the 3C level. Eventually I got hints and new names to consider, but no overlap with the Spollen tree names and the LaChance family. Actually, it's the "Pepin dit LaChance" family, due to 'dit' name nonsense.

So I began doing searches for Pepin rather than LaChance one day, and I stumbled upon a Pepin family tree with an Alfred in it, listing no birthday but with the same wife's and same parents' names as Alfred LaChance from the Spollen tree—but it was private and incomplete. None of the siblings had visible names and information except for one—"Joseph Ranel." Thought: Ccould that 'Ranel' Pepin/LaChance be my 'Ravil' LaChance?' So I wrote to the tree owner requesting access or information in May—no response, not even now.

Guessing, I put his wife Augusta Prud'homme as wife to my 'Ravil' in the Spollen tree anyway. Then I stared at the one Canadian census record for 'Ravil'—yesss! It could be 'Ranel' or probably 'Raoul' with a transcription error!

So I extended the Prud'homme family line back and placed you as a hypothetical grandson of an unknown son of Raoul Ravil Ranel Pepin LaChance. This would make you share great grandparents with WR Spollen, making you 2Cs.

It returned LaChance hints as before, but no Prud'homme.

Damn.

So I took a break away for awhile.

And I will stop here now.

Continuing next time with the breakthrough and all mirror trees falling in place. I will also send you the graphics with all the connections indicated (Philips and Schoenwandt results thrown in as well). A family tree chart as well. It should only be a day or so wait—most of that is already complete.

In the final email after that I will send you the contact information on the Grignon children and advice on how to make contact.

Until then,

Dave

Although the methods described herein were new and current at the time, genetic genealogy is a rapidly growing and changing field, and newer and more automated methods are now available. Since then the number of consumer DNA tests being performed has slowed, and companies such as Ancestry have modified their websites and data analysis methods and continue to do so. Use of the 'mirror tree' method as described is now discouraged in favor of newer methods involving data clustering analysis (based on the Leeds method and similar shared DNA match search aids). Building "quick and dirty" private unsearchable family trees is still necessary for unearthing connections to common ancestors with DNA matches. Some DNA testing companies and third party websites now offer clustering analysis tools online, such as Genetic Affairs, Gedmatch.com, etc. The reader is encouraged to search the web and Facebook for groups and sites specializing in genetic genealogy, in shared match analysis, and in helping adoptees find their birth families. (On FB: Genetic Genealogy Tips and Techniques, DNA Detectives, etc).

BOOK CLUB QUESTIONS

Who did you find as the more sympathetic character: Barbara, Elsie, or the narrator? What details and events described in this book led you to form your opinions about each of these characters?

Do you think Elsie had an inkling that the mental health issues suffered by her daughters could be genetic? Why or why not?

How was Barbara's mental disorder influenced by her upbringing—her social environment?

In 1936, Barbara wrote loving letters to her parents, extoling them on what magnificent parents they were. Years later, as she looked back, she reacted bitterly to that time in her life. Why?

What did Barbara's writing, both poetry and letters, reveal about her? What did Elsie's journal entries and letters reveal about her? What would your own journals, letters, emails reveal about you to a future generation?

Barbara was physically brutal to her mother, while her mother, Elsie, "rewarded" the behavior by buying her presents, taking her to expensive outings, and dining at high end restaurants. What might the outcome have been if Elsie had taken a different response route?

What clues or details in the story indicate that Barbara may have learned from her mother the habit of "modifying" history to justify her present circumstances?

What details might indicate that Barbara's intense dislike for her mother was a form of jealousy because her father's priority in life was his wife Elsie (Barbara's mother) over their daughters?

Why did the Grignon family so willingly accept the author into their circle? Did the author's own genetic quest inspire you in any way? If so, how?

Media links for Book Club discussion

The following interviews provide helpful context for book club discussions. Links to each of these items can be found at wendellaffield.com/media.

Television interviews: *Bemidji, Minnesota Man Finds his Roots, Local Veteran Honored with Award for Community Work*

Newspaper interview: *Finding his roots: Bemidji man connects with half-siblings through DNA testing*

Radio interview, Northern Community Radio: *Family History Discovered*

In addition, readers can also enjoy a recording of Barbara on her piano as she played the old Masters in the living room of the old farmhouse in Nebish, Minnesota.

ACKNOWLEDGMENTS

This book is the result of eleven years of exploration into my past. So many people have made important contributions to my research and the development of my mother's story that I cannot prioritize them—each illumination was of great value, so I say thank you in chronological order.

To my brother Chris who shared his memories of our time in New York during the 1940s, and my sister Laurel Affield Hofmann who made the first discoveries when she and I unlocked the chickenhouse door in 2010, and Laurel's late husband Jerry Hofmann who spent hours translating French letters, thank you. Early in the discovery phase, MaryAnne Wilimek, through a friend in Germany, translated a letter written in Latin. Jean Humeniuk, an amazing researcher, learned about my project at a book event, took an interest, and began exploring my mother's past. Jean shed light on my mother's time in Poland, uncovering details that had been mostly destroyed by the Nazis during their reign of terror.

My maternal roots are in the Pacific Northwest: In 2013, I reached out to Everett Museum of History for information about the "Fratt Mansion." They put me in touch with Saundra Cope and Walt Gillette. I am humbled by Saundra and Walt's dedication to preserving my great grandparents' home and our Fratt family history. Over the past ten years, Saundra and I have exchanged countless messages and documents as we explore the past. Thank you, Saundra and Walt, for the valuable insights you added to Barbara's story after reading the manuscript.

Late in the winter of 2017, my sister Laurel received an email from David Schmidt, an amazing man who changed the trajectory of our lives. Three years earlier Laurel and I had done DNA tests and registered them with Ancestory.com. David discovered Laurel's link to her paternal roots—overnight Laurel had a new sister and brother. Sadly, as I write this in January 2021, Laurel's new-found sister Grace recently died from Covid-19; her brother Frank died in 2018. I am thankful they all had a chance to get together a few times. When David learned that I didn't know who my father was, he began the search and two years later, I received an email. Laurel and I are forever grateful to you, David.

As I researched my mother's life during the 1940s, I was at a loss because she had moved from New York to the West Coast and cut communication with her parents. I reached out to several organizations for information, but records did not go back that far. On a long shot, I contacted 3rd Judicial District Court in Las Cruces, New Mexico, where my mother's first husband had obtained a divorce. Jodie Delgado, a court supervisor, sent me forty-two pages of priceless information, including a deposition that illuminated a very dark time in my mother's life.

I am thankful to the mental health professionals who have taken time to read and provide clinical insights into my mother's story. Thank you, Dr. Marsha Driscoll and Doug Lewandowski. A special thank you to William Petersen, MD, for his insights and for writing the "Foreword" for *BARBARA*.

Our writers' group, with whom I have, for many years, shared pages of my mother's story: Thank you, Marilyn Heltzer,

Sarah Teresa Vaughan, Polly Scotland, Mary Lou Brandvik, Doug Lewandowski, and Craig Benson. Sue Bruns, a member of our writer group, a special thanks for your years of help and the final close read of *BARBARA*. To all of you, your insights are priceless.

Thanks to David Schmidt's discoveries the summer of 2019, Laurel, David, and I traveled to the East Coast and met my father's family: Louis Grignon, Michael Grignon, Larry Grignon, Yvonne Grignon Adolph, and Guy Grignon. I didn't get a chance to meet Gene Grignon, but as I write this, Covid-19 vaccines are in the pipeline and my goal is to return to New York with Patti so she can meet this new branch of our family. Gene Grignon will be my first stop. Each of my new-found brothers and baby sister contributed a memory story about our late father, Guy Grignon Sr. Thank you—love you all.

To my beta readers and editors: Amanda Klejeski, Morgan Hess, Dr. William Petersen, Emily Enger, Peggy Nohner, Saundra Cope, Mary Lou Brandvik, thank you for your time and effort—you are all awesome. Emily Enger, thank you for your patience and work in bringing this book and the others to so many people through your marketing skills.

And my wife Patti—she has more patience than the Greek heroine Penelope. For more than a decade I have worked on my family history. Patti has listened to so many stories and read so many pages and kept the home fires burning while I was gone exploring my past. Thank you—love you.

If I have forgotten anyone, I apologize. Any shortcomings in this story are mine.

ABOUT THE AUTHOR

Wendell Affield, the third of nine children, grew up on a small farm twenty miles north of Bemidji, Minnesota. He was born in New York City in 1947 and moved to Minnesota as a toddler when his mother met his stepfather, Herman Affield, through *Cupid's Columns,* a singles publication. As a teenager, after his mother was committed to Fergus Falls State Hospital, Wendell lived in a series of foster homes. He dropped out of school, left northern Minnesota, rode the rails, and spent time in the Northwest, living in hobo camps. At seventeen, Wendell enlisted in the navy. In 1966, during his first Vietnam deployment, during down time, he earned his high school GED. In January 1968, he returned to Vietnam on a second deployment as the cox'n of a river patrol boat with the Mobile Riverine Force. On August 18, 1968, Wendell was wounded in an ambush and medevaced home.

After leaving the navy in 1969, he found work as a meat cutter apprentice in the Chicago area. A few years later he became a manager, a position he held with various companies for almost thirty years. In 1980, he and his family returned to northern Minnesota. After retiring in 2001, Wendell enrolled at Bemidji State University to learn the writing craft. Over the years, his Vietnam essays evolved into *Muddy Jungle Rivers* (2012). This memoir has been used in universities and reading clubs. The book led to reconnecting with men he hadn't seen in more than fifty years.

In 2010, Wendell's mother died. In the locked chickenhouse

on the farm where he was raised, he discovered thousands of letters, dozens of diaries, scrapbooks, and photo albums documenting his maternal family's history. He spent eleven years unraveling his mother's past. In the process, he came to understand her struggle with mental illness.

Treasures discovered in the chickenhouse and farmhouse attic opened doors to his past. He developed seventy-year-old picture negatives that awakened dormant memories. "Memory is like a shape shifter," Wendell says, "not to be trusted. But the cracked and faded childhood images don't lie. As I looked at the barefoot boy standing in front of the barn, I smelled fresh-cured clover in the open loft. I heard squawking chickens and bleating lambs."

Wendell encourages others to tell their stories. "Our life experience gives us the authority to tell our stories. For many individuals, a common regret near end of life is that their life story will die with them."

Today, Wendell works on his *Chickenhouse Chronicles* series, stays in touch with his New York family, teaches writing workshops, speaks to veteran groups about PTSD, and facilitates a Veteran's Writer Group at his local VA Clinic. He is a 2017 recipient of Minnesota Humanities Center "Veteran's Voices Award" for his work with the underserved in his community. Wendell and his wife Patti have two children and several grandchildren. Sadly, their third child, Jeffrey, died in 2015.

WENDELL AFFIELD'S BOOKS

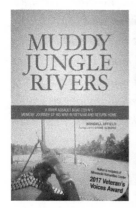
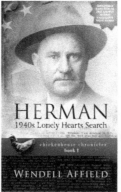

Books are available online at:

Barnes&Noble.com

Amazon.com

Walmart.com

WendellAffield.com

To learn more, go to: http://www.wendellaffield.com/

Dear Reader,

Thank you for exploring Barbara's tumultuous history with me. I hope you learned a lot about mental illness and Borderline Personality Disorder as her story unfolded. Perhaps it helped you make sense of a relationship in your life, as well.

Did you know that one of the best ways to help authors is by writing an Amazon review? This attracts more viewers to our books and helps us gain visibility. If you appreciated hearing Barbara's story, and my own subsequent genealogy quest, would you please leave a review on Amazon or Goodreads? Your feedback would very helpful to me!

Thanks so much,

Wendell Affield